Chicken Soup for the Soul.

Listen to Your Dreams

Chicken Soup for the Soul: Listen to Your Dreams
101 Tales of Inner Guidance, Divine Intervention and Miraculous Insight
Amy Newmark

Published by Chicken Soup for the Soul, LLC www.chickensoup.com
Copyright ©2020 by Chicken Soup for the Soul, LLC. All Rights Reserved.

Front cover illustration of sky courtesy of iStockphoto.com/Nongkran_ch (©Nongkran_ch), illustration of birds courtesy of iStockphoto.com/ksana-gribakina (©ksana-gribakina), illustration of mountain courtesy of iStockphoto.com/Vect0r0vich (©Vect0r0vich)
Back cover and interior illustration of woman in bed courtesy of iStockphoto.com/ Choreograph (©Choreograph)
Photo of Amy Newmark courtesy of Susan Morrow at SwickPix

Cover and Interior by Daniel Zaccari

Distributed to the booktrade by Simon & Schuster. SAN: 200-2442

Publisher's Cataloging-In-Publication Data
(Prepared by The Donohue Group, Inc.)

Names: Newmark, Amy, compiler.
Title: Chicken soup for the soul : listen to your dreams : 101 tales of
    inner guidance, divine intervention and miraculous insight / [compiled by]
    Amy Newmark.
Other Titles: Listen to your dreams : 101 tales of inner guidance, divine
    intervention and miraculous insight
Description: [Cos Cob, Connecticut] : Chicken Soup for the Soul, LLC,
    [2020]
Identifiers: ISBN 9781611590685 | ISBN 9781611593037 (ebook)
Subjects: LCSH: Precognition--Literary collections. | Precognition--
    Anecdotes. | Extrasensory perception--Literary collections. |
    Extrasensory perception--Anecdotes. | Dreams--Literary collections. |
    Dreams--Anecdotes. | LCGFT: Anecdotes.
Classification: LCC BF1341 .C455 2020 (print) | LCC BF1341 (ebook) | DDC
    133.8/6--dc23
Library of Congress Control Number: 2020935181

Chicken Soup for the Soul.

Listen to Your Dreams

101 Tales of Inner Guidance, Divine Intervention and Miraculous Insight

Amy Newmark

CSS

Chicken Soup for the Soul, LLC
Cos Cob, CT

Changing lives one story at a time®
www.chickensoup.com

Table of Contents

❸

~Early Warnings~

❹

~Listen to That Little Voice~

❺

~Messages from Heaven~

❻

~Prophetic Premonitions~

❼

~Comfort & Closure~

8

~Love Come True~

9

~Miraculous Bonds~

10

~What I Knew All Along~

Introduction

No one is you, and that is your superpower.
~Elyse Santilli

What are dreams? Are they a way of processing the day's activities and sorting out your thoughts? Are they a product of your subconscious telling you things you're too distracted to focus on during your waking hours? Are they sometimes a pathway to communications outside the constraints of your own capabilities?

Whatever you believe, this new collection of stories about dreams and premonitions will inspire you to remember and analyze your own. You may feel your dreams are generated by your own mind, or you may think that some of your dreams come to you via more divine routes. Either way, these tales of dreams remembered and advice followed reveal how incredibly powerful dreams can be — as a tool for redirecting your life, changing your relationships, and making you a happier person.

I'm a practical, fact-oriented person so I fall into the camp that believes that we generate our dreams ourselves, and that they are the products of our subconscious saying, *Hey you! Focus, please. Here's what I've been trying to tell you all day while you've been looking at your phone and doing projects and talking to people!*

Rebecca Radicchi, for example, shares one such tale in Chapter 1, "Personal Transformation." She had a recurrent dream in which a tidal wave would be roaring straight at her, and she'd stand there frozen, watching it approach. Finally, after years of this nightmare, Rebecca decided to analyze it. She realized something very important: "Those colossal waves had never actually overtaken me. Not once." Rebecca understood that no matter what kind of awfulness came at her, she would prevail. She says, "From then on, I viewed those walls of water as a gift. They reminded me to balance out my feelings with facts. They encouraged me to deal with challenges by facing them. And they reassured me that no matter what comes, I'll never be overcome."

Many of our writers found similar hope, courage, and confidence through their dreams. Others found new pathways for their lives. You'll read about people changing careers, homes, even spouses because of the direction they've received from their subconscious pointing out to them what they already knew. You'll read about people figuring out what the stressors in their lives are through their dreams, and deciding to do something about them. And you'll read about people sorting out their feelings for friends or family members — alive or dead — through their dreams.

In many cases, it's hard to imagine someone's subconscious was the source of their inspiration, when the advice they've received seems to come out of left field. That's what happened to Jody Sharpe after she lost her daughter Kate in a car accident. Her story in our chapter called "Listen to That Little Voice" is about a dream in which a voice told her to read *Charlotte's Web*. Jody had never read the book, and she had no reason to know its contents. But she went out and bought the book immediately, and in the last chapter she found the guidance she needed to move forward in her life, finding joy in her remaining children and her grandchildren despite her sorrow for Kate.

Have you ever had a premonition that something bad was about to happen? Perhaps you changed your day to avoid that bad event, or you warned someone else. You'll read plenty of tales of premonitions well heeded in these pages. One of our writers, Marya Morin, had so many dreams and premonitions come true that her parents warned her not to tell anyone. Her story in our chapter called "Prophetic Premonitions" concerns her discovery of her gift as a young child, and her later reluctance to tell the man she was dating about it, until they were about to have a tire blow out on a mountain road. She screamed at her date to stop moments before their front tire exploded. As they sat in the car on the shoulder of that treacherous road, trembling, she confessed that she had dreamed the night before about the tire and the ravine they would plunge into. Marya says that unlike her parents, "He expressed no fear or distaste — only relief for saving our lives and sympathy for the many omens I'd never disclosed to anyone." They've been married for decades now.

I learned a lot about the power of dreams and premonitions while I was making our two previous books on this topic — *Chicken Soup for the Soul: Dreams and Premonitions* (2015) and *Chicken Soup for the Soul: Dreams and the Unexplainable* (2017). If you're interested in reading more stories like these after you finish this book, I recommend those two volumes, which I put together with dream expert Kelly Sullivan Walden and her cadre of dream experts.

One of Kelly's recommendations in those books is to write down your dreams the moment you wake up. Even if you can scribble down a couple of keywords you'll have a better shot of remembering. How many times have you woken up, said "I had the most vivid dream," and then promptly forgotten it? That happens to me all the time. I did have two vivid dreams this spring, though, which I have managed to remember.

In the first dream, I was at the grocery store in a long line to check out. My shopping cart was completely empty — not one item in it — and yet I was forced to stand in the line. And everyone was crammed together, too, a no-no during this time of social distancing during the COVID-19 pandemic.

In my second dream, I was pushing a totally empty shopping cart again, but through the streets of the small city that is next door to my town. Apparently I had walked about ten miles from home pushing this empty cart, and now I was on a big city boulevard with lots of other people who were also pushing empty shopping carts. The road was divided and we had to walk in one direction on each side of the road. Everyone was obeying the one-way rule and trying to stay the proper six feet apart but it was difficult.

No one was wearing a mask in either of my dreams.

It wasn't hard to analyze those dreams. I started stocking up our usually empty kitchen back in February as soon as I saw the grocery-store lines in Italy. So by early March I was done, and I haven't set foot in any store of any kind since then. We're in a particularly hard hit area in the suburbs of New York City, so we are being extra-careful around here. After a few weeks of the shutdown, the grocery stores got more organized for delivery and parking-lot pickups, but during those early days it was almost impossible to get groceries if you weren't willing to walk inside a store. We ran out of some basics during that time. So those were anxiety dreams, plain and simple. No mystery there.

We have a dozen stories about dreams related to the COVID-19 pandemic in these pages. Most of them involve the stress of the pandemic causing epiphanies for our contributors, way more exciting than my very obvious dreams. Sergio del Bianco, for example, found that during the shutdown he was dreaming of people he hadn't seen in years. In his story in our chapter called "Miraculous Bonds" he describes what happened after he had repeated dreams about a woman named Gwen who had been kind to him at a part-time job he held in college many decades ago. He became fixated on finding her, figuring she must be in her nineties by now. After a prolonged Google and Facebook search, he found Gwen's daughter, who arranged a phone call for him. Sergio found himself crying tears of joy as he talked to Gwen and told her how much she had meant to him. A few days after that phone call, Gwen's daughter called to say that her mother had quietly passed away in her sleep, and that it seemed like she had hung on just long enough to hear from Sergio.

So, are dreams generated by your subconscious? Are they your connection to an unseen world? Whatever you decide after you finish this collection of 101 miraculous, thought-provoking stories, I know one thing: You'll want to listen to your dreams.

—Amy Newmark—
Editor-in-Chief & Publisher, Chicken Soup for the Soul
June 1, 2020

Chapter 1

Personal Transformation

The Boat

Don't wait for your ship to come in — swim out to it.
~Author Unknown

I was driving to an appointment with my grief counselor, and in my foggy state, I turned left instead of right. I didn't drive very far before I realized my mistake. While looking for a place to turn around, I drove past a boat on the side of the road with a For Sale sign. I had a fleeting thought that my son and I would have really enjoyed the boat.

He and I had loved being out on the water. We became certified as scuba divers when he was just thirteen and then re-certified when he turned sixteen. We loved to go fishing, kayaking, canoeing, sailing, snorkeling and scuba diving. We also liked going to an island near Tampa Bay to look for sharks' teeth.

I found a place to turn around and didn't think anymore about the boat. That night, though, my son came back to me in a dream.

He told me to buy the boat that I had seen. He was very specific about what he wanted me to do with the boat: provide boating trips to veterans, military service members and families who had endured the death of a warrior. He wanted me to take them to some of his favorite places in the bay and on various rivers in the area.

The dream woke me, but I was happy about having the dream. It was comforting to see him and hear his voice.

The next morning, over coffee, I told my mother about the dream. We both had a chuckle over the thought of me being a boat captain.

That night, I was awakened by the same dream. I had been diagnosed with PTSD, and it was very important that I got a good night's sleep so being awakened by the dream wasn't good.

For the next two nights, I had the dream again. My PTSD symptoms intensified due to lack of sleep.

On the fifth night when I was awakened by the dream I sat up in bed. I looked up to heaven and said, "Corey, please, please, please, don't make me buy this boat. You know why we always used to joke about them being called boats… 'Break Out Another Thousand!'"

After a few hours, I was finally able to drift back to sleep. The next morning, my mother asked if I had had the dream again.

I told her, "Yes, and if I don't get a good night's sleep soon, I don't know what I am going to do."

She suggested I call the doctor and schedule an appointment to see him. In the meantime, she told me to drive back to where the boat had been parked to see if it was still there. "If the boat is gone, maybe your dreams will stop. If the boat is still there, it sounds like it is going to be way out of your price range since you only have about $2,500. Maybe knowing you can't afford it will stop the dreams."

I was willing to try anything. After calling the doctor's office, I jumped in my car and drove back to where I had seen the boat. It was still there. I pulled in to take a closer look at the For Sale sign. There was no price listed, just a phone number. I pulled out my cell phone and dialed the number.

A man answered. "Hello."

"Hi," I said. "I'm calling about your boat. What can you tell me about it? Does it run?"

I asked a few more questions, and then the man said, "Lady, are you calling for your husband?"

"No," I answered. "I'm getting divorced."

"Well, have you ever owned a boat before?" he asked.

"No," I replied.

"Well, do you mind if I ask why you are interested in buying a boat?"

The question caught me off guard. My mind whirled. *What do I say?*

Do I tell him the truth? He will think I am crazy. Think, think, think... What can I tell him that will sound reasonable? I heard myself say, "It's a little complicated. Just tell me this: How much do you want for the boat?"

"Five thousand dollars for the boat and $2,000 for the trailer."

"Thank you for your time," I said. "That is way out of my price range. I'm sorry I bothered you."

I started to hang up the phone when I heard, "Lady, wait. Hey, lady, wait."

"Yes?" I questioned.

"You never did tell me why you wanted the boat." I sighed. I didn't think he would be able to send the people with the straitjackets after me, so I 'fessed up. "To tell you the truth, my son was killed in Afghanistan on September 20th, and he has been coming to me in a dream. He is very insistent that I buy a boat and provide boating trips to veterans, military service members and families who have experienced the pain of losing a warrior."

There was silence for a moment. Then I heard him say, "Lady, I am a veteran, and if that is why you want to buy the boat, I will sell it to you, trailer and all, for $2,000."

Wow, that's great! I thought. Then I began to wonder what was wrong with the boat. After all, he had just dropped the price by $5,000. "I am interested," I said, "but would you mind if I brought a boat mechanic friend of mine by tomorrow so he can look the boat over?"

"Sure," he said. "What time would you like to meet?"

"How about 2 p.m.?" I asked.

"Okay, see you then," he replied.

The next day, my mechanic friend and I went to look at the boat. Jeff gave it a good once-over and pulled me aside. "Buy the boat," he whispered to me.

"Are you sure?" I asked.

"Yes, buy the boat. I will donate my time to get it running. I think it just needs a good tune-up. I will bring you receipts for plugs and a fuel filter. If, after I get it running, you decide that you don't want it, I will reimburse you for the parts you have purchased plus give you $2,500 for the boat. You have nothing to lose. You will make $500 on the deal."

So, we left with the boat. Two weeks later, I conducted my first boating trip for a group of five veterans.

These boating trips led me on a journey to found a nonprofit organization called "My Warrior's Place." It has totally changed my life.

— Kelly Kowall —

The Cave

The purpose of life is a life of purpose.
~Robert Byrne

Like most people, I've had dreams so bizarre that even the most gifted psychologist couldn't decipher them. I've had recurrent dreams since childhood about seeing UFOs and moving objects with my mind. Lost loved ones have visited me, giving me information right when I needed it.

I've even had dreams that seemed to predict the future, like when I dreamt about an old friend I hadn't spoken with in over a decade and then received a phone call from him the next day. But until a few months ago, I never had a dream that left me so shaken that I called a friend who is a Christian minister and asked him to pray for me.

The dream started out very happily. I was riding a dirt bike along a sunny forest path. I came to a mountain and saw the entrance to a cave. I stopped, hesitant to enter, but then I thought it would be fun to explore so I rode in. I was my usual cautious self, entering the cave slowly and letting my eyes adjust to the darkness.

The cave was shaped like a tunnel. I could see a light far in the distance so I pedaled toward it until the wall on the left suddenly ended, opening to a giant cavern too deep and dark to see the bottom.

I was a little nervous but continued on. I was picking up speed when my right pedal suddenly collided with a small boulder, and I careened to the left toward the cliff. Before I could hit the brakes or turn away, I went over the edge, plummeting downward.

As I fell, there was no dreamlike quality. Every emotion I felt was exactly what I would feel in real life — shock, horror, panic, and sheer desperation to save myself somehow.

I saw a ledge approaching below. It was covered with rusty steel mining equipment. I knew if I landed on it, I would be broken to pieces, but at least I might survive. I had no control over my direction, so all I could do was hold onto the bike and hope I hit the ledge, but I missed it completely. With all hope lost and gaining speed, I hurtled deeper into the blackness that I knew would end with my crashing into the cold, hard ground with zero chance of survival.

I continued falling long enough to think about my wife and two daughters at home. My heart sank even further when I realized they would never know what happened to me. Nobody would, except perhaps some explorer years or centuries later who happened upon my bones and rusted bicycle. I cried harder, knowing with absolute certainty that my life was about to end.

Denial set in. This couldn't happen to me. I had such big plans. Worst of all, I would never see my family again. It couldn't be true, but it was. I was grieving my life while still living its final moments and thoughts. The wind in my face grew colder as I approached the cavern floor. I knew it would be the last thing I felt in this world. I saw a flash of the ground coming up, screamed, and hit it full-force.

I awoke with a gasp and sat up at the edge of the bed, struggling to breathe. My wife asked if I was okay. I couldn't answer. She turned on the light, growing concerned because I'd had a medical emergency a year earlier that had caused me to become disoriented, turn white, and pass out. At that time, my wife, who is a nurse, had to do chest compressions to revive me. Paramedics were called. I lost consciousness again at home and at the hospital. Each time, my heart rate decreased to less than thirty beats per minute.

A battery of tests was done. There was talk of pacemakers and epilepsy, but neither of those theories turned out to be correct. In the end, the doctors said I had a severe panic attack and gave me the usual advice — control stress and exercise more. Just my luck, I was exercising in my dream, and it got me killed.

My main source of stress over the past few years had been the loss of my father from complications due to Parkinson's disease and dementia. The last three years of his life were a trip to hell and back.

I had lost my only sibling more than twenty years earlier, and several friends along the way, but losing a parent was different. It made me acutely aware of my own aging process and mortality. I always looked and felt young for my age, but time had been catching up with me in the usual ways — more gray hairs, more difficulty staying in shape, and the mental spinouts that come with age.

I became a father late in life, so part of me still futilely wishes I could stay forever young for my children. I joke with friends that I looked young before I had children, but now I'm on the "Rapid Aging Program" caused by lack of sleep and worrying about them hurting themselves.

I was so rattled by the nightmare that I called my best friend Dean, a Christian preacher. He prayed on the phone with me. I felt better but still spent the next week or so unable to shake off the fear I had felt. It was more like a memory than a dream, as if it had actually happened and I had cheated death somehow. I kept seeing the ledge, my only hope of survival, passing me by, and the horrible blackness of death below.

But as time passed, I began to feel a strange sense of liberation, as one might feel after surviving a car crash or some other calamity. I was alive. I still had a chance to do everything I had planned. I could call my mother, who is still alive and healthy, and tell her I love her. I could be a better son, father, husband and friend. I stopped thinking so much about all the years behind me and focused on the decades I still have left to live, and all that I might see and accomplish if I can finally get out of my own way.

In his book *The Power of Myth*, Joseph Campbell wrote, "The conquest of the fear of death is the recovery of life's joy. One can experience an unconditional affirmation of life only when one has accepted death, not as contrary to life, but as an aspect of life... The conquest of fear yields the courage of life."

I concluded that, as horrific as it was, the nightmare was a warning to take better care of myself (avoid the cliff). It's easy for something bad to happen that we are unable to foresee (the boulder), and once the process of death is in motion (the falling), it's often too late to stop it. The nightmare became an important lesson. It had it all, even a "light at the end of the tunnel."

I have been given a second chance, and I'm making the changes I need to make. I have committed more than ever to loving and savoring the precious gift of life. I know death will come eventually, as it does for us all. When it does, I will rest easy knowing that I pursued my dreams fearlessly and, more importantly, lived and loved with all my heart.

— Mark Rickerby —

Turned Messenger

The key to life is accepting challenges.
~Bette Davis

Every sense in my body was on high alert with sheer terror. I stood fully frozen, unable to look away while I watched a dark, monstrous wall of water coming toward me. I was in a building of some sort with giant windows. Maybe a hotel? People I cared about were with me, but they were nameless. My feet betrayed me, frozen so that I couldn't turn and run away from the tidal wave. I stood there stunned, watching the water come and knowing I'd soon be pulled under.

Suddenly, I was awake, sweating, with my heart pounding and my mind racing.

The tsunami had first occurred in my dreams in high school. Though I can't remember that first nightmare, I remember that the waves came back to me uninvited throughout my teens and early twenties. Each time, I'd startle myself awake, trembling. The details were always a bit different, but the foreboding tidal waves that left me paralyzed were the same.

Somewhere along the line, I realized that dreams might hold meaning. They could be messages emerging from the subconscious to be interpreted. So, I sorted back through what I could remember, realizing that sometimes they had come just before the start of a new school year or other milestones, or when big work projects had loomed.

The interpretation was obvious. The waves represented my feelings of fear and uncertainty when I was overwhelmed or stressed.

Every year or so, the tidal wave would come back for me. I'd find myself once again standing in some sort of a shelter with large glass windows or on a beach with buildings just behind me. It always felt sudden, like the light turned to darkness without warning, without a hint of storm clouds. I'd turn around from eating or laughing with some fuzzy yet familiar faces to see that giant wave suddenly appear.

When I entered working adulthood, the dreams came a few more times. My faith and self-awareness had deepened as I weathered the normal storms of life. Even still, I never thought much more of them than as a sign of stress. They were just something funny to share when a leader asked about recurring dreams during a group icebreaker.

Then, one time when the dream came back I decided to analyze it. What I unlocked was a sweet and weighty realization. I'd felt all the negative emotions but had missed a very important fact.

Those colossal waves had never actually overtaken me. Not once.

Though the dreams were scary and recurring, they never went past a stunned awareness that all that awful water was coming for me. Never was I washed away. Never did the dream end with me bobbing wildly, sinking, or gasping for gulps of air in rushing water. Never did I feel even a drop of water. Never once did I run.

That awareness left me with a whole new understanding: In hard situations, I needed to balance my feelings with facts. The fact of the dream was that though I stood before something powerful and potentially overwhelming, the bad ending never came. And the fact that I stood there frozen? That was a good thing, not a sign of weakness. I was merely recognizing that I couldn't fight off every hardship or stressor. To properly deal with them, I must face them first — with courage.

I felt a profound faith lesson. In this life, I might have to feel all kinds of uncomfortable feelings, but I'd never be overcome.

As it turned out, those scary waves held all kinds of wisdom for me. From then on, I viewed those walls of water as a gift. They reminded me to balance out my feelings with facts. They encouraged me to deal with challenges by facing them. And they reassured me that no matter what comes, I'll never be overcome.

I haven't had that dream in years, but it stays with me still, a nightmare turned messenger.

— Rebecca Radicchi —

Tune In to Your Life

All our dreams can come true,
if we have the courage to pursue them.
~Walt Disney

I n my dream, I had contracted COVID-19. Since I have asthma, I was in the hospital. The nurse kept taking my temperature and saying, "You're holding steady at 103.5." I was lying in the hospital bed and kept telling myself, "103.5. I know I can beat this illness."

Upon waking, I couldn't remember much about the dream or even what the nurse looked like. However, I had a very vivid memory of the temperature, 103.5. I thought, *That sounds like a radio station.*

Looking for a change of scenery, I decided to go for a drive. I twisted the knob until it reached 103.5 FM. I wasn't even sure there was a station at that frequency, but curiosity was getting the best of me.

Sure enough, there was a talk show discussing how to make a career switch. I heard people debating the pros and cons of changing careers and how furthering one's education was beneficial.

It was eerie how relevant it was to my current state. I had been thinking about changing careers for some time but was afraid to take the leap knowing that it could require additional years of education.

It couldn't be a coincidence. I ended up listening to the radio channel for over forty-five minutes. It provided some additional resources that I will be using soon as I apply for the courses that will help me achieve my dream job.

—Jamie Wilson—

Real Diamonds

Better a diamond with a flaw than a pebble without.
~Devin Madson, The Blood of Whisperers

*T*he light hanging from the ceiling harshly illuminated the woman's body as I studied her from the corner of the room. She lay on her back on the exam table, cloths covering her face and private areas, leaving the remainder of her body exposed. Looking from afar at the woman's slim figure, I assumed she must be a model.

When I approached the table, however, I swiftly changed my mind. Her body was in fact littered with flaws. Pink stretch marks covered her hips like tiger stripes. Cellulite was clearly discernable on her inner thighs. Her calves were too thin, her tummy too bloated, her skin too blemished... My list went on and on.

As I completed my observations and concluded that her body was filled with imperfection, I removed the cloth shielding her face. The woman was me.

Then I woke up.

The dream made me enormously uncomfortable. There's nothing like examining someone's body and picking out each imperfection only to realize it's your own. It troubled me so much, that after documenting it in my dream journal, I deliberately sought to forget it.

Years later, when I stumbled upon the dream in my journal, its importance became apparent. I had been battling body image issues and poor eating habits for most of my life. Like an addict, I was obsessed. It was so bad that I became isolated, avoiding most social events. I was afraid to eat in front of other people, thinking they would judge my body and what I ate.

Even at age thirteen, I had looked at the calories and fat in everything. I even joked with friends, saying, "Hi, my name is Emily, and I have an obsessive nutrition label examining disorder." I shunned anything not labeled fat-free or low-fat. I avoided my mom's homemade cookies, brownies and fried dumplings like the plague. "Careful" doesn't begin to describe my behavior, and people began to notice.

The negative attention I received for my eating habits and resulting body made matters far worse. I remember sitting at my desk in my freshman English class when the boy sitting in front of me peered down at my bare legs and commented with surprise on how skinny they were. Friends teased me, unaware of the hurt they inflicted with their jokes. Although I was neither anorexic nor bulimic, when I left to use the restroom, they would stick their fingers down their throats as I walked away, suggesting I was going to make myself vomit.

My body image and eating struggles continued through most of my young-adult life as I lost and gained weight repeatedly, wavering between a gain and loss of almost fifty pounds. Yet regardless of how much I lost or how fit I became, I was dissatisfied with my body.

As I read this entry in my dream journal several years after it occurred, my heart sank. How horrible I had been to myself! Even my subconscious was criticizing my body. I felt overwhelming guilt for not only so harshly despising my body, but for the endless toils my body had endured for almost a decade as a result of my disgust. I knew I needed to not only forgive myself, but also make a diligent effort to change my outlook. I knew it would be no easy matter.

Changing my mindset is a chore I still struggle with every day, as my first instinct upon looking at myself in the mirror is still to let out a dramatic sigh as I view my perceived faults. However, I try to focus on the things I appreciate about myself, too. I think about my sapphire-blue eyes, broad shoulders and the genes that gave me my height. I highlight my fair complexion, natural rosy cheeks and wavy blond hair. I focus on the positives and grant myself grace for the areas I don't like.

My friend once passed on a sweet comment from her boyfriend. She was also critical of her body and overly embarrassed by the stretch marks on her hips. Sensing her self-consciousness, he asked her if she knew how to tell a real diamond from a fake. "A real diamond will have flaws," he said.

As I look at my perfectly imperfect body in the mirror, I remind myself that only real diamonds have flaws. From now on, if I shine a light on my body in a dream, it will be to appreciate the gift that is life.

— Emily Marszalek —

Shredding Sadness

To forgive is the highest, most beautiful form of love.
In return, you will receive untold peace and happiness.
~Robert Muller

Lately, I've been shredding documents I accumulated with my ex-husband. These always put me in a dark place. I have happy memories of Steve, but sometimes they get overpowered by the negative ones — the money I lost, the birthdays he missed, how sick he got, and the way I felt that he no longer truly loved me by the end of the marriage.

In all the years since Steve and I divorced, I had never dreamed of him. I spent enough of my waking time feeling guilty about our failed marriage; I had no need to do overtime at night. But just a couple of months ago, I dreamt of Steve.

He was off in the distance, walking across a field toward the building I appeared to be living in. I peered out my window and knew that it was him but couldn't figure out why he was there. Just as he got close, a noise in my real house woke me from the dream.

I remember how frustrated I was that I didn't get to see him face to face, didn't get to talk to him, and didn't get to understand why he was appearing to me.

Later that week, I missed a rare phone call from his son who was about to go into the Coast Guard. I felt frustrated about not getting to the phone in time or being successful in calling back. It had been four years since I'd seen Junior at his dad's funeral and seven years since I'd seen him prior to the divorce. All these years, I'd often lamented our break in communication. And now he would be unreachable for eight weeks of training — maybe even the whole time he would be in the Coast Guard. I thought back to the dream and began to worry. Did Steve know something I didn't?

Unexpectedly, though, two months after the dream and the missed phone call, Junior appeared at my door. He'd graduated from Coast Guard training and was on his way to report to duty. At first, it seemed he might stay for just an hour, but instead he ended up staying for two days.

The entire time he visited, we didn't talk about the difficult stuff of the past. Why fill what little time we had together with sadness? Instead, we laughed and hugged each other often, reestablished our connection, and vowed to keep it going.

After that, I had another dream of Steve.

This time, he was up close and personal. He pulled up in his blue pickup truck, pulling a large boat made of weathered plywood painted barn red — a ridiculous-looking thing with a large, enclosed captain's wheelhouse. I chuckled when I saw it.

"You didn't actually drive this thing all the way across the country, did ya?"

"Heck, yeah!" he said, puffing out his chest like a superhero.

I couldn't help laughing. "Are you sure this thing floats?"

"Guess we'll find out," he said, with a grin.

An instant later, we were at a table in a house I appeared to be living in. Steve came over to me with a big white bakery box. He took a birthday cake with lots of white icing roses out of the box, set it down on the table and dropped his head right down into it, taking a big bite. Next, using his fingers, he grabbed a huge hunk of icing and cake and joyfully shoved it into his mouth. His eyes sparkled. He was eating, laughing and joking.

"Now, your turn," he said, pushing the cake toward me while swiftly turning around and heading back over toward the other things he'd brought.

I hesitated for a few seconds and then said to myself, "Aw, what the hell," and dug in. Steve came back, grinning at my icing-laced face and fingertips. He laid another boxed cake on the table, one with big blue sugar-cream roses on it — just like the cake at our wedding some sixteen years earlier. He cut into that one, too, but with a fork instead of his fingers. I noticed there was a third cake on the counter in the distance, a white one with yellow roses around the edges.

He left the table again and came back this time with several documents. One was a blank check. Another was a proclamation honoring and memorializing my late father — with whom Steve had felt very connected. I looked up at Steve and, seeing his warm, gentle smile, I understood immediately all he was trying to say.

I would've liked to stay right there in that dream and enjoy what felt like a warm wave of healing, compliments of Steve. But like months earlier when I first dreamed of him, a sound in my real house interrupted my slumber. As soon as I opened my eyes, my pint-sized dog licked my face, saying "Good morning" in her own sweet way. Then my husband Mark rolled over to wish me a good morning, too. I must've seemed distracted because he did what he always does when he can tell I'm in deep thought. He asked in a lyrical, six-year-old-kid kinda way, "What'cha doin'?"

I laughed like I usually do when he reads me so well and answered with the same lyrical lilt, "Think'n." Then I proceeded to share with Mark the details of my dream. As has always been the case with Mark, he was touched by my story of emotional connection with my ex and was especially happy to see and feel my positive energy while I described the ridiculous boat, the cake-eating fest, and the loving kindness.

I spent the rest of the morning thinking about that dream and the many things that have been happening lately that feel like opportunities for healing. I thought about the symbolism of the dream, especially those cakes. The first one reminded me of a photo taken of Steve a week before he died. He was still in the hospital but felt good enough on Thanksgiving Day to ask for donuts, which he then ate with complete abandon, covering his face with white icing. The second cake reminded me of our wedding day. And the last cake, with yellow flowers, symbolized friendship.

Mostly, though, I remembered that I had loved Steve. And I remembered that he loved me, too — enough to drive a weird boat across the country to see me, and enough to bring me a blank check and three meaningful cakes. It was time for me to focus on the happy memories, to honor the love we had once shared.

And that's what I did today. I let go of any residual pain that came from loving Steve. I fed the last of my less-than-happy documents into the shredder, never to be seen again. With it, I shed the self-inflicted sadness that for so long kept me from fully living my life. I fully forgave Steve for all he'd done. But more importantly, I fully forgave myself for all I'd done, too.

— Susan Maddy Jones —

Leaving My Baggage Behind

No baggage — there was the secret of existence.
~Robert Louis Stevenson, The Wrecker

The winter had been long and brutal. I desperately needed a break, so I decided to book a last-minute trip to the Caribbean with a friend. My trip was just three days away, and it consumed my every thought.

I was planning to pick up some things for the trip during my lunch break, but at around 12:30 p.m., the company president came to my desk and asked to speak with me in the boardroom.

At first, I didn't think anything of it, but as I entered the room and saw the human-resources manager already seated, I knew it couldn't be good. Just months shy of my ten-year anniversary with the company, I was laid off.

As I left the office with an overflowing bag of my belongings, I was in complete shock — too shocked to even cry. I wondered how they could do this after everything I had done for them.

Canceling my trip wasn't an option, as I needed it now more than ever. But instead of picking out a nail colour for my pedicure or buying a new hat for the beach, I spent the next two days updating my résumé and standing in line to file a claim for unemployment insurance.

The night before my trip, I had a dream that my friend came to pick me up to go to the airport. I had two suitcases at the door — one that was packed and another that was empty. When I got to the airport, I realized that I had brought the empty one.

When I woke, I interpreted this dream to mean that I was leaving all of my "baggage" behind — and I did. I enjoyed and appreciated my vacation more than any others I had taken. And while I usually feel depressed about returning from a trip, I wasn't this time. Having had time and distance from my work break-up and a dream about getting rid of my old baggage, I was looking forward to returning and starting the next chapter of my life.

I knew I wasn't going to land a position in my narrow, competitive field right away. So when I wasn't working on my job search, I got back into doing one of the things I loved but never had the spare time to do: write. At the company where I worked, I was able to write, but it was ghostwriting. My president's name and picture were always attached to my work.

I had never been published under my own name before, but I wanted to try. I wrote a few pieces and sent them out to magazines and newspapers. Most amateurs would approach smaller publications, but I didn't. I swung for the fences and sent them to the bigger, well-known ones. No guts, no glory, right?

After several non-responses and rejections, my gamble paid off. The most-read newspaper in Canada agreed to publish one of my travel stories. I couldn't have been more thrilled.

I told my family and friends about my piece coming out but didn't know the full magnitude of it until after it was published. People I hadn't talked to in years contacted me to let me know they read my story. There was even a "Letters to the Editor" section that was published a few weeks later based entirely on feedback from my article. How flattering.

When I started writing after I got laid off, I did it because I liked it. What I didn't realize was that my first published story would open several important doors for me.

Being published in a major publication looked impressive on my résumé and led to interviews for writing positions at well-known organizations. It also led to more publications taking notice of the articles I submitted.

I am happy to say that now I work full-time as a corporate writer and have been published in a number of North American magazines.

Getting laid off was a life-altering experience for me that could have been devastating. I will be the first to admit that it was difficult to go through financially, emotionally, and socially. But there was something about that dream I had after it happened. That dream, in which I happily carried on with an empty suitcase, helped me put everything behind me and gave me the confidence to pursue new ventures.

— Debra Rughoo —

Loving Again

Change always comes bearing gifts.
~Price Pritchett

"I'm calling with exciting news. I'm getting married."

As my mother chatted about her engagement to a family friend I barely knew, I could only think one thing: *But Dad just died.*

Instead of congratulating Mom on her upcoming wedding, I blurted the most hurtful thing I could think of: "Well, I'll see if I can attend the ceremony. I can't make any promises."

Mom's giggly chatter, bubbling with the effervescence of a schoolgirl in love, ended. I'd shattered her fairy tale — the one where her daughter would congratulate her and she'd ride off into the sunset.

Our phone call ended in hurtful silence.

As I hung up, all I could think of was Mom and Dad listening to Frank Sinatra singing "My Way," the song they'd danced to at their wedding forty years earlier. Their love song was supposed to last forever. I'd heard stories about their courtship — how Dad was so smitten with her charm and good looks that he waited outside her apartment door, a melting half-gallon of White House cherry ice cream in hand, until her other suitors finally left.

His persistence paid off, and they married, raised two daughters, and stood by each other's side for four decades. They weren't the kind of couple to hold hands or go out on fancy date nights, but their love ran deep. Mom and Dad worked opposite shifts, so they spent weekends together rooting for their beloved Cleveland Browns, visiting Mom's parents on their family farm, and cheering for my sister and me at band concerts, music recitals, and skating competitions.

Dad's love for Mom was quiet but unwavering. Never a Christmas morning passed when there wasn't a bottle of Chanel No. 5 perfume waiting for her under the tree. Every Valentine's Day, Dad showered Mom, as well as my sister and me, with cards and giant heart-shaped boxes of chocolates. Never a day passed when I didn't hear Dad say to Mom, "You know I love you, honey."

In return, Mom's devotion was endless. Through Dad's five-year struggle with emphysema, she lovingly cared for him with infinite patience and tireless compassion. When Dad took his last breath, she was by his side, like always.

And now she was marrying someone else? I couldn't wrap my head around it.

"You should call your mother back," my husband instructed. "Talk to her."

But I couldn't. Losing my dad was the worst thing that ever happened to me. When I was in elementary school, Dad was my ice-skating coach, dinner date, and math tutor. When I tried everything from swimming to acting to Girl Scouts, Dad was always there. He helped me sell cases of Thin Mints and Do-si-dos, stood poolside and evaluated my diving form, and presented me with roses at my skating competitions.

Years later at my wedding, Dad didn't let his portable oxygen tank deter him from his fatherly duties. "I'm walking you down the aisle if it's the last thing I ever do," he said. And he did.

But now Mom was moving on. What would Dad think? Was this even okay? It had been only months since Dad died, so my grief was raw. Would I ever accept someone new at Mom's side? At twenty-eight, I was hardly a child in need of fatherly guidance. Why did I feel so confused?

Instead of talking things out with Mom, I slept on my worries. A deep sleeper by nature, I rarely remember my dreams. But that night, the answer to my concerns came to me so vividly I still can recall the dream sequence some twenty years later.

Right away, I knew I was looking in on heaven. There was a babbling brook, a lush green meadow, and bunnies happily hopping in the tall grass. In front of the brook sat my dad, happy and relaxed in his favorite cardigan sweater. To Dad's right sat Uncle Bud, a favorite relative who had passed away just a month after Dad. Instantly, I felt a palpable sense of peace. Everything was right in their world, and I awoke knowing everything would be fine in mine, too.

I couldn't explain it, but I felt a new sense of calm. I knew Dad was okay with Mom moving on. I could feel it in my bones.

Since heaven — and my dad — came to me in a dream, I was able to dance at my mom's wedding a few months later and open my heart to her husband Harry, a man my future children would call Grandpa. I never would have imagined learning to love a stepdad, but Harry, a man of deep intelligence and even stronger moral character, shared my deep faith and commitment to family. He attended my girls' concerts and birthday parties, ate their homemade applesauce at preschool, and welcomed them to his dairy farm, where they fed calves, chased kittens, and snapped beans. When my older daughter hit the "terrible twos," Harry presented me with a book of parenting tips. When I had my first story published — in a *Chicken Soup for the Soul* book — he not only attended my book signing but also invited several of his friends.

But by far, the best thing Harry did was love Mom with his whole heart. He gave her the happiest years of her life. Together, the two of them laughed, loved, and lived each day to the fullest. They made each moment count.

Nobody can ever replace my dad. But because of a dream delivery of peace and clarity, my heart was opened to a man who became my mom's greatest love, a grandfather to my children, and a supportive sounding board as I raised my girls.

Heaven came to me in a dream.

I'm thankful I heeded its message.

— Stefanie Wass —

The Climb

Dad, your guiding hand on my shoulder
will remain with me forever.
~Author Unknown

It always takes me a few minutes to realize that it is happening again.

As always, sweat is dripping down my cheek, and my breathing is fast. The weather is perfect. I'm on my bike, pedaling furiously up a steep climb, smiling and laughing despite the effort.

I know he's there, even before I look. As I near the top of the climb, I finally give in to the urge to turn and look behind. Dad is there, two or three bike-lengths behind. If he weren't so exhausted from the effort, I know his smile would be as wide as mine. Just as he's about to catch his breath enough to say something, I jar awake.

I desperately try to hang on to the dream and the feeling for a few moments longer, but it begins to fade. A new day is about to begin — another day without him.

Though it's been over twenty years, I still remember vividly when it wasn't just a dream.

Some fathers take their kids to play baseball, football, or maybe basketball at the park. My dad always took me cycling. For as long as I can remember, it was our perfect getaway — a time to get some exercise and talk about life. In the busy worlds of a social teenager and a working parent, it always gave us the opportunity to solve the problems of the world, or at least to understand them better.

Dad had always been a stronger rider than I was. I still remember the first time he took me up The Climb. He seemed to sail up the hill effortlessly, while I struggled and gasped for air, feeling like my lungs would explode at any moment. Gradually, though, I became a better climber, and eventually I was able to keep up with him.

Then, one day, it happened. As we neared the top of the climb on a perfect sunny day, I surged ahead, and he was unable to match my pace. It was the first time I had ever dropped him on a climb. When he eventually caught up on the downhill, he was smiling and laughing, patting my shoulder as he passed.

"Perfect," he'd say later. "Don't ever let up, not even for me."

Those were days when life made sense, and things were much simpler. It felt like we had all the time in the world, and he'd always be there to support, challenge and encourage me. But fate had different plans, and Dad was about to encounter a climb that he wouldn't be able to conquer. I still remember the first time I heard the word "leukemia." Dad fought hard, but within a year of his diagnosis he was gone.

Cycling, once intended to help me spend time with my dad, now became my escape. I began to ride longer and take more difficult rides. I competed in all the events that we'd planned to do together.

The first time I had the dream was a restless night before my first 100-mile "century ride." It wasn't long after his death. I had been a bundle of nervous energy in the days leading up to the event, but the dream gave me a sense of calm and comfort. From the moment I woke up, I knew it was going to be okay. The ride went well. In a way, I felt like Dad was along for the ride, chasing me up the climbs.

After that, the dream would recur every few months, often before cycling events as I pushed to 150- and 200-mile rides. I would also have the dream after difficult days or when I was contemplating or encountering major changes to my life.

The dream happened the night before my wedding. It happened when each of my sons was born. It happened when my wife was in the hospital—and again a few days later when she came home. It happened the night before I started a new job.

I've spent years trying to understand the dream. Is Dad trying to connect with me, to assure me that he's still watching over the family? Is he reminding me to never let up, to never give in, to never give less than my best? Or is it just my subconscious, conjuring up a treasured memory when life hits unexpected bumps or critical forks in the road?

I have no idea, but I do know this — there are climbs in everyone's life. Some are literal, some figurative. Some are pleasant and mild, while others are cripplingly steep. Climbs seem less severe when we have someone to accompany us on the journey. For whatever reason, the dream always finds me when I need to see my dad. It never disappoints.

Ironically, I still ride my bike up that same climb every few weeks, though not as quickly as I did in my youth. The dream — and Dad — are never far from my mind. Even after all these years, occasionally I'll still look back over my shoulder, half-expecting to see him chasing me up the hill.

Someone once theorized that the dream is just a manifestation of residual grief. They explained that even though many years have passed, I'm still grieving for my dad, and that I'll stop having that dream eventually.

Just between you and me, I hope that day never comes. I don't ever want to stop doing that climb with him.

— Rob L. Berry —

Here to Shine

You have to be self-interested in order to be selfless.
You have to put yourself first if you want
to be of use to other people.
~Rachel Bartholomew

As an accounting professional, I know there are a few time periods each year when my life will be crazy. I can't schedule a vacation then, and I won't see much of my family or friends. I accept it and deal with it, as this is my chosen profession.

But when COVID-19 hit the U.S., my world flipped upside down.

Instantly, my role as a bookkeeper morphed from helping clients reconcile their ledgers to becoming their counselors. I became a shoulder to cry on. In some cases, clients felt I was their only hope to make it through the pandemic. They felt alone and scared, and they leaned on me.

The weight of that realization was so heavy I could hardly move. I was chained to my desk and computer for six weeks straight — ten- to twelve-hour days, seven days a week.

The enormity of what was happening took its toll. I couldn't let people down. I couldn't let clients lose their businesses because I didn't help. I couldn't leave them to fight this battle alone.

Nightmares became a regular part of life. I'd wake up in a cold sweat looking around the room, trying to snap back to reality. I lost weight. I didn't eat. My body felt as if it had been in a car crash. I didn't talk with friends or family. I just worked.

But one night I had a dream that not only changed my entire way of looking at this virus, but also changed the way I look at myself.

In my dream, I was running from someone — a stranger. I was running from room to room in an unfamiliar house. I didn't know where I was going. I was just running.

Random people from my work life appeared in my dream and said, "What are you doing?" Then I'd run out of that room and into another.

Someone else would say, "But wait, what are you doing?" Then I'd run out of that room, over and over, trying to find my way out.

The odd thing that stood out the most was the song playing throughout the dream. It was "Firework," written by Katy Perry and Ester Dean.

I woke up singing it. Okay, who doesn't love Katy Perry? But I found it curious. Why that song? In my nightmare?

I Googled it: "What does it mean when you dream about music?"

According to Dream Bible, "To dream of hearing music represents a theme to the type of emotions you are feeling."

These are the first lines of the song: "Do you ever feel like a plastic bag, drifting through the wind, wanting to start again. Do you ever feel, feel so paper thin, like a house of cards, one blow from caving in. Do you ever feel already buried deep, six feet under scream, but no one seems to hear a thing."

I felt chills. I'd heard that song a thousand times, but for the first time I listened to what it was saying. I actually heard the message.

It's easy to get lost in all the "have-tos" and "must-dos" in our lives. It's easy to get overwhelmed by the needs of others and want to help them. Until that moment, I felt that if I didn't drop everything and help someone in need, it made me a bad person.

But does it really? I run around on empty all the time, trying to fill up other people because that's what a good person does, right?

Maybe not.

My whole life, I've heard the saying: Love yourself before you can love others. It took a pandemic for those words to sink in.

My clients, friends and family are everything to me, but nowhere on that list of most important people is *me*.

I have to make time for me. I have to make time for what's important to me. And I have to find a way to be okay with that.

I'm starting to see that it's not an act of selfishness to take care of myself. If I take care of myself, I am a better, healthier, happier person for my friends, family, and clients.

I'm here to shine, but I can only do so if I take time for myself first. I need to make time for what lights me up so I can then shine for others.

I have to remember that I'm a firework. Fireworks are fragile. We have to handle them with care, or we could get hurt.

Now, I handle myself with the same care. Only then can I truly shine.

—Diana Lynn—

Who's Standing Beside My Bed?

You must take personal responsibility. You cannot change the circumstances, the seasons, or the wind, but you can change yourself.
~Jim Rohn

It's not often, thank goodness, that I dream someone has broken into my house. When such nightmares occur, the intruder is always a stranger — except for the unforgettable night when a person I knew better than anyone in the world was standing beside my bed.

The man I'd been married to for thirty-five years.

I found out my husband Greg was cheating on me in the worst way possible. I walked in on him and his girlfriend. He couldn't deny it. He couldn't say I misunderstood. He couldn't claim I hadn't seen what I most definitely saw.

I moved out. Filed for divorce. Tried to figure out how to live on my own for the first time in my life.

I won't pretend that navigating the world as a single woman was easy, especially at the age of sixty. Nights were the worst. Every little sound set my nerves on edge. The wind blowing through the trees. The cat scratching at the back door. The icemaker dumping a giant load of cubes into the bin. Those were the noises I heard before I climbed into bed. When I turned out the light, my unfamiliar new house became even more frightening. Some nights, I didn't sleep at all. On nights when I did, it was never deep enough to dream.

Until the night Greg came calling.

I had fallen into a blessedly solid sleep, only to awaken with my heart pounding. The streetlight shining through my window blinds cast just enough light to see a shadowy figure standing beside the bed. I knew I should reach down and grab the baseball bat I kept under the bed. Or open the nightstand drawer and pull out the can of wasp spray. Or find my phone and call 911. But I couldn't do any of those things. My body wouldn't move.

"Who are you?" I stammered. "And why are you in my room?"

"It's me," the figure said. "I can't believe you don't recognize me."

Of course, I knew his voice as soon as the words were spoken. "You're not supposed to be here!" I shouted. "Get out of my house!"

Greg laughed in a mean kind of way. "I don't see what you're getting so worked up about," he said. "I won't hurt you. You know I've never lifted a hand against you."

That's when I went from scared to angry. "No," I said. "You've never harmed me physically. But how dare you say you've never hurt me? And I'm not just talking about her." I went on to list the times I'd felt used, ignored and taken advantage of. I told him things I'd never said while were married, things I would have told a marriage counselor if only he'd agreed to our seeing one. How financially selfish he'd always been. How controlling. How emotionally unavailable.

Greg just stood there and listened.

"And one more thing," I told him. "When we got married, you promised to take care of me forever and ever. What about that?"

"Now it's your turn to listen," he said, in a voice so low I could barely make out his words. "Those days are over. We're finished. It's not my job to take care of you anymore. You're going to have to learn to do that yourself." And with that, the shadowy figure of the man I'd once loved with all my heart vanished into thin air.

Slowly, my arms and legs began to move. I opened my eyes, reached out from under the covers and turned on the bedside lamp. My heart rate calmed, and my breathing slowed. There was, of course, no intruder in my bedroom. I was alone. Maybe forever, maybe not.

But I knew one thing for sure: Greg's visit had been a dream, but it hadn't been a nightmare. He had said the very words I needed to hear.

"You're going to have to learn to take care of yourself."

And you know what? I have.

—Jean Morris—

Chapter
2

Divine
Guidance

Chicken Soup for the Soul

Kathy's Dream

*We have the choice to use the gift of our life to make
the world a better place — or not to bother.*
~Jane Goodall

I was working on a middle-grade novel based on the lives of chimpanzees, a fanciful and magical rendition of what one might expect to find in the jungles. In order to expand the reality of chimpanzees while writing my book I needed to understand them. I devoured almost every book written by Dr. Jane Goodall, a famous primatologist.

After stalking her website, I went to Washington, D.C. to hear her speak about her experiences with chimpanzees. One day, while perusing her website, I stumbled across the opportunity to complete a six-month internship with the Jane Goodall Institute (JGI) in Tanzania, East Africa.

Something welled inside me—a blend of longing and knowing. Despite having a full-time job as a consultant, a car payment, a mortgage, and a boyfriend, I just knew I had to go.

I was offered an unpaid internship after applying.

My logical mind interceded. "You can't leave. It's not feasible, not logical. What are you going to do with your house and your life?" The whispers were relentless, so I hesitated and prayed.

I wanted a definitive answer to my questions about why this trip meant so much to me. Why did I have so much fear, and what would happen if I let go of my current version of life?

Weeks went by, and my mind and heart remained in conflict. With just two and a half weeks before I was due to leave, I had not made a decision. I had only told a close circle of friends. If I am honest, I probably would have let indecision play out until it was too late to take action. But then came the dream — Kathy's dream.

I arrived at work on a Monday still gripped by paralyzing fear. My co-worker Kathy said, "Hey, when you have a second, come to my office because I have the weirdest dream to share with you. It makes no sense at all."

"Okay." I laughed and told her I would return.

Later, I plopped into her office chair. She again prefaced the conversation by saying it didn't make sense, but she felt she had to tell it to me.

"You left work very quickly and without any notice," she said, launching *into the telling of the dream.*

Being aware of my two-week window to leave, I leaned forward with growing interest, especially since she and my other co-workers had no idea I was considering quitting my job and heading off to Africa.

She continued. "Everyone at work began getting upset and nervous about your whereabouts, and I was assigned to lead the search committee. I searched in grocery stores, restaurants, shops — everywhere — but I could not find you.

"Finally, I found you on a huge yacht running a large enterprise. People were moving all around you, packing boxes and sending them off the vessel. Your skin was glowing, and your hair was flowing in the wind. You were the most beautiful version of yourself.

"I told you that you needed to return to work, and people were worried about you. But you responded that there are things more important than work, and you needed to take a leap because life was about taking chances. You said that you would never return, and you didn't care that people were sad because you were living in your truth."

She said that I often stopped my interactions with the team to encourage her to join me, but she refused. She said, "You would call me spineless and explain that life is short, and I needed to join you in taking a chance and stepping into purpose."

My mouth fell open. That dream answered every question that I had been praying about. It was unbelievable. When I informed Kathy, she joined me in puzzlement. The message had been delivered, and I would never be the same.

At first, I wondered why the dream had not come to me, but then I remembered that I was so full of anxiety that I was having nightmares instead. Such a dream probably couldn't manifest through the clutter of my mind. Why didn't it come through a close, personal friend? One of my friends helped me realize the answer. She explained that if she had said it to me, it would not have been as powerful because she knew all about my potential trip. No, the best, most convincing dream was the unsolicited one by the unknowing co-worker.

That dream clinched it. That same day, I drove to my company headquarters and met with my manager to hand in my resignation. I had no way to pay any of my bills and no plan for doing so. But I did have a knowing in my heart to walk through my fear, take on a new adventure, and become more aligned to my purpose. I was going to answer the call no matter what.

Within two weeks, I had posted my house for rent on Craigslist, moved all of my essential items into storage, packed for my six-month trip, said goodbye to bewildered friends and family (some who thought I was making a mistake), and boarded a plane to Tanzania.

I remember that twenty-four-hour trip. My heart pounded with nervousness and excitement — unsure of who or what I would find at my destination.

During my six-month internship, I slowly filled my soul. I met wonderful friends and completed several community projects for JGI, including teaching at an orphanage and building a community garden. I also visited Gombe and the wonderful staff there who took us chimpanzee tracking, sometimes on our bellies and elbows through the thick brush to view the chimpanzees I had only read about.

I learned basic Swahili, went on safari, and lived some common experiences of being in Tanzania, like squat toilets and crowded, colorful open-market places. For me, the icing on the cake was that I got to stay in the house with Jane Goodall for two weeks. Initially, I was told she would not be arriving during my stay, but then she decided to spend what little time she had off visiting with her family who lived at the compound where we stayed.

Although we interns respected Jane's space and understood she was introspective by nature, I was honored to be welcomed to some of her dinners where she purchased local Indian cuisine and hosted various innovative and interesting guests. It was like having a seat at a table of masters, or so I felt.

I will always carry the lessons and the light of those memories in my heart. I experienced immeasurable growth in learning how to listen to the desires of my soul, how to vanquish fear and being open to new adventures.

Despite the wishes of some family members who called me often to encourage my early return home, I learned what I was made of, who I was as a person, and what I was willing to sacrifice to reset my life and direction.

Those six months solidified what I only faintly believed to be my calling. I was now sure of my purpose to help and love people, and to document those lessons with words — either through my writings or my podcast, which was inspired by my experiences there. I was meant to shift people's consciousness in a similar way to which I had been transformed.

Looking back, I don't think my journey was specifically about the trip itself as much as it was about learning to own my own power. I had to travel thousands of miles to do that because my previous life and the rat race of it all would not have allowed for this reflection. So much happened during my stay, and all of it contributed to the most wonderful unfolding of my highest life lessons — all set in motion by Kathy's dream.

— Keisha M. Reynolds —

A Dream About a Dream

Pay attention to your dreams — God's angels often
speak directly to our hearts when we are asleep.
~Eileen Elias Freeman,
The Angels' Little Instruction Book

My family immigrated to Canada when I was about a year old. In those early years, we didn't have much. Our home was a simple rented apartment furnished with hand-me-downs and thrift-store finds. There certainly wasn't enough money for expensive outings, so our weekends were filled with simple pleasures we could do for free, like picnics, bike rides, and my favorite — trips to the library.

Thanks to the library's children's section, I fell in love with stories — silly ones, moving ones, and even educational ones. I'd have my parents read the books we borrowed over and over until we needed to return them, or I'd page through them myself, imagining the stories in my head, even though I was too young to read the words.

When I was about five years old and finally starting to read on my own, I had a curious thought: I knew we could get books from the library or buy them in stores if we had the money, but where did books come from?

I asked my mother this question, to which she replied that the stories I loved were created in the imaginations of people called "writers." These people then wrote them down so they could be shared with others.

Four decades later, I still remember that moment. It was as though I'd been struck by lightning. Then and there, I knew my purpose in this world. I would be one of those writers. I would create stories and share them with the world.

As a young child, I began by making up stories about animals or my toys, dictating them to my grandmother since I hadn't yet mastered the skill to write them down myself. When I grew a little older, I filled countless notebooks with words and illustrations. For a time, I even published my own little newspaper with a circulation of my immediate family.

I didn't know a thing about the writing profession or the skills involved in the craft, but I kept writing all the same, figuring I'd somehow learn these things over the years.

As I grew into adolescence, I did start to learn some of the required skills. I learned grammar and basic story structure first in school, and then through writing books.

Meanwhile, I watched my peers struggle with what they wanted to do once they were grown. I knew I was luckier than they were. I'd always known what I was meant to do in life, and I kept at it, getting my homework done quickly each day so I could write for the rest of the evening. In this way, I completed my first attempt at a novel by fourteen. It was a challenge to see if I could write a book-length story from start to finish, even if it wasn't very good.

Despite my dedication to this dream, I'd heard repeatedly from the adults in my life that writing was a difficult way to make a living. One day, I'd have bills to pay, and I'd need a reliable income to do so.

The research I did into the writing business seemed to confirm this. Sure, there were writers who were very successful — some even rich and famous. But most spent years trying to succeed and generally did so while working "day jobs."

I began to think that maybe I should have a backup plan. I began to doubt my dream.

One thing I knew was that whatever I did, it would have to be in the arts. Art was the one thing I was good at. I considered several options, ultimately settling on photography. It was something I'd been doing as a hobby already, and I could see myself working as a nature photographer while writing on the side.

After graduating high school and working for a time to save up money to supplement my student loan, I went off to college to study photography. This was still in the days of film and dark rooms, and I enjoyed the challenge of developing and printing in total darkness. College was very demanding, though, and didn't leave me a lot of spare time. Because of this, my writing fell by the wayside a little — and then a lot.

Eventually, I graduated, and it came time to find that job that would allow me to pay my bills. But there weren't great jobs available where I lived for someone fresh out of school. All I could find was work assisting other photographers, mostly shooting things like weddings or school pictures — a far cry from the nature photographer I'd imagined I'd be.

I was the child of immigrants, though. I knew sometimes you had to start at the bottom and be patient getting to where you ultimately wanted to be. If I just kept at it, in time I might start my own business and photograph what I wanted. I had college loans to pay back, after all.

But the truth was, I wasn't happy. Work became a slog, and I stopped writing altogether. Then one night, I had a dream.

I saw myself back in college, in the old dark room. I moved through the room toward the chemical trays in which we developed prints. As I approached, I could see the various chemical baths, photo paper already in them. But then I noticed that instead of photo paper, the paper in the trays were the printed pages of a novel I'd been working on before I'd stopped writing. The chemicals were damaging them. I could see the ink running and the paper falling apart.

I woke up and immediately understood what my dream was trying to tell me. I was focusing on this photography career while my dream of becoming a writer fell apart. It wasn't making me happy. It wasn't what I was meant to be doing.

This dream changed everything. I quit photography and went back to college to study journalism. There I met my husband. This course gave me the skills that got me work as a copyeditor after graduation, first for a major magazine and later as a freelancer. These skills were also transferable to writing fiction.

After a few years of helping to pay the bills, I was able to quit my day job and dedicate myself to writing fiction full-time. Today, I have several published stories out in the world for others to enjoy. One day, I hope to publish a book. But I wouldn't be where I am if it hadn't been for that dream that reminded me about a little girl's certainty of her purpose in life and the importance of living your dream.

— P.A. Cornell —

14

What Dreams May Come

Words could never tell the joy an uncle brings.
An uncle is a bond of faith that even time can't sever,
a gift to last all of our lives. An uncle is forever.
~Irene Banks

U ncle Gary was one of my favorite people. He had a cowboy mentality and was a hard worker. He could fix anything and always had grease- or motor-oil-stained fingertips. He had a quiet strength about him.

He was like a second father to me, and to my husband he was like the father he always dreamed of.

My husband, Daniel, and I had a roller-coaster marriage. It was bumpy. Our hardest year was our fifteenth. We stopped talking. We fought constantly, and I was ready to call it quits. I had completely checked out of my marriage. My husband had, too. We knew that if we didn't fix what was broken, divorce was the next step.

Uncle Gary also passed away that year.

One night, I had a dream that Daniel and I were at Uncle Gary's house. The sounds and smells were so real that I felt like it wasn't a dream at all. My uncle said, "You two come outside with me and let me show you what I've been working on."

We followed Uncle Gary to his shop table where there were parts to something scattered all around. He picked up a few pieces and tried to puzzle them together. He handed a piece to Daniel and then a piece to me.

He looked straight at us and said, "If you don't have the right tool, you can't fix it. It can't be fixed without the right tools." He kept saying this to us until we assured him that we would find the right tool.

I had this dream four nights in a row — exactly the same dream every night.

Since my husband and I were barely talking to each other, I didn't tell him about the dream. On the fifth night, Daniel mentioned that he was really missing Uncle Gary. Having a wall up, I shrugged and said simply, "Me, too." After a few moments of silence, Daniel began to tell me about a dream he had about Uncle Gary every night for the previous four nights. Every detail, every word was the exact dream I had.

We both broke down and sobbed uncontrollably. Then, we did something we hadn't in years: We talked all night. We fixed what was broken, and the right tool was communication. My uncle knew we wanted to fix it. We just needed a little bit of help.

— Lindsay Brown —

15

Love and Purpose

In the process of letting go you will lose many things
from the past, but you will find yourself.
~Deepak Chopra

"Is everything okay?" Trina asked as we walked toward the park. I wasn't sure how to answer, but I couldn't say that everything was fine. Trina knew me better than that.

"I had a weird dream last night," I told her.

Trina looked concerned. "What was it about?"

I stopped for a minute, trying to figure out how to respond. There weren't any scenes or events in the dream. That's why it had felt so strange, almost not a dream. "It felt like a bunch of voices speaking a language I couldn't understand, but somehow I knew what language it was."

She cocked her head and raised an eyebrow, waiting for me to finish.

"They were people from India," I told her.

"Do you think the dream meant something?" she prompted.

I felt tears spring to my eyes unexpectedly. Blinking them back, I started walking again. I was afraid of the meaning, but I couldn't deny it. "I got the feeling I'm meant to go to India," I told her. I had had dreams of moving to Ireland or Scotland, maybe becoming a midwife like my mom. But India? I had no plans to even visit.

My friend didn't laugh. We were both daughters of former missionaries, both entering our adult years, trying to figure out our direction in life. My parents had lived in India when I was very young, but I hardly remembered it. I had mainly grown up in central California and moved to Southern California the previous year after graduating from high school.

There was another impression the dream had left me with, but I didn't have the courage to share that part with Trina. It felt too personal and specific. I decided to keep that part to myself.

"Why don't you give it some time?" Trina suggested. "Maybe talk to a few others about it. What about Angie?" Angie was a mutual friend who had spent a year in southern India and had recently returned.

"I'll do that," I told her. I had mixed feelings, but as the days went by, I couldn't forget the dream or the strong impression it made on me. I started making plans to visit India. To my delight, Trina decided to come along. A few other friends joined us, and it felt like an adventure as we landed in Bombay (now called Mumbai) and adjusted to the changes in weather, culture and lifestyle.

Then, almost before the adventure started, it was nearing its end. Trina had only gotten a three-month visa, and our friends decided to stay only as long as she did. When they returned to California, I stayed in India, somehow knowing this was what I was meant to do. Although I began volunteering my time in tutoring and other social work projects, I felt aimless and homesick.

One rainy day in early monsoon, I got a phone call from a friend of Trina's. Her voice broke as she told me the news. Trina had been bicycling on a mountain road and had been hit by a truck. After twelve hours in a coma, she passed away. My vision clouded, and it felt as though someone had sucked the oxygen from the room where I sat, unable to respond to the voice on the other end of the line. I managed to get out a word or two and ended the call.

The next few days passed in a haze. I couldn't get through a conversation without crying. I had no appetite. I just wanted to go home, but I knew nothing would be the same again, no matter where I went.

Why did she have to die? The question burned inside me. There was so much she wanted to do. She had talked about adopting a dozen boys or starting a school in some remote place where children didn't have the chance for education.

One night, tossing and turning in the oppressive humidity, I fell into a restless sleep.

I woke with a start, knowing I had had a dream, an important one, but I couldn't remember the details. It was beautiful, but not a single scene remained in my mind. All that stayed with me was a single phrase spoken by a voice I knew well.

Trina's voice.

She said, "If you only knew..." She didn't finish the thought, but the feeling behind her words was full of joy and awe. I knew that she was in a place of perfection and beauty.

I sat up in bed and looked outside my window at the early dawn in a land that I didn't call home. One day, I would be home, but I knew I couldn't leave India. If nothing else, I had to make a difference for Trina's sake. I had to live as she would have lived — with a sense of purpose. I needed to do it for both of us, even though I was comforted by the thought that she was happy and content.

I traveled to southern India to attend a conference for young people, many of them foreign volunteers looking for a place to settle in and a ministry to devote themselves to. I attended a workshop by a man named Ajay from New Delhi who worked with deaf people. He mentioned that there were over ten million deaf people in India, and that many of them did not have opportunities for education and training. He had started more than a dozen deaf friendship clubs in and around New Delhi, where deaf people could join a community with others who had shared common experiences. They also received training, education, and various kinds of assistance from Ajay and his co-workers.

After the workshop, I approached Ajay and introduced myself. I told him I had taken several classes and knew some American Sign Language.

"Why don't you come visit us?" he asked. "There are plenty of ways you could get involved in the work. You really could make a difference."

He sent his friend Daniel to pick me up by train so I wouldn't have to travel to New Delhi alone. I went for a visit, but I ended up staying. India became my home for the next decade.

Remember the part of the dream I didn't want to share with Trina? I had been embarrassed because it seemed like nothing more than a young woman's foolish hope: that India was the place where I would meet my future husband, and that he was waiting for me there.

Two years after Daniel picked me up at a crowded train station not far from Bombay, he took my hand, and we exchanged vows. He had been waiting for me.

— Bonita Jewel —

16

What They'll Remember

I have a wonderful shelter, which is my family.
~José Carreras

A few days before COVID-19 took center stage in the United States, we self-quarantined our family of seven. At the time, I was having confusing dreams and waking up in the middle of the night covered in sweat. An avid dreamer, I often find confirmations of my waking intuition in my dreams. Still, confusing dreams are unusual for me.

That whole week, my dreams had a recurring theme. *I was staring in the bathroom mirror. The "other" me smiled and spoke calmly, but I couldn't understand what she was saying.*

Later that week, in the wee hours of shared concern, my husband and I agreed it was time for our family to react to (what was clearly becoming) a national pandemic.

We are no strangers to action plans for respiratory illnesses. Many members of our family, including my husband and me, have compromised health. Congenital heart issues, autoimmune disease and asthma are all part of our family's everyday lives.

Last year's case of strep throat had exasperated our most medically compromised child's health and landed her in the hospital. We were worried. For our family, a pandemic could literally mean life or death.

"There's no longer a way of shielding them from how serious this is," I said.

In the middle of the night, ahead of the rest of our nation, we made a drastic adjustment to our lives. We wouldn't wait for the anticipated school closures. We would pull our five kids from school immediately and self-quarantine our entire family.

We sat in the silence of the monumental decision. We knew we were experiencing a significant moment in history and in the story of our family.

"You okay?" my husband asked.

"Yeah," I sighed. "It's just a lot of pressure. They'll remember this their entire lives."

My mom brain was going a mile a minute. I was barely managing a full-time at-home job, five kids, our medical needs and our everyday lives. How would I add the stress of a pandemic and virtual schooling without totally losing it?

That night I had trouble falling asleep. My mind was preoccupied with our forthcoming conversation with the kids about the situation. Anxieties over health and mortality were already a stress on our children. Sharing the severity of the situation — without frightening them — was going to be like walking a parenting tightrope. This conversation (and the weeks to follow) would be a defining moment in their childhoods and my motherhood. They'd remember how we loved, fought, prayed, cried and laughed.

Once I fell asleep, I dreamed again of looking in the bathroom mirror. The "other" me was smiling again, and this time, when she spoke I understood her.

"Remember," she said.

I woke myself up screaming, "Remember what?"

I quickly jotted "Remember" in my nightstand journal. The following day, I worried that I'd missed an important item on the to-do list from my subconscious.

That afternoon, our youngest daughter interrupted me while I was working in the bedroom.

"Let's bake something," she said. "I want to learn to make frosting!"

"This isn't a vacation," I snapped at her. "I still have to work, and now you're all here all day! I can't bake on a workday."

Her face fell. Her bottom lip quivered like it does when she's trying not to cry. She stomped out and left me with my computer, feeling like a failure. It was day one of the quarantine, and I had already snapped at a child about how stressful this was for *me*.

Usually, I like to jump right in and help, with either a solution or a reminder that most problems aren't that bad. I needed to analyze my own behavior. I recalled my dream and pulled out my journal to examine the question I had written. Below "Remember what?" I added: "Remember that this virus is contagious, and so is my reaction."

I felt relieved and ready to "reset" our quarantine. I had figured out what the "me" in the mirror was trying to say, and I had a plan for my attitude about the pandemic.

I called my daughter back into the bedroom, and we researched cream cheese frosting recipes. When she found the perfect one, she grabbed my nightstand journal.

"Can I write it in your important notebook, Mama?" she asked. "You write all the things you promise you'll do in there."

She took my journal and diligently copied the recipe.

That night, I went to bed feeling confident. Then, I had the dream again.

I woke up feeling defeated and frustrated. I thought I'd figured out my dream and my approach to the quarantine.

Again, I wrote "Remember WHAT?" in my journal. This time, it was next to a recipe for cream cheese frosting.

Throughout the first weeks of the quarantine, I had some version of that dream a few more times. About a month in, on a particularly difficult day, my husband was especially frustrated. The homeschooling, working, uncertainty and fear had overwhelmed him. He was grumbling at the kids about some minor issue.

"When you get like this and I know you need a break, what do you want me to do?" I asked.

"Just tell me to remember," he said. "In these moments, I need to remember how trivial the things that upset me really are."

I was taken aback. I hadn't told him about my dreams, so I was surprised at his wording.

As he left the room to take a break, I noticed our youngest daughter sitting on the couch, paying close attention.

"I'll remember, Mama," she said.

Oh, no! Another parenting fail, I thought.

"We make cream cheese frosting and bake in the kitchen a lot now," she said.

"Really, honey?" I responded. "That's what you'll remember about this whole thing?"

"Yeah, Mama," she said. "I'll remember dessert every night!"

That night, I opened my journal. Right next to that frosting recipe (in my daughter's handwriting), I crossed out the question mark and completed the sentence: "Remember dessert."

I haven't had the dream since, but we've eaten a lot of dessert with homemade cream cheese frosting.

— Holly Rutchik —

17

Gentle Nudges

Never stop dreaming.
Wake up and chase your dreams.
~Gift Gugu Mona

Two years ago, my husband took a new job, requiring us to move from our home in Texas to Washington, D.C. It wasn't an easy move, and that's saying a lot since we are a retired military family and used to moving often.

The family part was the problem. No one would be moving with us. All our children were grown and on their own. This move would be different, just the two of us, my husband and me.

We left behind our grown children, beautiful granddaughters, and aging parents. It felt worse than being an empty nester because I believed my husband and I had flown the coop and abandoned everyone! When we sat down for dinner in our new home, just my husband and me in our big, empty house, I thought the quiet was going to swallow me whole. I didn't know how to navigate and survive this transition.

Then the dreams began.

At first, I tried ignoring them. After all, how many times can a person be accepted to graduate school, run away from the opportunity, and hope to knock on the door again?

I had discovered my passion for writing thirty years ago while working on my English undergrad degree. I fell in love with children's literature and knew that's what I wanted to do with my life: write for children. But life kept me busy, and my dream was shoved to the back burner.

Two decades later, I thought working toward my MFA would jumpstart my writing or at least hold me accountable and make me sit down and write. So I applied and was accepted into a low-residency program. The workload, however, seemed daunting in light of our constant moves and busy family life, so I declined.

Then I spent years vacillating, looking at and applying to MFA programs. Twice, I even began programs and went to first residencies. The second time, I hightailed it home after only a few days and knew I would never apply to school again. I had closed that door.

So why, just months later, shortly after we'd moved to D.C., was I dreaming of school again? Was I losing my mind?

The dreams persisted. One morning, I awakened from dreaming that I had contacted the last university's writing department, asked to rejoin, and was reinstated. The dream had shaken me. It was too vivid to ignore. So, before I even crawled out of bed or could change my mind, I reached for my cell phone and dashed off an e-mail asking what I would need to do to reapply, certain they'd scornfully laugh at me for even contacting them again. Hours passed. No reply, as I expected.

Later that afternoon, my husband and I went to the grocery store. In the produce aisle, I admitted I had looked into re-applying to school. He wasn't angry — that isn't our relationship at all — but normally we talk over such big decisions beforehand. He went one way to think. I went the other.

Minutes later, in the dairy section, my cell phone rang. Hamline University. I answered, expecting the program's administrative assistant I'd e-mailed to be on the other end of the line. Instead, it was the program director. By the end of our five-minute conversation, after I explained the turn of events in my life, the dreams, and how I needed the program, she invited me back. I would begin coursework in January, exactly as my dream foretold.

It's funny how life works when we keep moving forward, listening to and honoring our dreams — those from our sleep and those we aspire to in our waking hours. My husband and I are a little more settled in our new home and, at least for a while, have family to share it with, too! Our son is redirecting career paths and is temporarily living at home. One of our daughters has recently moved much closer as she embarks on a career, thanks in part to a leadership program with her dad's employer.

Although we see our other daughter and the rest of our family a little less frequently than when we all lived in Texas, we still get together often and keep in touch via phone, e-mail and texting. And my husband has been my greatest supporter as I have worked toward my goal. I am in the last semester of earning my MFA in Writing for Children, working on my creative thesis. The program has helped me grow in ways I never realized I needed to grow and has allowed me to work under many wonderful mentors and make lifelong friends in the process.

Has the road been easy? Not at all! The work has been every bit as challenging as I expected it would be. Plus, first semester, I cracked a tooth munching on popcorn while studying and had to have it pulled. Second semester, I contended with a bout of kidney stones. Third semester, our son had back surgery, and I developed clots in my legs from all the hours I spend sitting and writing. And last summer, as I was preparing my critical thesis lecture to present during residency, our younger daughter ended up in the hospital. I flew to Texas, brought my work with me, and completed it while sitting at her side, all the while not knowing if she would be well enough for me to attend residency and present my lecture.

I was able to attend residency and presented on my topic of Hope in Children's Literature. From this study, I learned about the importance of setting goals and achieving them through pathways (the actions and roads we take to reach our goals) and agency (the willpower to keep going despite tough times), and how we have to be proactive and take charge of and responsibility for our own lives and happiness.

I've also learned that not everything we view as setbacks are setbacks. Sometimes, they are opportunities in disguise, like the move with my husband to Washington, D.C., the catalyst that sent me back to school and allowed me to finally realize a lifelong dream. Life is not meant to be stagnant. Life is meant to be lived, for us to keep learning and growing.

And dreams? I don't know from where our dreams come, especially those that guide and direct us. Maybe they're from our Creator. Or, perhaps, from angels or our ancestors keeping watch over us. Maybe it's just our own soul whispering what it already knows. But I do know that dreams can be gifts, gentle nudges that keep us moving forward.

— Tracey Sherman —

18

Flying with Red

The wind of heaven is that which blows
between a horse's ears.
~Arabian Proverb

When I was a teenager, I was besotted with horses. We lived in the city, so owning a horse was just a fantasy. Still, I read all the horse storybooks, and my daydreams and night dreams were of racing across meadows or jumping high fences. In my dreams, I tamed the Black Stallion, befriended Flicka, or raced a stampeding herd across a prairie.

In real life, I was a bit shy around horses. I went to a place where one could rent a very tame horse. I would ride for an hour or so in a group with a guide. Knowing the immense power of the animal under me had me shaking. But, in my dreams, I was one with my wild stallion, my hands gripping a lashing mane as we raced along.

I did have one disturbing dream where I was not in control and hung on for dear life to my out-of-control steed. My only thought was "Don't fall off." We raced along rocky dirt roads, and jumped bushes and logs through a marshy, mucky place. I was terrified.

I woke from that dream in a cold sweat, and every muscle in my body ached with the dreaming effort of not falling off the horse.

I was a bit reticent after that terrifying dream to even try the rent-a-pony rides I was used to. But after a month or so, when autumn was ablaze and the weather was unseasonably warm, my mother took me out to the trail-riding place.

"I know this might be your last ride before snow," my mother said, letting me out of the car. "But the weather is perfect, and the leaves should be glorious out there along the river. Pick your favorite horse and enjoy your outing. I know you love them so. I'll be back afterward to pick you up." And she drove off.

The ranch was crowded. Everyone must have had the same idea to ride along the river path while the leaves spangled the trail with their last color before the coming winter. Most of the horses were already picked by other riders. My favorite, an extremely gentle old guy named, of all things, Buckeroo, was already carrying another rider.

"You've been out here a lot," our guide said, as I looked over the remaining horses. "I saved Red for you. You should be up to it."

Red. Not my favorite. He was a younger horse who shook his head a lot, whipping his mane around when his rider might want to go a certain way and he did not. And Red was fast. If the horses got it into their heads to hurry back to the barn at the end of the ride, Red was always first.

The guide led us out onto the trail. I knew this trail. I had ridden this trail often during my summer outings. And, for once, Red seemed to be listening, paying attention, as I tested his response to my leg and hand signals. He sometimes fidgeted along, prancing, tossing his head.

Suddenly, there was a commotion behind me. I had not seen the horse at the end of our line do anything wrong, but the rider was on the ground.

The guide stopped us and went back to see what was wrong. The rider, a girl of ten or so, was on the ground, not moving much, but something was clearly wrong. Her friends, who had come with her on this ride, said the girl was diabetic. She sometimes had her sugar out of whack. Her friends gave her some of the sugar tablets she always carried.

"But someone needs to go call her parents to come and pick her up," one of her friends said.

The guide sought me out. "Take Red back to the barn and have someone there inform her parents." He had already turned back to tending to the girl and never heard my silent plea. *But I'm afraid…*

I spent a moment in terror before turning Red toward home. I gave him the slightest tightening of my leg, which he understood not as "Go a bit faster," but "Run like the wind!"

He broke into a full-out gallop, and I hung on for dear life.

His head was low, and his hooves thundered. Sticks and leaves flew up at our passing, and I barely got my head down in time to avoid getting whipped by low branches. I knew I was going to die.

I hung onto the reins and managed to guide Red along the right trail to the barn area. He plunged through the mucky part, and I thought I would fall, but I didn't. My brain, somehow, remembered lessons from the guide, and Red was obeying. My legs gripped his sides, my hands held the reins and guided his headlong dash — and we flew. I was living my dream. Tree branches swooshed by, and leaves twirled in our breeze.

It seemed like no time at all had passed as we raced into the barnyard. The girl's parents were in their car, waiting, and dashed out when I brought Red to a plunging halt. Everyone there hurried into action, and the farm truck took the girl's parents out to the trail.

Things quieted down. I dismounted and patted Red.

"Well done, my friend," I said to him, giving his sweaty neck a hug.

The girl was okay. Her parents always carried insulin and other medicine with them. The riders and the guide came back, the horses' saddles were taken off, and the horses were turned out into a pasture. The other riders met their rides home and left. My parents came for me.

"Good job," the guide said to me as I started toward my parents' car. "Who d'ya want to ride next time?"

"Red," I replied. "He's my dream horse come true."

"Gotcha," he said, touching his hat brim in a salute.

— NancyLee Davis —

19

Golden Faith

*Believe in your heart that you're meant to live a life full
of passion, purpose, magic and miracles.*
~Roy T. Bennett, The Light in the Heart

isney's Cinderella proclaims that a dream is a wish your heart makes when you're fast asleep. That line rang true for me when I was going through an exceptionally difficult time in my life. On top of my own cancer diagnosis, my brother was rapidly declining in his own battle with the disease. There was little hope that he would survive the week.

A friend invited my husband and me to some dirt-bike races to take our minds off things. For the most part, I dressed casually and comfortably for the event. There was one exception. I wore a chain with a solid gold groundhog on it because it bore a special dual meaning to me.

First, February 2nd — Groundhog Day — was my due date according to my mother. I was born weeks late, but still felt there was something significant about that day. That was confirmed when I began my spiritual journey with the Lord on that day as an adult. My friend knew the special significance of that day, so had the pendant made for me.

We had a long but fun-filled day spanning over twelve hours. During that time, whether it was walking or driving an all-terrain vehicle, we covered between fifty and 100 acres. It wasn't until nearly midnight that I discovered my gold groundhog had fallen off its chain.

To say I was devastated was an understatement. On top of all the loss in my life, I felt like I had lost a part of myself as well. It was almost like it was a further assault on my life.

Everyone close to me, sensing my distress, helped me search for my lost treasure, but it was no use. It was dark, and other than the dim lights from the stars, it was just too difficult to see. Even though they promised to resume their search at first light, I headed home with a heavy heart, knowing that it was impossible.

Fortunately, sleep came quickly that evening. But there was one interruption. *I dreamt that I was back at the racecourse. While I didn't see anything odd in my dream, I clearly heard a voice say, "If you return, you will find it."* (Yes, I know this is reminiscent of the movie *Field of Dreams*, but take that up with the dream master, not me.)

The next morning, I got dressed and prepared to head out to the hospital to see my brother. I had written off my dream as nothing more than wishful thinking. But even as we traveled down the road, I could not shake a nagging feeling. Finally, I convinced my husband to head back to the race site.

When we pulled up, we saw about twenty people walking around. A few approached me as I exited the car. "We've been looking for hours. You just aren't going to find it. It is worse than a needle in a haystack," they said.

I knew they were right. Sighing, I walked a few feet from the car to stretch my legs before continuing my journey to the hospital. As I turned around, I saw a glimpse of something shiny in the dirt that caught my attention. It was the groundhog! Despite overwhelming odds, it had made its way back to me.

I knew I still had a long and trying road ahead, but somehow finding my treasure renewed my hope and faith. I knew that no matter what happened, I was going to be okay because I had a greater power watching over me.

A dream had turned into a miracle. The impossible had become possible. And just like Pennsylvania's Punxsutawney Phil often predicts, my groundhog showed me that my spring was just around the corner.

— Pastor Wanda Christy-Shaner —

20

House of My Dream

Don't be pushed by your problems.
Be led by your dreams.
~Ralph Waldo Emerson

My husband and I bought what we thought was our dream home — a Frank Lloyd Wright–style house in Texas with a gorgeous live oak tree gracing the front yard. After extensive renovations, we moved in. One week later, our joints started aching, and we felt as if we'd aged ten years. The culprit? Extreme allergies from live oak pollen. We desperately needed to find a new home — fast.

Thus began the dreaded search for a house with no live oaks, an almost impossible task in a city where these enormous trees shaded nearly every yard. Our caring, enthusiastic real estate agent was determined to find the perfect house for us. But as eager as we were to leave the terrible allergies behind, we were equally determined not to be pressured into buying another home that was not a good fit for us.

That resolve was underscored one Sunday morning at church after several exhausting weeks of nonstop house hunting. Our desire to hold out for the ideal house had begun to wane, and I felt myself starting to cave in to our highly motivated salesperson's timetable.

As I stood to sing, a strong voice rose inside me: "Don't buy a house just to buy one."

It was a clear directive.

However, our successful "top sales" agent thought we needed to accomplish the goal of finding a new house quickly. When that failed to happen, her caring morphed into pushing. Because our goals no longer aligned, we made a mutual decision to part ways.

A few days later, this recent parting occupied my mind as I stumbled back to bed following a middle-of-the-night bathroom trip. I sent a heartfelt petition heavenward, asking for help in finding a new real estate agent. When my alarm went off, I was jolted out of a deep sleep. Stunned, I awoke to something extraordinary.

I lay still, my mind flooded with the memory of a vivid dream — rich details of pulling up to a two-story home and entering a lovely foyer. More images emerged: elegant arched doorways, hardwood floors, high ceilings. "This is exactly the house we have been looking for!" I cried out in my dream.

I reached over, picked up my notebook, and recorded as much of it as I could remember. Believing God speaks through dreams just as He did in biblical times, my husband and I had kept dream journals for years.

I was beyond excited. I had lifted up one prayer, but God had answered an even bigger one. There was just one problem: I had no address. How would I find the house?

Hoping to locate it, I scanned listings online — even For Sale by Owner homes that are occasionally advertised — but nothing came close. I called my husband, who was out of town on business, and shared the dream with him. The next afternoon took me to a nearby doctor's office for a weekly allergy shot. On the way back, I asked for guidance to the house of my dream. Slowly, prayerfully, I turned down one street and then another, scanning for vital "For Sale" signs in yards of two-story homes. Nada.

Then, I rounded a corner and saw it — a stately, two-story yellow brick house with a For Sale by Owner sign in front. Could this be the one? With my hand shaking, I copied down the phone number and then drove straight home and called the owner.

An answering machine took my call. After several anxious hours, an older woman called back and set up an appointment for the next morning. As we were about to end the conversation, she asked, "By the way, what time did you see the house?"

Not an odd question, perhaps, except I'd heard it before — spoken in my dream!

"Around 4:30," I responded. "Why?"

"Great," she said. "You saw my For Sale by Owner sign before I listed the house with my friend at 5 p.m. That means I can sell it directly to you and save the commission."

I hung up, taken aback. Our conversation precisely mirrored a mystifying one in my dream and explained why it was not listed online. Yet, I was miraculously led to the house anyway. I slept very little that night.

It felt like déjà vu as I walked into the entryway the next morning and looked around in wonderment, enveloped by beauty and light. It was an enchanting old home built in 1927, full of the now familiar arched doorways, original floors, tall ceilings and windows from my dream. As I walked through the home, it checked almost all of the boxes on our wish list. Clearly, it was the dream house we were meant to find. My excitement was tinged with mounting anxiety because the house was now listed in the Multiple Listing Service, and the whole world would know about this delightful gem.

I called my husband as soon as I returned home. "What do you think we should do?" I asked, barely able to breathe.

"Make an offer on it today!" he practically shouted.

My heart was pounding. Things were moving way too fast.

We had no real estate agent and needed one quickly — the reason for my early morning prayer in the first place. One whom I had recently met and trusted came to mind. I called, and she agreed to work with us on negotiations.

After my husband returned the next day, the three of us toured it. Even though our current house had not yet sold, we made the tough decision to buy the new one. We never regretted it.

We loved living in that beautiful home with its thirty-two tall, elegant windows that filled it with natural light — and no live oaks in the yard. We made significant upgrades, and it grieved us to sell it twelve years later to move to another state. We believed it was a gift given to us in a dream, after all, and we wanted to pass it on to someone who would treasure it as much as we had.

We left a "What We Love about This House" flyer on the dining-room table for potential buyers, describing its numerous assets, and included a special reference to finding it as the result of a dream.

The third couple who came to see it bought it. A few days later, we sat in the real estate agent's office feeling a little sad about selling when a letter arrived from the buyers containing their deposit. Also included was a thoughtful note expressing their love of old homes and the careful restoration they had done on their current home. The letter closed with, "We saw a number of other homes in our search but were totally convinced this was the house we wanted. One of the biggest deciding factors was that it had been given to the owners in a dream."

The blessing of the dream that had set in motion our purchase of this wonderful home was now carrying it forward through another sale and blessing the new owners. A priceless gift had come full circle.

— Ruth Rogers —

21

Saved by a Rooster

The power of intuitive understanding will protect you
from harm until the end of your days.
~Lao Tzu

We were living in a war zone in France. Our Alsatian farm on the outskirts of a village near Strasbourg was considered so dangerous that we were relocated to a distant outlying region that was somewhat safer. We were unfamiliar with this town, so we had to figure out what was what and where to hide in case of an attack.

I was just a girl during World War II, trying to help my mother take care of my four siblings and my grandparents while my father was serving as a French soldier. We seemed to always be worried about where our next meal was coming from and how to duck the next terrifying onslaught of bombs.

I had been doing plenty of dreaming and having lots of nightmares, and scary images of roosters featured prominently. Our precious egg-laying chickens and their rooster mates had recently been stolen from our farm, probably by people even hungrier than we were. Perhaps that's where the dreams were coming from. It felt like the rooster dreams were trying to warn me about something. But during the petrifying war, everyone I knew reported having some sort of weird or awful dream. So, I tried to put them out of my mind.

The rooster is the unofficial National Animal of France, used to symbolize vigilance. In the 9th century, Pope Nicholas I decreed that all churches must display the rooster on their steeples as a symbol. The ruling was forgotten as centuries passed, but roosters remain on Protestant church steeples in France, distinguishing themselves from Catholic churches that exhibit a cross.

As I was exploring the new town where we had been placed, the air-raid sirens started wailing, sending adrenaline coursing through my system. I needed to run. But where? I saw a solid-looking church in the distance, but as I scampered toward it, I noticed the ominous-looking rooster on its steeple. Screeching to a halt as I remembered my dreams, I dove into a culvert without thinking and crawled into the sewer to take cover.

Bombs rained down on the village, trilling loudly as they fell. As if getting bombed wasn't scary enough, engineers designed whistles to be attached to the bombs, making them even more frightening as they noisily whistled their way to earth. Explosions occurred everywhere, spraying dirt and debris wherever they hit. Finally, things subsided enough that we could hear the engines of the bombers fading in the distance. Peeking out from my hiding spot, I peered through the floating dust to check out the damage in the area. The church that I had been running to for safety had been hit, its ceiling and front wall disintegrated. I could have been injured, or worse, had I made it inside to hide.

The war ended soon afterward, and we returned home to find our farmhouse and outbuildings totally destroyed. But I was very much alive and couldn't wait to roll up my sleeves to start rebuilding it all. The first thing I replaced was the family rooster. Those dreams about roosters had saved me and given me the chance to start over again and live my life to the fullest.

— Denise Del Bianco —

Chapter 3

Early Warnings

22

Living the Dream in Paris

Our inner wisdom is persistent, but quiet.
It will always whisper, but it will never
stop knocking at your door.
~Vironika Tugaleva

lass exploded in my face as the deafening percussion pounded my ears. "GET DOWN! GET DOWN!" Brad screamed. "THEY'RE SHOOTING AT US!" I dove to the floor of the Mercedes, just as a big, hairy hand reached menacingly toward me. My fantastic dream had just turned into a living nightmare!

We were driving in the middle of Paris, heading toward the huge international airshow there. The French presidential entourage was ahead of us, jamming traffic as far as the eye could see. It would take us forever to get through the gridlock. I found myself muttering under my breath at the delay while praying for patience. The French military and Paris police were guiding the President of the Republic through the mess as quickly as they could. Once he was clear, the rest of us could finally follow.

I had been looking forward to this airshow for a long time. Our aviation university had a booth and chalet booked there, and I was part of the team organizing our share of the massive event. We had rented several huge Mercedes Benz limos to haul our staff and our printed material and other promotional items to the show. My vehicle had Mike and Brad in front, two burly Air Force veterans who had been doing the heavy lifting, while I rode in the back, jammed in with packages of brochures and lots of giveaway goodies.

Since I had been excited about this trip for a long time, it wasn't surprising that I was having recurring dreams about it. The dreams were generally convoluted yet pleasant, except for one repeating theme. I would see a door at the end of a hallway that seemed ominous. I chalked it up to stress and didn't let it ruin my trip.

Our group had made all the preparations and were now putting our plans into action. However, we hadn't expected that the President of France would be going to the show at the same time and on the same road. It made sense, of course, since he would be delivering the opening speech at the Paris Air Show. There was nothing we could do but sit in the traffic jam until it got moving again.

That's when the windows exploded in the car we were in, and we hit the deck, fearing the worst. The hairy hand that I could see reaching toward me through the pulverized glass grabbed my bag and hauled it out through the smashed window. I couldn't believe what I was seeing. I was being robbed. My whole life was in that purse.

It turned out the robbers hadn't actually shot at us; they had run through the packed lanes of traffic to the back of our rental car and smashed in the windows with hammers. By the time we reacted, they had grabbed what they could and escaped on foot through the gridlock.

I had been worried about being stuck in traffic, but now I was covered and nicked by shards of glass, and all my important documents had disappeared with the criminals. My passport, cash, credit cards, cell phones, official documents, personal stuff, and laptop computers were all in that bag. It was a terrible blow. I didn't see how I could recover.

Mike and Brad felt sheepish about misinterpreting the attack and not being able to catch the robbers. There was nothing we could do except wait out the traffic jam, as I shook broken glass out of my hair in the back seat of the car and Mike dug through the emergency kit for bandages.

Once finally clear, we found a police station to make our report.

They said that this type of crime was common in blocked traffic. Their police force had been concentrated on protecting their President, so we got some sympathy but didn't receive a lot of help. Next, we headed to the rental agency to file a claim and exchange our damaged vehicle. Finally, we headed to the American Embassy to start the paperwork to replace my passport.

The whole day was shot. I was exhausted and devastated by the loss of my bag. The documents, credit cards, and ID would be difficult to replace, and some of the data on the stolen laptops was irreplaceable. I couldn't even think about what had happened without breaking into tears. I tried to pull myself together as I walked through the lobby of my hotel. I had to repeat the whole sordid tale to the staff at the front desk as I requested a replacement key for my room. I had checked in on our arrival first thing that morning but hadn't seen the room yet since we rushed straight off to the airshow. I was past caring if I had a decent room. I just wanted to try to get some sleep and for this horrible day to end.

Finally accommodated, I walked to the elevator like a zombie with leaden feet. I was totally fried and could barely make it to my room. The elevator ascended, the door slid open, and I found myself staring at the same ominous door at the end of the hallway that I had seen in my dream. The number on the door confirmed it was mine.

This was unbelievable. I froze, and the elevator door shut again in front of me. Composing myself, I hit the button to reopen the elevator despite my dream about that door. I needed to get some sleep.

The elevator opened again, giving me another view of the hallway. In the same instant, amazingly, my room door at the end opened! Out popped the same hairy man who had stolen my bag earlier that day! He clearly had taken the original key from my bag and found the hotel and room from the writing on the key fob, boldly setting himself up for another score. Our eyes locked as he recognized me and raced toward me.

I frantically punched the Close Door button, just before he had time to reach me in the elevator. Inside, I held down the Ground Floor button, screaming at the elevator to move faster. When it opened on the lobby, I ran shouting to the staff in the reception area, alerting them to what had just happened.

We never saw the crook emerge. He must have taken the back stairs into the alley to make his escape. I was chilled to the bone thinking about what could have been.

My persistent hotel hallway dream had made me pause just long enough to save myself from a dangerous situation. From then on, I learned to listen to my dreams and trust my gut instincts, no matter how odd they may seem.

—Donna L. Roberts—

23

Feelings

*All a skeptic is is someone who hasn't
had an experience yet.*
~Jason Hawes

I was getting that uneasy feeling again, the one I always got when something was about to go wrong. At first, the strange sensation came on intermittently. Some days, I didn't experience it at all. But as time went by, I noticed my anxiety was increasing, especially during my husband Bill's daily commute.

Bill drives over sixty miles in heavy traffic to and from work each day. He's got an excellent driving record and keeps his car in top shape. Still, sometimes I worry. Most days, I keep my thoughts to myself. Yet now I knew I had to tell him about my concern.

"Um, Bill," I started as we sat eating dinner, "is everything all right with your car?"

"What do you mean?"

"I mean, have you noticed any funny noises under the hood or anything else odd while you're driving?"

"Oh, I get it," he scoffed. "You're having one of your 'feelings' again."

After twenty-five years of marriage, my husband was well aware of my quirky intuitions. It baffled me, though, that after seeing how many times my premonitions were correct, he still didn't give them the credence I thought they deserved. I decided to drop the whole thing… for the time being. Yet, in the coming days, during his commute times and whenever I was a passenger in his car, I became more and more certain something was awry with his vehicle.

As I sat in his passenger seat one evening, I decided to broach the subject once again. "When did you have the car inspected?" I asked nonchalantly.

"Relax," he smiled. "There's nothing wrong with this car. It passed inspection with flying colors a few months ago. I had all the fluids changed, and I even had a new set of brakes installed. Enough with your 'feelings.' The car is fine."

Still, I could not be convinced. My instincts were too strong.

Then one night I had a dream.

Bill and I were driving in his car with three friends sitting in the back seat. We were all having a pleasant conversation when Bill decided he was too tired to continue driving and asked me to take over the wheel. He pulled to the side of the road, where we switched seats.

"Be careful with the brakes!" Bill shouted at me as I pulled into traffic. "You have to tap them lightly. You can't hit them hard."

Normally a soft-spoken man, Bill's loud directive took me by surprise, and I experienced a sense of unease. I did continue driving but with added vigilance. We were going along well when suddenly the car in front of me stopped short, and I slammed on the brakes. There was a loud crack, and the car seized right there in the middle of the road.

I wasted no time in waking Bill from his sleep and told him about the dream. He hesitated for a moment and then finally replied. "Okay. I'll make an appointment with the mechanic for Saturday."

Bill knew better than to ignore one of my dreams.

And it was a good thing, too. When the mechanic took a look at the brakes he had installed only a few months earlier, he discovered a defect in the mechanism that was causing them to wear unevenly. At this point, the problem was easy to remedy. Had this defect been discovered during the car's next annual inspection — or later — it would have been a different story.

Does Bill still scoff at my premonitions? Not anymore. Now, after all these years, my husband is finally in touch with my "feelings."

— Monica A. Andermann —

24

A Welcome Second Warning

Our life is composed greatly from dreams,
from the unconscious, and they must be
brought into connection with action.
They must be woven together.

~Anaïs Nin

It concerned me when my husband Harold announced, "I think I'll turn in." It was only 8 p.m. We both had colds, but he insisted he was feeling better. Observing his pale face and tired expression, I had my doubts.

"Why don't you take a day off to rest?" I asked, even though I knew what his answer would be. Harold worked twelve hours a day as a car salesman, often going in on his days off. If the dealership was open on Sundays, I'm certain he would go in on that day as well. Working for commission only, he is a hustler. He insisted he would be okay to go to work and went off to bed.

My head was congested and throbbing. I decided to head to bed soon after Harold. A good night's sleep was what we both needed to feel better. Unfortunately, I had a very restless night. I tossed and turned and couldn't get comfortable. I looked at the clock on the nightstand. It was a little after 5 a.m. I had been up most of the night. Harold was thankfully sound asleep. The alarm would be going off soon, and I prayed I would get just a little more sleep.

I don't know what time I eventually fell asleep, but I finally nodded off to a disturbing dream. The dream was so realistic that I thought I was awake.

I was walking around my house. I made my way to the kitchen to get a snack. All of a sudden, I heard a loud noise that sounded like running water, like a waterfall pelting against rocks. Walking down the hallway, the sound of the water got louder to the point where it was unbearable. The sound seemed to be coming from behind the bathroom door.

I ran down the hall. That's when I heard a faint voice inside the bathroom. It was hard to hear and understand since the rushing water was so loud. It was a man's voice that sounded garbled as if he was underwater. His voice was unsettling and desperate. I didn't want to open the door for fear of what was on the other side. The voice got louder. This time, I clearly heard him say, "Help." I held my hand on the doorknob as my heart raced. "It's only a dream," I repeated several times until I willed myself to wake up.

I sat up in bed sweating. My heart was pounding, and I couldn't catch my breath. The house was quiet and still. Harold was still sleeping peacefully. I looked over at the clock to see that I had only been sleeping for fifteen minutes. I tried to go back to sleep, but it was impossible. I was afraid the dream would return.

By day's light, it was a normal Saturday morning. Harold claimed he felt better and left for work. I, too, was feeling better despite my lack of sleep. Good thing because my day was filled with errands. I called Harold a few times throughout the day to see how he was feeling, but only reached his voicemail. It wasn't unusual for him to be too busy to answer while at work, so I wasn't too worried.

Driving to my last errand, I was caught in a sudden downpour. The rain was so bad that I decided to pull into a parking lot to wait it out. While sitting in my car, the rain became more furious and loud as it pelted on the windshield like a waterfall. I got chills down my spine when I realized the rainwater was deafeningly loud just like in my dream. A sudden fear washed over me, and I decided I needed to drive home right away despite the torrential rain. Miraculously, as soon as I started to drive, the rain stopped as quickly as it came.

When I drove up to our house, I saw Harold's car parked in the driveway. He had come home from work. I had a dreadful feeling. Running into the house, I heard the shower running from the hall bathroom. My nightmare seemed to be coming true. I tried to stay calm as I knocked on the bathroom door. "Harold, I didn't know you were coming home. Are you okay?" There wasn't an answer. I stood a few seconds with my hand on the doorknob. Just like my dream, I was fearful to open the door. But this wasn't a dream. I knew I had to face my fear. What I saw nearly made my heart stop. Harold was sitting slumped in the shower, unconscious under the steady stream of the shower, which had run cold.

Harold spent the next few days in the hospital for severe dehydration and the beginning of kidney failure. After everything settled down and he was released from the hospital, I had time to reflect. At first, I was unaware that my dream was a premonition of what was to come, so I simply went about my day as usual. The rain that appeared so randomly out of nowhere gnawed at me, nudging my inner sense of intuition into action. It compelled me to head back home immediately. I'm so grateful I was given a second warning that spurred me into action, preventing what could have been a heartbreaking outcome.

— Dorann Weber —

25

Ready for Action

Forewarn'd, forearm'd.
~Benjamin Franklin

My heart was racing, and I was trembling with fear as I stood at my back door looking out into the yard. I heard a voice say, "You have to get him out of your house!" I felt like I was in a life-threatening situation although it wasn't clear who was in my house or what exactly was happening. I didn't know who was speaking, but I knew instinctively that the voice was right.

At that moment, I awoke with a gasp and in a cold sweat. I lay awake and wondered where the dream had come from. I hadn't watched anything on TV that night that would have affected me that way. I tried to figure out if it was a premonition or warning of some sort, but couldn't make sense of it. I finally drifted back to sleep, but the memory of that dream haunted me for several days.

Weeks later, I came home in the afternoon after running some errands. I carried my groceries into the house and shut the door behind me, not bothering to lock it since I needed to make another trip back to the car. Suddenly, there was a knock on the door. I assumed, being that time of day, it was one of the neighbor kids wanting me to buy something for a school fundraiser, so I just opened the door without looking out the window first.

Without warning, a tall, muscular young man abruptly pushed

his way into my house and shut the door behind him. All of a sudden, I was standing face-to-face with a stranger who said, "You have to help me! There are people with guns chasing me!"

I was stunned and speechless for a moment, thinking, *This is how it happens on a TV crime drama, and usually the homeowner ends up dead or worse.*

Finally, I summoned my voice and said in a strong, authoritative manner, "You have to get out of my house." He just looked at me for a moment and seemed shocked that I didn't want to save him. I knew I needed to get him out of there as soon as possible. Somehow, I spoke fearlessly even though I was terrified. I said again, "You HAVE to get out of my house!" My palms were sweaty, and my heart was racing just as in my dream, but I looked him in the eyes and stood firm.

He peeked out the front window to see if his pursuers were coming, and then he said to me, "Do you have a back door?"

"Yes!" I showed him where the back door was. The back fence was low enough he could get over it and, if they came to the front door, he could be long gone before they realized what happened. So, he bolted out my back door and over that fence.

With shaking hands, I dialed 911 on my phone but was frustrated when it was answered by a machine and I was put on hold. I thought to myself, *I could have been dead by now!*

Then there was another knock on my front door! Apparently, the pursuers figured out which house he had gone to and were trying to find their prey. I was dismayed that my drama wasn't over yet, but for whatever reason, the pursuers went away and didn't even try to come in, even though the door was still unlocked.

My 911 call was finally answered, and when the police arrived, I learned that my big adventure was due to a "drug deal gone bad" in the neighborhood. There were indeed people with guns chasing my intruder. That the pursuers didn't even try my unlocked door made no sense. After all, whoever heard of polite bad guys? But maybe they just figured he wouldn't be hiding so close by.

When things calmed down, I said a prayer of thanks. I know I was protected that day by the premonition/dream that gave me strength and the right words to say to convince my intruder that he needed to leave, and by keeping the people with guns from entering my unlocked house.

— Stephanie Pifer-Stone —

26

Banana Land

I believe that there is an explanation for everything,
so, yes, I believe in miracles.
~Robert Brault

I don't recall every detail of the dream I had forty-five years ago. But I do recall the intense uneasiness that engulfed me when I woke up the next morning.

In my dream, my then-husband Ron and I were driving home from a three-day holiday weekend. We both needed to be at work the next morning. Ron was a graduate student/teacher, and I was a grad student/ dormitory director at the same college. But, tragically, we didn't make it home safely. We had an automobile accident instead.

Although the dream was deeply disturbing, my demons were quickly forgotten as I went about my morning routine. Since I was a new dorm director — and Ron and I were, in fact, leaving the next day for a long weekend five hours south of campus — the Dean of Women had scheduled a meeting with me to see how things were going and to discuss my dorm's coverage in our absence.

The dean was a lovely woman. I always enjoyed our talks. Heading across campus to her office, I felt carefree, excited at the prospect of three full days away with my husband. My earlier dream never crossed my mind until our meeting ended. Then, abruptly, it resurfaced.

"Dean Walawender," I began hesitantly, "if something were to happen to me this weekend, and I was unable to return to work Tuesday, who would oversee my dorm?"

Then I told her about my dream. Although not generally prone to surreal drama, for some reason this dream resonated deeply. And, given my new job and responsibilities, I needed to know what would transpire on campus should the unthinkable happen. The dean quickly eased my mind, assuring me that contingency plans were always in place should emergencies arise.

Relieved, I put the foreboding dream out of my mind once and for all. Ron and I and our two cats spent a delightful three-day weekend in the Adirondack Mountains. On Monday, we piled back into our Volkswagen Beetle and headed north. That's when the unthinkable happened. Just fifteen miles into our five-hour journey, we rounded a notoriously dangerous ninety-degree turn that we'd driven countless times before. This time, a light rain was falling. We were talking, the cats were wandering about, and all was well. But as we made the turn a little faster than marked, Ron and I both sensed something amiss. Although the nose of our car was heading forward, the engine-heavy back of the Beetle was failing to make the curve with us. It just kept sliding outward into the opposing lane.

Before we could fully register what was happening, we were fishtailing back and forth across the road as a monstrous, fully loaded logging truck approached from the opposite direction. Stunned and incredulous, we continued weaving perilously, certain we would collide with the semi. But somehow, miraculously, the truck sped past us as we headed straight for the right-side ditch. There was an abrupt impact — amazingly soft, I remember thinking — and then I was airborne, hurtling through the air eight feet above asphalt. Helpless, certain I would crash and die on impact, I suddenly heard a clear directive: "Land like a banana!"

WHAT? I shrieked silently.

The words came again: "LAND LIKE A BANANA!"

Instantly, I relaxed my body, shoulders rounded forward, head and knees bent toward my chest. A second later, my entire left side slammed down on the asphalt, and then rebounded so hard and high that I managed to stumble to a semi-standing position.

My body was screaming and I could hardly see, but I did spot our car upside down in the ditch twenty-five feet away, facing the direction we were traveling. My dazed and shaken husband was struggling to exit a side door. Our cats were nowhere in sight, having beelined, we later learned, into the neighboring woods. Ron and I hadn't been wearing seatbelts — they weren't mandatory back then — and, as pet owners, we hadn't yet evolved to the point of caging our cats while traveling. But everything changed that day. Seatbelts and cat carriers became staples in our lives going forward.

We could never fathom how that massive truck managed to miss us, or how our car managed to flip over and turn ninety degrees as it did. But, to our vast relief, our cats were uninjured, albeit traumatized. Getting them back safe and sound was the day's high point. A deputy soon arrived, perhaps contacted by the trucker who hadn't managed to stop to help us. Although our car was totaled and we were stranded, a kind neighbor took us in, fed us chili, and helped us arrange for transportation back to school.

My husband, thankfully, suffered no physical injuries. But the damage I sustained that day continues to haunt me all these years later. Initially, I was told I'd broken my neck. But, fortunately, that was not the case.

Upon our return to campus one day later than planned, the Dean of Women immediately sought me out.

"I'm so glad you're okay," she said, hugging me gently. "It's amazing that your dream actually came true."

Hearing her words, I felt sucker-punched. Incredibly enough, I'd forgotten all about my dream! I hadn't lived in fear of it going into our trip, and my thoughts hadn't returned to it after we crashed. But, upon hearing the dean's reminder, my heart swelled with gratitude for all the help we'd received from above. Although I hadn't fully heeded my dream's advance warning, I had felt compelled to mention it to the dean — which greatly eased my job worries when disaster struck. Miraculously, our tiny VW had been guided safely past the grill of that monster truck. A voice out of nowhere had coached me on how to land as safely as possible in a dangerous situation. And, last but hardly least, Ron and I and our sweet felines were alive. Battered, yes, but not broken.

To this day, I remain humbled and awed by the fact that a dream could so accurately foreshadow real life. That long-ago incident marked the first of many times over the years when, inexplicably, I've felt guided to act in some way that was not, intrinsically, initiated by me. I can't say that I live each day actively watching for signs from other realms. But when they do appear, either in dreams or wakefulness — with that uncanny sense of urgency that cannot be overlooked — I pay far closer attention now. And when directions are given, I do as I am told.

— Wendy Hobday Haugh —

27

My Own Soundtrack

Music gives a soul to the universe, wings to the mind,
flight to the imagination and life to everything.
~Plato

It all started when, out of curiosity, I decided to write down my dreams first thing in the morning. My family and I used to love sharing our dreams over breakfast, and I had heard that journaling them might help me remember them. It did. But it also opened me to new perspectives.

When noting my dreams every day, I started to notice something. Every night, the dream I would wake up to was filled with music. The music was different every time, mostly pop music. It would grow louder and louder as the dream progressed, reaching its climax seconds before I woke up.

To say that I was surprised to discover music in my dreams would be an understatement. I was not a music person. It's not that I didn't like music — I did — it's just that I didn't love music. I had never felt the need to listen to music when alone or commuting. I would listen to music chosen by someone else in a group but would never be the one to turn on the radio. I didn't dislike any kind of music, but I didn't especially like any kind either. Yet, my dreams were full of it. What's more, it wasn't even the kind of music I would have naturally gone to. I wrote the name of the song every morning anyway, when I knew what song it was.

Once I started writing down my dreams and noticing the songs, that music started following me during the day. Not happy with just filling my dream at night, it was filling my head all day!

Sometimes, I loved it. If the song was uplifting, I was happy to carry a little piece of my dream with me during the day. It felt like being linked to the psychic world while being awake. That was quite exciting, especially if I liked the song. But when I didn't like the song—and I couldn't help but wonder where and why my mind had picked up on that one—I wished I could just forget about it. Still, I liked to remember my dreams in the morning and to read them again later on. Most of the time, the songs were okay, so I continued with my journaling habit.

With time, I realized that when I was waking up to a happy song, an exciting one, and no matter whether I liked it or not, my day was the most amazing it could be. I was happy. The world was happy. Everything was exciting.

But when I woke up to a sad song or gloomy music, no matter whether I liked it or not, my day would go on as the song from my dream. Gray. Dark.

Not happy with just filling my dreams and my head, the music was filling my heart, too.

At first, I thought it was a coincidence, but it happened every time. All day long, every day, I would feel in me the mood of the music from my dreams.

How was it possible that waking up to a dream playing "Hey Ya!" by Outkast in my head would lead me to a day of fun, free cakes, good grades and good news from everywhere around me, including the news on TV? And why did waking up to a dream full of "Cry Me a River" by Justin Timberlake mean a day filled with crying friends, bad grades, and bad news around the world?

I woke up to "Walking on Sunshine" the day I met my now husband.

I woke up to "Mad World" the day my grandmother died.

While I was looking forward to the happy music dreams, I started to dread waking up to a dream filled with sad music. I tried to ignore them, not noting the name of the song in my dream journal and pushing the music from my head. But it was still in my heart. And it still showed in my days.

While I talked about my dreams from time to time with my family, I never told them about the power of my music dreams. I was convinced they wouldn't understand, and it made me feel terribly lonely to face these kinds of premonitions with no one to talk to about it.

One day, I decided I couldn't keep going like that. I couldn't live my days knowing from the start how badly or well they would unfold. So, I stopped writing down my dreams. I stopped journaling them, and I stopped trying to remember them. It took time, but eventually I couldn't remember which music had accompanied my dreams and I was liberated.

I went back to living my days without knowing what would happen from the start. I had a chance to believe that every day could be a good day. I like that better.

But even now, from time to time, I can't help but remember the happy songs from my dreams. And I spend the day on a cloud.

And from time to time, I can't help but remember the sad songs from my dreams. And you know how that day will go down...

— Élise Dorsaine —

The Holding Room

Dreams are the guiding words of the soul.
~Carl Jung

I pulled my car into the familiar driveway like I'd done a thousand times before. As I stepped out of the car, I glanced over at the mature maple in the middle of the yard. I'd watched that maple grow since it was just a sapling. Letting myself in, I climbed the hardwood stairs to find Mom fixated on the computer screen.

"Hi, Mom," I said in my usual upbeat manner. My mood quickly shifted as she turned to face me. I could see in her eyes that something was terribly wrong.

"Dad has been diagnosed with a serious lung condition." We sat together, dumbfounded, staring at the computer screen as we read the shocking words from Mom's Internet search: progressive... hardening of lung tissue... incurable. No! It couldn't be! Unbelief and denial set in despite the hard medical evidence.

Dad looked fine and seemed like his usual self, so I tried to ignore what I knew was coming. It went on like this for a year or so. The only hint of his dire condition came from occasional shortness of breath.

However, Dad had not put it out of his mind. At my father-in-law's funeral, Dad turned to me as we stood at the gravesite and said, "I'm next." His words sent a jolt through me. Unable to formulate a response, I pretended not to hear him.

A few months later, I froze when I heard Dad violently coughing. The sharp sound pierced my thick veil of denial.

At the end of a visit on one overcast morning, I stood at the front door to say goodbye. Dad shocked me by saying, "I want to talk about my demise." Regretfully, I could not meet him in this place of terrible truth and death. I mumbled something placid, dismissive and falsely upbeat like, "Don't say that, Dad. You are doing great." He had dared to speak the unspeakable. I refused to allow it in.

Soon after, in hushed tones, my mother shared grim stats with me. Extremely low oxygen levels, more coughing, decreased stamina, increased shortness of breath. And then, the undeniable delivery of dark green oxygen tanks accompanied by long, plastic tubes, his new lifeline.

His symptoms spoke the plain, painful truth: Dad was dying.

But still, I found ways to push it away. I busied myself with chores. I floated through life in a numb state. And I avoided visiting him.

I frequently drove past my parents' house in my travels around town. As I passed by, I'd think to myself, *I really should stop in and visit Dad.* But a stronger force often convinced me to wait until another day. On occasion, teetering with indecision, I'd park across the street and sit in my car. My belly sick with dread, I'd ask myself, *Do I have the courage to face him today?* I would quickly come up with excuses to put off the visit and find myself driving away.

And then I had a dream.

I was sitting in a small, plain "holding room" across the street from my parents' house. The room was filled with people who were crying in grief about Dad. I felt their heartache as it mirrored my own. I sat together with them, crying and crying.

Later, I imagined myself back in the dream, sitting alongside the crying people. A well of grief from inside became unlocked. With these difficult feelings emerging came a clear realization: It was time to get out of the holding room, face these feelings and go be with my dad.

This dream shifted me. It opened me up to the depths of despair and pain that I'd been working so hard to push away. And so, I began visiting Dad regularly. No longer did I dismiss his words. I sat with him and listened as he spoke of getting his things "in order." He wanted to make sure my mother would be taken care of—a new roof for the house, a new car, a list of repairs and more.

During one of our visits, Dad looked me in the eye and told me how much our relationship meant to him. Time paused briefly as I met his eyes and gratefully absorbed his words.

At the end of another visit, we stood to hug goodbye. The words "I love you" slipped out of my mouth as we embraced. Although we had never been in the habit of saying this to each other, Dad immediately replied, "I love you, too." A threshold was crossed for both of us that day. And once crossed, we always finished a visit or a phone conversation with those heartfelt words.

During a break at work one day, my step quickened as I excitedly proceeded down the school hallway toward my office space. My parents were traveling home from a trip, and I'd be seeing them soon! I plopped down on the swivel chair and reached for my phone. Immediately, the space around me began to close in. Multiple missed calls. Repeated texts that read: "Call me right away!" Heart pounding wildly, I rushed back into the hallway and dialed my husband. Gazing out a small, unclean window, I heard his shocking words. "Your father just died. I am so sorry."

In that moment, I lost track of place and time. I immediately began screaming out "NO, NO!" as tears of anguish overwhelmed me. Hearing my cries, a co-worker ushered me into a nearby "holding room" away from the hallway of classrooms. She sat with me as I telephoned Mom. Her voice shaking, Mom explained that Dad had died at a rest stop on their trip home from the beach. Dragging his oxygen tank behind him, Dad had found his way to a bench next to a newly planted tree. He sat to catch his breath. My mom was waiting in the car and watching in shock as she saw him keel over on the bench. She rushed to help him as people gathered around shouting, "Call 911!" It was a chaotic, traumatic scene. He died right there on the bench.

In the week after my father's death, I visited my mother. Stepping out of the car, I paused and stood next to the empty space in the middle of the yard. The faithful maple of my childhood had recently fallen and been removed. Staring at the circle of wood chips, I felt tugs of grief upon grief. I stood and reflected upon Dad's and my precious visits together over the last year — visits that likely would not have taken place if not for the dream of the "holding room." Thankfully, the dream had cut through my haze of denial and procrastination, urging me to be with my dad. And when I thought back to our last conversation, I felt a rush of gratitude as I remembered our parting words to each other: "I love you."

— Kat Samworth —

29

Off the Rails

Never apologize for trusting your intuition.
Your brain can play tricks, your heart can be blind,
but your gut is always right.
~Rachel Wolchin

I n the early 1980s, I moved from home to attend college in Toronto. A few months into my first semester, I was introduced to a slightly older guy who was the best friend of one of my class-mates. Although Jake was a laborer with little education and I had serious literary aspirations, we grew close and then began dating.

Jake worked on the railroad, laying and maintaining tracks. Part of his work was emergency-related, and he'd been a member of the crew that headed out after a massive train derailment only a couple of years previously. It could be dangerous work.

Meanwhile, I was a student, often studying and writing papers late into the night. I always had my nose in a book. Jake and I usually only saw each other on the weekends, when I didn't have classes and he was free from work.

One rare weeknight, Jake happened to stop by while I was study-ing, and we had a quick visit before I politely kicked him out. He had to be at work at 6 a.m., and after he left, I put away my books and went to bed.

I fell asleep almost immediately, but I tossed and turned all night. Horrible dreams disturbed me. I kept seeing train tracks and hearing screams. Train tracks, blood, and metallic screeching. I'd wake up only to fall back to sleep and dream the same horrific scenes.

Finally, at about 3:30 a.m., I jumped out of bed and woke up my roommate. I couldn't ignore the dreams anymore. I explained that I'd had these visions, and I sensed that something terrible was going to happen on the railroad. My roommate asked if I wanted to call Jake to make sure everything was all right.

"Call him and say what?" I asked. "My Spidey sense tells me there's going to be an accident, so pay attention to your surroundings? Or just, hey, have a good day at work and be careful out there?" It seemed so ridiculous to call just because I had a bad dream.

This was long before cellphones and texting, so calling Jake in the middle of the night meant that I would wake up his mom and dad. I hesitated, made a cup of instant coffee, and sat thinking. I was worried. What if I didn't call, and Jake wasn't extra careful and was killed? My mind was racing. I wasn't overly superstitious, but I believed in intuition and gut feelings, and I had a nagging premonition that he was in danger.

At 4:15 a.m., I couldn't wait any longer. My roommate sat with me while I dialed Jake's number. It rang several times, and finally his mother picked up and said hello. She was a wonderful lady who genuinely liked me, but she was alarmed and annoyed that I'd call at that hour. Nonetheless, she called Jake to the phone.

"Jake, hey, sorry to call…" I started. Then I realized I had no idea what to tell him. "Sorry to wake you up, but I… had a dream."

Well, that sounded stupid, I thought. I almost hung up in embarrassment.

"A dream," he sighed. "Okay…?"

"I dreamt that there is going to be an accident on your shift today, and all I could see was an arm and an empty glove on the tracks. And blood. And there were screams. And…"

"You woke me up for this?" he asked, impatience coloring his voice.

"Promise me you'll be careful," I whispered.

"I'll be careful," he answered. "I'm always careful. Nothing like that happens. Go back to sleep. I'll call you tonight."

"Promise?"

"I promise."

I crawled back into bed, my mind a little eased that I'd alerted Jake to any potential danger he might face at work. Later, I hopped on the bus and went to class, eventually arriving home by early evening.

I called Jake when I got home. His mom said he hadn't come back from work yet. I was frantic.

I waited and waited. At 9 p.m., I still hadn't heard from him. Again, his mom answered my call; she told me she'd just spoken with Jake, and he was at the hospital.

"Apparently, there was an accident on the tracks today," she explained. I froze, and it felt like I'd swallowed a ball of lead.

"One of his co-workers lost three fingers in a freak accident," she continued. "Jake stuck around to drive the guy home from emergency. He's on his way home now."

At that point, I told Jake's mom about my dream, and I apologized for the early morning call.

"Oh, Cat, you must have been terrified!" she exclaimed. "Jake told me you'd had a bad dream, but he didn't tell me what it was about. Good god, thank you for telling him to be careful."

Jake called me when he arrived home. It turned out a piece of machinery they'd been using slipped into reverse, and his co-worker had been working almost prone on the tracks when it sped toward him. He'd rolled away just in time but lost his fingers in the process.

"Luck of the draw," he said. "I was doing the same job about twenty minutes before it happened."

—Catherine Kenwell—

30

A Series of Dreams

Follow your intuition, listening to your dreams,
your inner voice to guide you.
~Katori Hall

aster was less than a week away. I worked nights, and before I went to bed each morning, I watched the news and checked out the weather. I remember thinking it looked like the warm weather would hold for Easter.

Dream One: Tuesday Morning After Working Monday Night

It wasn't a spectacular dream, and I just ignored it. I figured it was caused by something I had watched on TV before going to bed, like the weather. It was no big deal. *I dreamed of a bad storm, and there was the sound of a train in the background. I heard the word "closet."* There must have been more, but all else was forgotten as soon as I opened my eyes.

Dream Two: Wednesday Morning After Working Tuesday Night

I had the same dream. I remembered more this time. *There was a terrible storm. High winds, heavy rain, the sound of a train, and a voice in my head saying, "Safe in your closet." I saw a flash of light out my bedroom window. Getting up to look, I saw skid marks right outside my window in my perfectly manicured lawn.*

When I woke up, I even looked out the window. Lawn undisturbed. Sky clear. Weather warm. I hoped it would stay this way for a few more days. Easter was this Sunday.

Dream Three: Thursday Morning After Working Wednesday Night

There were high winds and heavy rains. A tornado had been spotted overhead. The sound of a train was getting louder and louder. As my doublewide began to shake, I heard a voice say, "Safe in your closet."

Needless to say, this dream left me shaking. When I got to work, everyone was talking about the coming weekend and their plans for Easter. I had a three-day weekend coming up, and plans with my kids, and I quickly forgot about the dream… until I returned home and prepared for bed. Would I dream again?

Dream Four: Friday Morning After Working Thursday Night

I worked Thursday night. I was off from Good Friday through Easter. But Friday morning, after working all night, I still needed a few hours of sleep before going to a bridal shower that afternoon. Would I have the same dream? I couldn't have been asleep long when it started.

The high winds, heavy rain, thunder, and lightning. The flash at the window. I got up and looked out. I saw a huge angel struggling to hold down the house, fighting against the wind. I could see ridges in the mud where the angel slid. That corner of the house held steady.

Suddenly, I was back in bed. I heard my daughter calling and felt her shaking me. "Mom! Mom, wake up! This is not a normal storm!"

My eyes popped open. I sat up and, without thinking, said, "Safe in the closet."

Once we were inside the closet, I added, "We are safe. We need to pray for the neighbors."

The sound intensified on the other side of the closet door, and the floor beneath us began to shudder. It sounded and felt like we were in a tunnel with a train passing through. It seemed to go on and on.

We lived in an area with mostly single trailers and doublewide homes spread out on five-acre lots. We began to pray for protection for each neighbor by name.

The storm passed as quickly as it came. When we came out of the closet, everything was a mess. Things were tossed around; storm windows were blown inside; walls were lopsided; cabinets had been emptied; furniture was thrown around. The cement pilings from under the house were pushing up through the floorboards but not breaking through the carpet in every room except the one where we were.

The house was warped, and the outside doors would not open. I could see that our three large covered decks and three-car carport were all gone. I opened the bedroom window and climbed outside. Our well house was gone. The wooden play set, with swings, slide, sandbox and a fort, was missing. The room under the home was smashed. I would have thought that would have been the safest place if not for the dreams. That's where we would have sheltered if the dream hadn't told me to go in the closet.

Neighbors, emergency crews and sightseers began arriving. The area had to be closed to traffic. Even though it was Good Friday and school was out, there were no injuries. Every family we prayed for remained unharmed and had minimal property damage. There were two families we did not know and missed praying for. Both singlewide trailers were destroyed. One flipped, and one blew apart from the pressure. Thankfully, neither family was home when the storm struck.

Yes, it took four dreams, but I learned to listen.

— Debbie Sistare —

31

Defensive Driving

Trust your instinct to the end,
though you can render no reason.
~Ralph Waldo Emerson

It was a usual quiet weekday morning. I was watching the news while drinking my coffee before getting ready for work. As always, the news was filled with the latest accidents and criminal activity, most of which I ignored. However, one particular traffic accident caught my full attention.

A vehicle had run a red light and T-boned another vehicle. As I watched the replay of this accident, I thought to myself, *What could the driver have done to lessen the impact of being hit broadside like that?* I visualized that a sharp turn of the steering wheel might have helped.

Not thinking much more about it, I finished my coffee and got ready for work. I headed out the door for my twenty-two-mile drive to work. As I approached the intersection that I had traveled through countless times before, I saw out of the corner of my eye that a black SUV on my left was not slowing down to stop at the stop sign. It was actually speeding toward me...

I was now living the exact scenario that I had played out in my mind less than an hour earlier. So, I did exactly what I had planned and cut the wheel sharply to the right. I was not able to avoid the accident and the SUV did hit my car. It tumbled down the road before it came to a stop. Somehow though, my car ended up in the grass on the other side of the road. To my amazement, after what had just happened, I was completely unharmed.

I believe with all my heart that I watched the news that morning for a reason. I don't think that I would have reacted as quickly as I did if I had not been through that practice run in my mind first.

— Bonnie Collins Wood —

Chapter 4

Listen to That Little Voice

32

Learning to Trust My Intuition

Intuition is a spiritual faculty and does not explain,
but simply points the way.
~Florence Scovel Shinn

One hot San Diego day in mid-July, I slumped in the waiting-room chair of the car dealership, my hand resting on my pregnant belly. As luck would have it, my oil change finished early. I realized I was only minutes away from the thrift store where a friend of mine had worked, so I headed over with renewed energy.

When I stepped into the store, though, my heart became heavy with grief. It had only been a few weeks since the world had lost such a kind person. He was only thirty-two years old.

A part of me refused to believe he was really gone.

I found myself drawn to the used-book section in the back of the store. I had a strong sense there was a book I needed to find.

Running my fingers along the uneven spines, I scanned the titles, asking for my friend's guidance. My hand finally stopped on a book wrapped in a blue jacket. Carefully sliding it out from the bookshelf, a smile stretched across my face.

This was it — a book I'd been hearing about over and over in a recording from an inspirational speaker I'd seen the previous year. "Dr. Wayne Dyer wrote a book some odd years ago — not 'you'll believe it when you see it,' but *You'll See It When You Believe It*," Esther Hicks had said. I'd vowed to read it someday. Well, that day had come.

As I thumbed through the pages, I couldn't help but notice that the book remained in pristine condition despite being published in 1989. My jaw dropped as I discovered words scrawled across the title page: Wayne Dyer's signature.

I'd always believed in the power of intuition, and that loved ones continue to guide us long after they physically leave our sides. But I'd never been 100 percent sure. As I held the book to my chest that day, I silently thanked my friend for the sign, trying to trust in it.

My elation grew as I randomly opened to a chapter titled "Synchronicity" — the idea that seemingly coincidental events happen for a deeper purpose. That was reinforced just a few days later by a post on Wayne Dyer's Facebook page: "Read the books that mysteriously show up in your life." Another sign.

A month later, I heard the devastating news that Wayne Dyer had passed away from a heart attack in his sleep. I became overwhelmed with a mix of emotions: immense sadness for the Dyer family; disappointment that I'd only just discovered Wayne's work; gratitude that his teachings would continue to change people's lives long after he'd left the Earth.

As excited as I was to read it, I was so busy preparing for my daughter's arrival that I didn't get around to finishing the book. And as soon as she was born, I wanted only to rest alongside her, inhaling her baby scent and watching her as she dozed. Not to mention, a book with such deep concepts probably would've gone right over my head on so little sleep!

I didn't read the book until almost a year later. Near the end, I came to a part where Wayne described his anger over a legal battle that had haunted him for nearly two years — until he realized he was going about things all wrong. He let go of the anger that tormented him, replacing any negative feelings with love. He sent flowers and copies of his books to the people who were suing him, and miraculously, just like that, the case was dropped. Forgiveness, he explained, was the key.

Reading this sparked something in my mind. I recalled a post that

Wayne's daughter had shared on her Facebook page about a similar experience she was going through with a legal situation.

Maybe I'm supposed to share this with her because she needs the reminder, I thought. *Maybe I didn't finish the book last year for a reason.* Had I finished the book a year ago, I might not have even made the connection. While I wasn't sure how to contact her, or if my revelation would even matter to her, I set it aside. Months passed, and while I occasionally thought about writing to her, one day I decided I'd just do it. But would she even care?

"Hopefully, everything's been resolved, and you don't need this message after all, but sending it anyway with love," I wrote after telling her the story. Then I pointed out the page numbers and nervously hit Send, trying to trust my intuition.

The next day, I was surprised to see that she'd answered. My eyes welled with tears as I read her words. About three weeks prior, she wrote, her father had come to her in a dream, urging her to read *You'll See It When You Believe It* because the answer to the legal situation was in the book. She'd told her sister about the dream, and they both planned to read it, but hadn't done so yet.

"It makes me laugh to think that my dad was probably trying so hard to get me to understand this message, first by visiting me in my dream and also by urging you to send the message to me. He must've thought that I'm so stubborn he won't even try to get me to read the whole book, so he'll have to settle with just pointing out the page numbers! I can't tell you how happy this makes me! Thank you so much!"

I couldn't help but smile through the tears streaming down my face. And then it hit me: It's so easy to dismiss an intuitive thought as just a thought — something meaningless we made up. And we can convince ourselves that it really wasn't our lost loved one sending us a sign or showing up in our dreams, letting us know they're okay. That despite the pain and emptiness we feel without them, we'll be okay, too. It may not be the words we yearn to hear in our loved one's familiar voice, but I knew in the moments after reading her response that the guidance we receive is as real as words will ever be.

I vowed then to never take my intuition for granted. Even if doubt starts to creep in, I'll always remember Wayne's wise words and his message: "If you really, really want to see it, first you must truly believe."

— Danielle Soucy Mills —

Flashes in the Fog

I have been a seeker and I still am,
but I stopped asking the books and the stars.
I started listening to the teaching of my soul.
~Rumi

The blissfully foggy moments between sleep and wakefulness can offer unique insights, according to some of history's creative geniuses. Beethoven, Edison, Dali, and Poe all noted flashes of invention and understanding during those transitions. I now count myself among those who have learned to pay attention during those fleeting moments. Insights I've gained haven't revealed me to be some kind of genius, not by a long shot. But they did push me to pen the novel I never wanted to write.

Before I learned to notice those creative flashes, I spent six years researching and writing my first book. A historical novel called *Risking Exposure*, it is the fictional tale of a Hitler youth named Sophie. Because of the novel's setting and subject matter, I'd spent hundreds of hours immersing myself in the darkness of that time and place.

Nazi Germany wasn't good for my soul; I knew that. When the book was completed, I happily put it on a shelf. My attention turned to more pleasant topics.

It wasn't long before readers contacted me, asking for more of the story. Some reviewers said the novel ended too abruptly. Even my own mother registered her complaint. "You can't leave Sophie and her friends alone on the verge of war!" she said.

I ignored them all. Instead, I wrote and published a humorous children's picture book. I penned short inspirational articles, a few of which were accepted to magazines. I blogged about people who positively impacted others. I cleansed my palate, so to speak, of the bad taste of Nazi evil. I grew content with my writing life.

One night, a couple of years after *Risking Exposure* was published, I was lounging in the comfortable fog between sleep and wakefulness. A man's voice startled me. It was not speaking audibly, of course, but speaking to that subconscious part of my mind. Keeping my eyes closed so as not to disturb the flow, I listened. The man was an elderly grouch, and he was telling me a story. Details were coming fast, so I hurried through my darkened home to my computer. There, I began to record his words.

About 500 words in, I realized he was in a residential care facility where nothing suited him. Another 500 words in, I realized he was an unrepentant Nazi. Not only that, I recognized him. This was an octogenarian version of Werner, the antagonist from *Risking Exposure*. He was telling me his account of what happened back in 1938 when he'd been a young man in charge of Sophie and other Hitler youth. My stomach sank.

Before breakfast, I had dutifully taken a few thousand words of his dictation. I had no idea what to do with his narrative, filled as it was with blame and excuses for his horrible behavior decades earlier. And the idea that he was unrepentant so long afterward, well, I couldn't bear it. I shut him out of my mind.

I didn't mention the disturbing incident to my family. My fictional characters speaking to me in the night? They'd think I'd gone crazy. Maybe I had.

But Werner was relentless. Each night over the next week or so, his voice invaded those moments between sleep and wakefulness. He spoke of what he'd done during the war and afterward, who he'd met, where he'd lived. And each day, I stumbled to the computer and documented his words. Even as I did so, I'd shake my head. Why was I writing about a grouchy old Nazi? And who would want to read it?

In finally talking about it with my husband, I confessed that I didn't have the stomach to immerse myself in the Nazi era again. We agreed that I had two choices: find a second story, one with a narrator who behaved decently to counterbalance Werner's evil, or let this story die on my computer. I voted for the latter.

My muse had other plans. A few nights later, a different voice filled the muddled transition between sleep and wakefulness. I recognized her right away as Renate, another character from *Risking Exposure*. She was, in fact, Werner's younger sister and Sophie's best friend. But Renate wasn't narrating her story in retrospect the way Werner was. She was telling me her tale as it happened, beginning in July of 1938 when *Risking Exposure* ended.

Renate's clear-eyed version of events during those dark years was exactly what I needed to counterbalance Werner's rambling lies and twisted facts. Reluctantly, I reopened myself to that time and place.

Over the next couple of years, I wove the siblings' stories together — Renate's narration of events as they happened in 1938, and Werner's version as he looked back from the year 2005. The finished novel, *The Path Divided*, went on the shelf alongside its partner, *Risking Exposure*. Again, I cleansed my palate and announced that I was done writing about Nazi Germany. I meant it.

A year later, I was again lounging in that delicious state between sleep and wakefulness when I heard voices. I tried not to listen for fear it was another Nazi-era story, but after several minutes I caught words that drew me in.

Bigfoot. Cupid. Fairies.

I started to giggle, waking myself completely. My imaginative muse was speaking with a human woman who was married to Sasquatch!

The situation was funny, absurd, and a delightful change from my earlier dream inspirations. I happily grabbed my phone and narrated bits of the interview into its voice recorder. That morning's flash of insight grew into "The Spouses Club," a short story that won second place in the Bethlehem Writers Roundtable contest.

As I've lounged half-awake in recent months, a number of other quirky characters have told me bits of their stories, so I'm expanding the original idea into a humorous book series for middle-grade readers.

The series will include fairies and Bigfoot, of course, and also Jack Frost, the Loch Ness Monster, the Sandman, and the Yeti.

It's clear that the foggy moments between sleep and wakefulness are my imagination's fertile ground. Like others before me, I've learned to listen while I inhabit that space. Best of all, I get to tap into that creative resource from the comfort of my own bed!

—Jeanne Moran—

34

The Giveaway

An effort made for the happiness
of others lifts us above ourselves.
~Lydia M. Child

I had finally accepted the fact I would never walk without assistance of some kind for the rest of my life. It came to the point that I could not go anywhere without someone to help me get around. The pain kept getting worse.

Nothing seemed to help, but I didn't want to be a shut-in. One day, I called my mom and asked if she'd like to go out to eat.

That was a momentous decision, because after our meal, as we were leaving the restaurant, I saw an older man using a thin metal cane. The rubber stoppers were missing. The cane was slipping on the floor and almost caused him to fall a couple of times.

I always carry extra canes because I don't want to be caught without one if I misplace one. I had a four-legged cane in the back of my car, so I asked my grandson to get it for me. I called out to the man and asked if I could talk to him for a minute. He looked perplexed and kind of scared, but he stopped.

I gave him the cane and told him that I was afraid his was going to cause him to fall. He looked at me with watering eyes and asked if I was sure. I nodded.

Once I was in the car, my mom asked, "What was that about?"

"God just told me to do it," I said.

The next day, I had to pick up my medication. As I was turning my car into the parking lot, I saw a man on the side of the street walking with a broken broom handle. He was using it as a cane, and it wasn't helping him much. Once again, I heard, "Give him a cane." I pulled to the curb and waited as he got close. I asked my grandson to get me a cane out of the back of the car. He came around to my side of the car and said, "Grandma, there are no more in there."

As plain as day, I heard, "Give him the one you are using." I hesitated for a second. How would I get around if I gave away my cane? But I decided the Lord knows best, and we should always listen to him. He would not steer me wrong.

As the man approached my car, I called to him to please come over. He hesitated and looked around, confused and cautious. Then he came over, and I handed him my cane. I told him, "You need it more than I do." He called me an angel and walked off smiling. I will never forget the look in his eyes. I decided I would use a shopping cart as a walker until we got in the store. They didn't have any motorized carts available, so I continued using the shopping cart.

I got what I needed and pushed my cart back to the car. I helped my grandson put some stuff into the car, pushed the cart to him to put it away, and then stepped into the car. It wasn't until I cranked the car that I realized I had walked around the store and gotten into the car without help or pain. I felt tears running down my cheeks.

I have not used a cane since that day.

— Donna Faulkner Schulte —

35

I'll Tell Him Tomorrow

When you listen, it's amazing what you can learn.
When you act on what you've learned,
it's amazing what you can change.
~Audrey McLaughlin

It was the last period of the school day, and the last group had just finished showing their project to the class. We were wrapping up our unit on rhetoric and the art of persuasion. This group had created an infomercial showcasing the use of Aristotle's logos, ethos, and pathos to advertise a green tea that could improve your skills at anything you wanted.

The video they made showed a student on a basketball court shooting an airball. Then he drank some of the green tea and unleashed a barrage of swish after swish. Then it showed a close-up of my student Sean drawing stick figures. He took a swig of the green tea and frantically scribbled all over the page. Seconds later, Sean held up his art piece, revealing the Mona Lisa, and the whole class erupted in laughter.

Sean was good at making people laugh, even though he wasn't good at putting effort into his grades. But he was as smart as any student and wiser than most adults.

I was so proud of Sean. His group had hit a grand slam, and I was excited to inform him that he had just earned his first A. He once told me that he had never received an A before.

The bell rang just as their video finished, and I started to walk from my desk over to Sean, who was walking toward the door. There was the hustle-and-bustle energy of school being out for the day, and I was maneuvering my way through students to reach Sean. I wanted to make a big deal of him getting his first A. I was going to high-five him, congratulate him and let him know what a stellar job he had done. He was about to reach the door and I almost shouted out his name to wait, but then the thought in my head said, *I'll just tell him tomorrow.* I let Sean walk out my classroom door without ever saying a word about how great I thought he was.

I had the dream again that night, the same one I'd been having the last several nights. I usually didn't remember my dreams for more than a flash of a second, but this one had stuck with me each day when I woke up.

In my dream, I was speaking at a funeral. I never saw the face or heard the name of the person who died, but I knew it was a student's funeral, and I was surrounded by strangers who were grabbing onto me as if I could heal them of their pain.

The next morning as first period was about to begin, a girl from my fifth-period class (Sean's class) burst into the door. "He's been hit! He's been hit!" she frantically shouted.

"Who?" I replied.

She collapsed onto my feet and cried out, "Sean! A car hit Sean, and his body is still in the street."

Four days before his sixteenth birthday, one block away from Fountain Valley High School, Sean was hit by a car while riding his bike to school. That night, when I was finally about to leave campus after hours spent consoling grieving students, I stared at Sean's empty desk and wrote down a few words about Sean on my Facebook page. Those words would go locally viral, and they reached Sean's parents. They printed what I wrote in Sean's funeral program and asked me to speak.

I will always regret that I didn't pay more attention to that recurring dream. Never make my mistake and delay expressing your love or appreciation until tomorrow. Don't let someone walk out the door without giving them their "A."

I cry when I think of Sean's death, but I smile when I think of Sean's life. Sean was a master at turning strangers into friends and was always happy and smiling. When I start to feel down about life, I think about the boy who never lost his smile because he was always giving it away to others. Sean said, "The purpose to life is to enjoy your life and to make friendships and take notes."

Sean was a genius at making friends, but he didn't write down any notes in his classes. Standing next to his hospital bed, holding his hand while machines kept his body pumping even though he no longer had brain activity, I realized the notes were not for him to take — but for us to take *from him*.

The final words Sean wrote in my class were: "Revolt. Rebel. Love. What is truth? We're all killing ourselves. There are too many fakes in the world. We need real leaders who have values. Every life matters, yet some act as if some lives aren't worth as much. People need to take their eyes away from TV to enjoy what's around them. War is created because of how people treat each other. We all need to be more aware and stop paying attention to less important things. There's always someone who needs help. I think you just have to accept some things. Think of Sisyphus. Maybe he's happy because the task is supposed to punish him, and since he's a rebel, he's going to be happy to make the gods mad."

I made a promise to Sean's mother that I would share his story with my classes every year because when you speak someone's story, they never fully die. Due to the global pandemic from COVID-19, our school was shut down in the spring of 2020, and I hadn't shared Sean's story yet.

I'm glad I can share it here even though I missed my opportunity with my students. Sean lives on in every person who reads his story and decides to speak love more loudly. Sean lives on in all the people his organs gave new life to. And he lives on in all the people who learned to speak their truth and their love because of him. We all take notes… from Sean.

At the beginning of each class, I say these words to my students:

"I love you big, giant, much!" There was a kid named Sean Dylan Severson in my English Language Arts class, but I was not his teacher; I was his student, and I continue to take notes.

— Steve Schultz —

36

Following My Heart

Forget about the fast lane. If you really want to fly,
harness your power to your passion. Honor your
calling. Everybody has one. Trust your heart,
and success will come to you.
~Oprah Winfrey

aring Hearts! It seemed that the name was shouted at me. As I wiped the sleep from my eyes and looked at the clock, I saw that it was only 5 a.m. What in the world?

I awoke with the clear message that I should start a business called Caring Hearts. Was this a dream?

When I went to bed the evening before, I had tossed and turned as I tried to think of a job I might like. My father had passed away in March, and here it was June. I had enjoyed the time I spent as a caretaker for my father as his health declined. Visiting the residents of his residential building when I went to care for him was enjoyable, too. I realized I didn't want to spend the rest of my life working at a job that was not fulfilling.

As I drifted off to sleep, I thought maybe I would like to be a paid caregiver. The only problem was that I would have to take a considerable pay cut. When I awoke with such strong feelings and thoughts about this business, I decided I better get up and write down my thoughts because I didn't want to go back to sleep and forget it in the morning. After all, that voice had shouted "caring hearts" at me.

Listening to this dream has been wonderful. I researched the business, and I started a home-care agency with the help of my husband in October 2012. The name of our successful business is Caring Heart Companions, Inc. Sometimes, you just have to listen to your dreams!

—Lori Reed—

37

Voice of an Angel

Love knows no limit to its endurance,
no end to its trust, no fading of its hope;
it can outlast anything. Love still stands
when all else has fallen.
~Blaise Pascal

My daughter Kate had just passed away in a car accident, and I was beyond despondent. I didn't think I could go on those first few weeks. But the angels had the most beautiful messages in store for me.

One night, I had a dream that changed everything.

A clear, calming voice, neither male nor female, said one sentence to me. "Read Charlotte's Web. *There will be a message in it for you.*"

That was all. I woke up astounded at such a strange dream, realizing I had never read the children's book *Charlotte's Web* by E.B. White. I knew my children had seen a cartoon version when they were young years before.

That morning, I went to a bookstore and bought the book. I sat down and read the classic children's book all afternoon long. E.B. White's beautiful imagery of life on the farm swept me into a bucolic world. He wrote of the wonderful friendship between Wilbur the pig and Charlotte the spider. Charlotte even saved Wilbur's life at the state fair by staying near him and weaving words like "Terrific" in her intricate web.

But as I read, I couldn't find any message that pertained to my own grief for Kate's passing. It appeared the story was focused on Charlotte and Wilbur's enduring friendship. Where was the message?

Amazingly, it was on the very last page. Charlotte, the spider, had died, and Wilbur was very sad. Yet the great writer had written a most loving passage: "Wilbur never forgot Charlotte. Although he loved her children and grandchildren dearly, none of the new spiders ever quite took her place in his heart."

These simple, wonderful words changed my thinking that very moment. No one could ever take Kate's place in my heart, but I could and would go on loving my children and husband who were still living. I had a life to fill with happiness and giving to others.

That beautiful message has stayed with me for twenty-four years now. My children are grown, and I have grandchildren to love. Because of my love for Kate, I've written a series of novels about angels. This all happened because of a dream in which I heard an angel's voice with a life-changing message for me.

— Jody Sharpe —

38

Urgent Serenity

We have all a better guide in ourselves, if we would
attend to it, than any other person can be.
~Jane Austen

Staring upward through a thin pane of 1890s glass, I saw white pastel wisps against a cobalt backdrop. Fluttering leaves along the periphery confirmed it was blue sky. In this tranquil place, I felt a sense of wholeness.

A slight surprise occurred when a ripple disrupted the view, and I thought, "This is not glass. I'm looking through water."

I was immobile a few feet below a pond's surface, looking upward, suspended, but I felt indifferent about it. The fact I wasn't facing downward or swimming through water with arms pumping and legs kicking did not faze me.

The water temperature was not warm or cold. There were no thoughts, sensations, or need for air. It felt as if time stood still.

I heard a gentle whisper: "Up."

"What?"

It became clearer. "Up!"

"It's nice here. I am staying here," I thought, wanting the whisper to go away so I could continue to enjoy this serene environment.

Charcoal clouds began to edge into view.

The voice came through more demanding now. "Get up now!"

"Get up? Swim?" I said. "No, I like it here. It is peaceful. I am staying." There was no rising or shift in my body. My arms and legs did not move as I faced the sky. I felt serene, and inert.

"Get — up — now!"

I started to feel a need to breathe and I heard the command more insistently: "GET UP NOW!" I still didn't want to leave.

I wanted to go back to that calm pond, but I couldn't find it. "Where's the pond? Can I go back to the pond?"

And then it was over. My eyes opened to a hospital room. I wondered why it was so hard to breathe. I was bathed in sweat and my heart was racing. I was awake and I was in distress.

I slowly pulled on the bedrail to half-turn myself toward my dad. He slept in a reclining chair-bed to the left of my hospital bed during my surgical recovery. It was three in the morning. With great effort, I hoarsely said, "Dad, I think I have to be up."

Then I heard an authoritative voice say desperately, *NOW! Get up. SIT UP! UP! UP!*

My dad woke and leaned toward me as he righted his recliner.

"Something is telling me to be up," I whispered to him. My movement was slow, but the urgency inside my soul felt frantic.

My dad helped me to a sitting position in the bed and said, "Are you okay? Can I get you something? Would you like some water?"

I nodded.

I felt weak and shaky. Breathing was laborious, and there was a new pain in my chest.

Call for help, now — NOW! Press the nurse button!

This direction was not coming from my dad. I was looking right at him. He was pouring the water in silence.

I paused. *If I press the button, the medical team is going to tell me I'm already receiving treatment and to relax.*

The voice shrieked, *PRESS THE BUTTON!*

Winded, I managed to say, "Dad, something's not right. I just pressed the nurse button."

I stared at a nature picture on the wall above the foot of my bed while waiting for the nurse to come. I counted shallow breaths in silence, "1, 2, 3…" While I did this, a confident knowing blanketed me. *You're going to be okay.* And I believed it.

Help arrived and chaos erupted. Liquid coming from my kidneys was creeping up and around my heart. What if I hadn't listened, if I hadn't sat up, if I hadn't called for help...

— Sheri Lynn —

39

An Unshakable Dream

No matter where I am your spirit will be beside me.
For I know that no matter what,
you will always be with me.
~Tram-Tiara T. Von Reichenbach

I had given birth to my daughter in late September, but I was determined to finish my senior year of high school. I knew it was going to be difficult. However, almost two months after school started, a classmate died in a tragic drowning accident. A few days after his funeral, I had a dream that would haunt me for the next seven months.

The dream was crystal-clear. My mother, thirty-nine years old and healthy, was lying in a casket in the same funeral home I had visited with friends only a few days earlier. I was standing next to the casket looking down at my mother, yet I could see the entire room. It was filled with people offering condolences. The room was overflowing with flowers. I saw my grandparents sitting on a couch in a far corner and my mother's five sisters sitting together on folding chairs. My mother's closest friend was standing alone in the back of the room, and my uncle was standing next to me.

I awoke terrified and sweating. My mother wasn't ill; she didn't have any health problems. Why would I dream something like that?

Usually, if I dream, it's quickly forgotten, a fleeting memory. But for the next several months, I couldn't shake that dream. It was so vivid, and my mother's face so clear. I was concerned she would be in an accident or diagnosed with a terminal illness.

I never said anything to her about my dream. I told myself it was fear emerging from my subconscious, a fear of losing her at a time when I needed her most. But I couldn't shake it or stop thinking about it. My mother was my best friend, my biggest supporter. She was the one pushing me to finish high school so I could go on to college. She loved watching her granddaughter and was the happiest I had ever seen her.

Eventually, Christmas came and went, winter turned to spring, and somehow in the chaos of life, I managed to tuck the dream away.

The following April, on a morning when my mother wasn't coming over to watch my daughter, I felt an overwhelming urge to call her, but I didn't. Without her morning help, I was running late for school. I had to get my daughter up, dressed and fed, and take her to my in-laws. In my rush to get ready that day, I told myself that I'd call her later.

She passed away around ten that morning from a cerebral aneurysm. I received a call at school to go to the emergency room. My dream had become a reality. Two days later, I was standing in that same funeral home beside her casket.

Flowers were everywhere. My grandparents were sitting on a couch. My mother's five sisters sat together on folding chairs. Her closest friend stood in the back of the room. My uncle stood close by, wiping tears from his eyes.

I believe God gave me that dream to prepare me, a glimpse into the future perhaps. I believe He was also urging me that morning to call my mother, but I didn't listen. Since then, I have learned to listen and heed that quiet but insistent voice when I hear it.

I've never had a dream that vivid since, but I have heard that quiet voice many times. I have always heeded the instructions, like sending a card or flowers, even though I don't always know why. Once, I took a bag of potatoes to someone, feeling a little silly, but I found out later it was exactly what they needed. I listen now. I may not always understand why, but it doesn't matter because my experience has proven it's the right thing to do.

—Dana D. Sterner—

40

Woman to Woman

It takes a great man to be a good listener.
~Calvin Coolidge

"**B**ut, honey, it's 2:18 a.m." I patiently tried to reason with my agitated wife, who had shaken me awake and ordered me to go get my mother and bring her to our house. "I'll go in the morning, at a reasonable hour."

"You need to go right now," she insisted. "You need to bring her here now and bring her yarn and medicine — lots of it."

When I finally calmed her down, she told me she'd just had a vivid dream where my ninety-year-old mother insisted that we come get her in France and bring her to our house in Germany. In the dream, Mom was clutching her knitting yarn in one hand and her medication in the other.

My wife is generally not a fan of long-term houseguests, especially strong-willed mothers-in-law, so I knew something was different this time.

With my mother living about two hours away, I normally visit her every week or so. I check on her health and make sure she has everything she needs — groceries, medicine and yarn for her numerous knitting projects. The COVID-19 stay-home restrictions had just begun to take effect in various communities around Europe, and I wondered if my trips to see my mother would be delayed for a couple of weeks.

"Go!" my wife continued to insist. "Now!"

And so I dragged myself from my comfortable bed and headed to France. It was an uneventful trip that early in the morning. I noticed there were extra guards at the border, but I passed through without incident.

I was concerned about arriving at my mother's apartment in the middle of the night. I hoped the neighbors wouldn't think I was an intruder and demand an explanation or call the police. How would I explain that I was there because of my wife's insistent dream? I also worried about rousing my mother. She was a heavy sleeper and not easily awakened at reasonable hours, let alone before dawn.

I needn't have worried. When I arrived at her door, she opened it immediately, fully dressed with her bag packed, bursting with yarn and medications.

"I hoped you'd come for me," she explained. "I've been anxious and having bad dreams."

"Donna insisted I come right away. She had a dream about you and was worried."

Next thing I knew, she thrust a huge box of groceries into my arms.

"We're taking a bunch of stuff from the pantry," she insisted. For the second time already that day, I found myself at the mercy of a strong-willed woman's whims.

My mother had kept a full pantry for her whole life, following the experience of going hungry as a girl during World War II in occupied France. There was so much to pack into the car that it took over an hour before we were ready to head to Germany.

It was now almost 6 a.m. and had been a long day already. This time, we were stopped at the border and asked where we were going. When I explained, the guard sternly told us that the borders were being closed in an hour, and we would not be let back into France.

Because of my wife's insistence that we pay attention to her dream, I'd made it just in time to pick up my mother and bring her to Germany to ride out the pandemic with us. My mother had always said that my wife was more in tune with the metaphysical than the rest of us, so it made sense that Mom's urgent message was picked up by my wife in her dreams.

The lockdown orders continued throughout Europe, but we remained together with plenty of yarn and groceries, thanks to the power of dreams.

— Sergio Del Bianco —

41

Prompted to Shop

God strengthens those hands that serve others.
~*Apoorve Dubey*, The Flight of Ambition

I was in the vegetable section in my local supermarket, picking the ingredients I needed for my weekly meal plan. I hadn't been there long and was still at the beginning of my shopping when the face of a lady in my church appeared clearly before me.

"Do her weekly shopping." I heard the gentle but insistent voice in my heart very clearly.

I knew it was divine guidance, but to my shame, I stubbornly resisted. The church I attended had around six hundred members, and I hadn't been attending that long. Although I had seen this lady, I didn't really know her. Sure, I knew she was married and had two small daughters, but that's all I knew. I wouldn't have a clue what to buy for her, and I was worried she would be offended by my charity.

I finished shopping, buying the things I needed for myself, and went home. I felt a heavy weight inside. I knew I had not obeyed, and I felt bad for the rest of the day. But I had no spare time left that day. I was booked up and couldn't get back to the supermarket even if I had wanted to. That evening, I felt decidedly uncomfortable. It's hard to pray to God when you know you haven't obeyed what He told you to do!

Eventually, I told God that if He would walk around the supermarket with me and tell me what to buy, I would go the next morning. Then, by faith, I got up the next day and went shopping.

I really did feel guidance as I put things in the trolley — meat for the week, fruits, vegetables, toilet paper, snacks and biscuits for the girls. Eventually, the trolley was full, so I went to the checkout. I had found out from someone at church where the family lived. I hoped they would be in because I had no space for any of these items in my own fridge or freezer after doing my own big shopping the day before.

I pulled up near their house and noticed they had a disabled parking bay outside. I hadn't known anyone in their household was disabled. When I rang the doorbell, there was no response. The house was silent, with no noise of kids playing or the sound of TV. I got a sinking feeling. What was I going to do with all this stuff? Then I heard someone shuffling down the hallway. The husband opened the door. He looked somewhat confused and a little unsteady. Recognising my face from church, he told me his wife wasn't home yet.

I took a deep breath and then explained my visit. I told him that I needed to buy them some groceries, and I hoped they wouldn't be offended. He wasn't offended at all and willingly accepted the bags, taking them into the kitchen. He told me he'd recently had an operation to remove a brain tumour and hadn't been able to work as the surgery had left him epileptic. That explained the disabled parking bay outside their home. He thanked me for the groceries, and I left.

At the next church service, his wife sought me out to ask if I was the one who had brought the shopping over. She said her husband had memory lapses and couldn't remember who had blessed them, but he did remember it was a white lady. As most of my church is black, I guess that narrowed the search down a lot! As she thanked me, she became very emotional while telling me that they had no money to buy food or groceries, and she had been praying for provision. She said I had bought the exact brands she would have bought, even down to the same toilet paper. I had bought them a lamb joint, which she had told God she wished she could buy as a treat for the family. And I had chosen the exact biscuits that her daughters had picked out the week before, but she had told them she couldn't afford to pay for them and put them back on the shelf.

I was so grateful that I had the opportunity to help that family. We became friends, and when I got married a few years later, this lady was instrumental in helping us find our first home. God really did come shopping with me that day. But more than that, He showed me firsthand how He hears the prayers of those who cry out to Him in their need, and He moves others to respond, even when we have no idea why!

—Carolyn Akinyemi—

42

Bearing a Miracle

Miracles are not contrary to nature but only contrary
to what we know about nature.
~St. Augustine

I lost my first baby due to an ectopic pregnancy a few days after conception. It was heartbreaking, to say the least. Some people thought it shouldn't cause me sadness since the baby wasn't born. So, I suffered in silence and cried by myself.

I was not getting any younger. My husband and I were in a long distance relationship. He was based in the U.S. and I was still in the Philippines. He could only spend three weeks a year of vacation with me. And with only one fallopian tube remaining, conception proved to be difficult. For three years, we prayed and waited.

During our third year of trying, we finally went to a well-known IVF specialist since my OB/GYN told us that our chances of conceiving naturally were very low. We were informed of the financial, physical, and emotional cost. Conceiving with IVF is not a guarantee, but we decided to go for it anyway. We just needed to come up with the money.

A few days after that appointment, I felt pregnant. The intuition was so strong that I didn't feel I needed confirmation at all. I just knew. However, I took a pregnancy test as my husband wanted to be sure. And there it was, confirming what I knew all along: a double line. I went to my doctor, and all she could say was, "Indeed, you are!" She was amazed that we were able to conceive naturally, despite the odds. Our prayers had been answered.

However, I started to worry. I had been pregnant before and rejoiced too soon. When I went to have an ultrasound this time, the sonologist told me that it was a blighted ovum and I would need to undergo a D&C. I left the ultrasound room, walked to my doctor's office, and scheduled an appointment for the procedure. I walked out of the hospital in a daze. How could I not be pregnant when every part of my body was telling me I was?

When I got home, I cried. Nothing made sense.

Two weeks later, when the date of the D&C arrived, I didn't want to go to the hospital. I didn't even want to get out of bed. I didn't want to believe the ultrasound. I was sure there was a baby growing inside me. I must have fallen asleep crying because it felt like someone whispered to me and woke me up.

"Get up and see me."

I can offer no explanation why I felt my baby was talking to me. Perhaps I was used to talking to my baby all the time since I had learned I was pregnant, so it didn't seem weird to assume my baby was communicating back. I got up, even though my mind was telling me, "Are you crazy? You really believe someone told you that?" I got up because my heart told me to believe.

I went to my doctor and asked for a second ultrasound. She didn't see any problem with that and did the ultrasound herself. Then she looked at me, confused but smiling.

"I don't see any problems! You are pregnant. The baby is in your uterus, not in your tube. This is a sure thing."

"Are you sure?" I knew how I had felt all along, but I needed to hear that she was sure as well.

"Look… That's your baby!" She circled the image on the screen. "Do you want to hear the heartbeat?"

I nodded.

I heard the heartbeat, loud and clear. It filled the room for a while, and then I felt my cheeks wet with tears.

"It's a girl," I whispered to myself. "She's a girl."

I felt it. I knew it. But I didn't say it. Nobody would believe me anyway. I was just six weeks pregnant, but I was secretly thinking of girls' names.

One night, I dreamed of my baby. She was sitting by the window, watching some kids playing outside. She looked like she was around two years old. She asked me to tie her hair in a ponytail. She had long black hair. I told her I just needed to go upstairs to get a comb. When I returned, her hair was already tied up neatly. I asked her who had fixed her hair. She replied, "The Blue Fairy." Her lips pursed in an exaggerated way as she said the word "blue."

During my seventh month of pregnancy, I found out her gender. Yes, indeed, she was a girl. I saw her move around during the 4D ultrasound. It was surreal.

I gave birth to her two weeks before my due date. I finally saw her. Her eyes, ears, fingers, toes and, of course, her thick black hair. But it was only after a couple of weeks when I noticed that her favorite expression was pursing her lips in an exaggerated way so that her upper lip almost touched her nose, just like in my dream when she said, "Blue Fairy." I also loved to tie her hair, which was always sticking up in tiny fountains on top of her head.

She is my answered prayer, a dream come true — the one who told me to get up and see her. She is my testimony that miracles happen.

— Lut M.D. Evangelista —

Chapter
5

Messages from Heaven

43

Going to Paradise

Perhaps they are not stars, but rather openings
in heaven where the love of our lost ones
pours through and shines down upon us
to let us know they are happy.
~Author Unknown

isneyland was hot. I stood with my kids, sweating in the June heat, waiting for the Aladdin parade to begin. Suddenly, I shivered when a rush of goose bumps shot up the back of my arms. I glanced my watch: 4:15 p.m.

After a crowded Friday afternoon at Disneyland, we returned to our hotel for a swim. I told my husband I'd be in the gift shop. I wanted to get a book to read at the poolside. I chose a story about a man who went missing. A psychic told his daughter to look in a body of water; his car had crashed near a bridge.

The next day, Saturday, my mother called and asked us to come home. She spoke fast, and I could tell she was frantic. "We haven't been able to find Grandma and Grandpa," she said. My heart fell. What did she mean?

Mom's sister had called, asking if my grandparents were with her. When Mom said no, they called their brother. He hadn't heard from them either. It was unusual for my grandparents to go away without telling anyone, so they knew something was wrong.

On Sunday, with still no word from my grandparents, Mom, her siblings, and my dad drove out to my grandparents' house. They lived about twenty miles away in West Marin. Along the drive there and back, they searched along the side of the road, in gullies and ravines—anywhere a vehicle might have tumbled off the highway—but found nothing.

"He wouldn't have left his medicine," Mom said. I thought this bugged her because she said several times, "It's new, and I could see that she (my grandma) kept track of it on the calendar. It hasn't been marked since Thursday."

Dad noticed that their pick-up truck was missing when he'd checked the garage. He searched the entire house, even the basement. "I knew I had to check the freezer," he said. "But when I lifted the lid, thank God, only Grandpa's venison and duck filled it."

Tuesday night, my mom went on the six o'clock news. Holding a framed photo of my grandparents, she made a plea for the public to call the Marin County Sheriff's Department with any information.

A woman stated that my grandma had complimented her little girl at the grocery store that past Friday. "She told my daughter she was pretty. She seemed like a nice lady." That tip verified they'd been in San Anselmo. From the grocery store to their home, family and deputies traveled the roads back and forth, looking for my grandpa's truck. No one mentioned foul play, yet it crossed our minds.

By Thursday, still unable to eat or sleep, I imagined my grandparents stranded without food or water, perhaps injured or trapped. I pushed the dreadful images out of my mind and prayed for good news. That night, I had a dream.

I found myself inside an airport, near a terminal. When I looked around, I saw my grandparents, and they waved to me. I was filled with joy. "I found you," I said.

They didn't speak to me, but they intuitively messaged that they were on their way to "Paradise."

"Hawaii? You're going to Hawaii?" I asked in disbelief. Their eyes beamed, and I was relieved. I couldn't wait to tell my mother that I'd found her parents. But I noticed something odd: Grandma's sister, who'd previously passed away, stood beside them.

The following day, a week after my grandparents disappeared, a fisherman came into Point Reyes Station. Drinking at the local bar, a reporter overheard him boast about finding a six-pack of beer along the shore of the Nicasio Reservoir. "Take me to where you found the beer," said the reporter.

When the fisherman and the reporter scoured the lakeshore, they found a watermelon and other food. Within the hour, the Marin County Sheriff was notified. The road was examined, and it was determined that the guardrail had been damaged — an indication that, "It's likely a vehicle careened into the lake."

That evening, gathered around the television set at Mom and Dad's, we watched breaking news. My grandfather's longtime friend, the same man who sold Grandpa his pick-up, pulled the truck out of the water with his tow-truck winch. The process took a while; their vehicle had settled seventy-five feet below the water's surface. "I just gotta know there was nothing wrong with that truck," Grandpa's friend said, the despair evident in his voice.

Dad cried when the obituary segment mentioned that my grandpa had driven a school bus for forty years without one incident.

At their funeral, my husband squeezed my hand and expressed how he found both tragedy and beauty at the sight of my grandparents' caskets positioned side by side at the church. I knew that Grandma had sent me that dream to tell me she and Grandpa were okay and together.

After the funeral, the coroner completed his report. He offered answers for our family. Grandpa had suffered a stroke and lost control of the vehicle. The cause of death for both of them was drowning. He assured us that even though it's scary to let go of that last breath, once you do, drowning is a peaceful way to die.

Before the coroner left, he gave my mother the wristwatches my grandparents had been wearing. I stared at them and got the chills. Both watches had stopped at 4:15 p.m.

— CM Riddle —

44

Phone Call from Heaven

While we are sleeping, angels have
conversations with our souls.
~Author Unknown

I was twenty-one when my dad passed away, seven months after having a severe heart attack. The doctor had warned us that, due to the damage to his heart, he wouldn't have much time left.

During his remaining time, my dad tried to prepare my mom for his passing. He had always taken care of everything. She knew nothing about their insurance, pensions, or investments. She had never paid a bill, much less balanced a checkbook! She had so much to learn and so little time to learn it.

Apparently, he ran out of time telling her everything because almost a year after he passed away, I had a dream giving me even more instructions.

In the dream, I was at a party, laughing and having a great time. I heard the phone ring, and someone yelled, "Vicky! Phone for you. It's your dad, and he says it's important." I ignored the person because I knew my dad had passed away. I thought he was either mistaken, or it was a different Vicky at the party. He yelled for me again to come to the phone, and I yelled back, "No, it's not my dad... My dad passed away." But he was insistent and wouldn't let it go. After several times, I became more emotional because it just seemed cruel at that point.

I finally gave in and made my way to the phone, saying angrily, "Who is this?"

I could hear the voice on the other end say, "You have to listen to me. Tell your mom the money in the closet is worth more than she realizes. Don't get rid of it!"

I said, "Who is this? Please stop it. My dad passed away!"

Again, the voice insisted, "Please, Vicky, tell Mom!"

It sounded like my dad, but I knew my dad had passed away, so it wasn't possible. I just shook my head and said, "Whatever." I hung up the phone and went back to the party.

After I woke up, the dream stayed with me. It had been so vivid! I remembered everything clearly. After about a week of it gnawing at me, I finally found the courage to tell my mom. I hated bringing it up and bringing his death back to the forefront of her mind, but I remembered the urgency in his voice.

I couldn't look at her when I told her. I felt ridiculous even bringing it up. I explained everything about the dream. I had tears in my eyes as I finally turned to look at her and said, "I'm so sorry. Do you think it means anything?"

I will never forget her face. She was white as a sheet, and tears filled her eyes. She said, "Vicky, I was cleaning out the closet in my room last week and found a coffee can full of coins that your dad had hidden back there! I never told anyone because I thought it was just a can of old coins, and I was going to get rid of them."

I knew then that it really had been my dad. I now understood his insistence on letting my mom know about the coins. He was still taking care of her... even after his death.

— Vicky Webster —

45

A Visit in the Night

Face what you think you believe and
you will be surprised.
~William Hale White

I had recently moved to a new home with my two children, in hopes of giving them a better life. The area that we moved from seemed to be going downhill fast, with increasing violence in the community and bullying in the hallways of the school.

However, at our new home, things quickly got much worse. I was hit from every direction. The job that I was supposed to have fell through the second day I was there. My relationship with my boyfriend Jack started to fall apart. Soon, his best friend, Paul, began telling me bad things about him. I was crushed. I tried to hide that I was sad because I did not want to upset my kids. Since I had moved so far away, I did not have any friends or family around to lean on for advice or support.

I struggled to get back into the workforce, causing my finances to get tighter and more difficult every day — another fact I tried to hide from my kids. But I noticed that they were lonely, too, for their old friends. So, I tried to fill their days with as much fun as possible. Not knowing our way around town made this difficult, so Paul often helped. He was a good person, or so I thought. I did not connect the fact that often the things I argued about with Jack stemmed from conversations that I only had with Paul.

I started to yearn for the wise counsel of Captain Robinson, my pastor from when I was a child and attended church. At one point, he was more than just my pastor. I lived a violent life of turmoil with my abusive father and stepmother, and he was the only one who comforted me and gave me strength on really bad days. Captain Robinson was the man I needed now. But how could I find him? I hadn't seen him in twenty years.

I called my former church, hoping that someone there could help me find him. Maybe the new pastor was still in touch with him. I called the church almost every day for over a week, but no one called me back.

One night, I broke down. I lay in bed and cried myself to sleep. I quickly found myself in a dream.

I was sitting on a couch in a light-blue room by myself. There was nothing on the walls, just me in this room. I cradled my face in my hands and was crying. Suddenly, Captain Robinson was in front of me. He was the way I remembered him as a child. It was as if he had not aged a day.

He pulled my hands away from my face and said, "I'm here. I'm here. Shh, I'm here." Then he sat next to me with his arm around my shoulder and said, "Shh, it's okay. I'm here. Tell me everything that's wrong." I spilled out every aching thought inside me, sharing everything that was happening. He just nodded his head and let me vent.

It seemed like he already knew what was happening, but talking about it helped me feel better. It felt like he was scooping out the jagged pieces of my life that were tearing me apart inside while giving me that listening ear I needed so badly. At the end, I was just a shell — a hurt shell — but all the bad stuff was gone from inside me.

He told me that I needed to go back home — that where I was now would never be home for me and my kids. I needed to let go of Jack and Paul. What Jack and I had was not love, and Paul was not a friend and never was.

He explained I was being told many lies. It would take too long to sort out the lies from the truth, and trying to do so would only make things worse. He told me again to take my kids and go home — rebuild our lives from there. We would be happy again once we made that move.

Then he said he had to go and could not come back again. He told me not to try to find him anymore. He needed to make sure that I would be okay and stressed that he was only allowed to come and see me this one time. His last words still play over and over in my mind. He said, "Don't try to find me anymore. You won't be able to find me. I died of a heart attack over a year ago, but I'm still here listening."

That was in October. The next month, I moved with my children back home — to the town they had lived in when they were born. Finally, we had everyone back in our lives that we needed so much.

In December, I learned that my childhood church — the one where Captain Robinson preached — was having a toy drive for Christmas. It was late notice when I found out about it, but I bought two toys and went to the church to deliver them and volunteer my gift-wrapping skills. I debated about whether I should do this, but I still wanted to see the new pastor and make one last attempt to find Captain Robinson, even though he had been insistent in my dream that I not do that. But then again, it was just a dream, right?

At the church, I had a long talk with a woman who was wrapping gifts alongside me. She also knew Captain Robinson. She said that, at one point, her daughter was married to the Captain's son. And then I heard these words from her own mouth: Captain Robinson died almost two years ago — from a heart attack!

There they were, his own words, echoing back through her. "Don't try to find me. I died over a year ago." It was true, and it was him in my dream! He was there, next to me, to comfort me and carry me through to the next stage of my life. Sometimes, I still talk to him. Although I know I will never see him again, no one can take away the fact that he rescued me on one horrible night — in one glorious dream!

— Charlotte Hopkins —

46

Lost Letters from Vietnam

A dream which is not interpreted is like
a letter which is not read.
~The Talmud

I was dreading the next day. It had been awhile since my grandparents passed away, and their house was being put up for sale. Tomorrow would be the last time I would go to Mamaw and Pappy's. So, when I dreamed of my grandmother that night, it was a sweet salve for my aching heart.

Mamaw Elsie and Pappy lived in an approximately 900-square-foot house, with three tiny bedrooms, a single closet to share, and one bathroom. Somehow, every holiday, there was room for all five kids and their families to gather and visit.

In my dream, Mamaw's smile greeted me as I entered through the back door, as usual. All my family was clustered at their house, singing together around the piano that used to sit in the "middle bedroom" (so-called because we had to walk through it to reach the "back bedroom"). I saw a ghostly, semi-transparent image of my grandmother sitting on the end of a plaid couch that impossibly fit into the 4x3 hallway in front of the bathroom.

"Shh," I told everyone. "There's Mamaw. Come see her!"

She looked me in the eye and started to say something, but when my family turned to see her ghost, she joyfully smiled and faded away.

Then I woke up feeling comforted, almost like I had really visited her. I wished I had thought to ask her where my dad's letters from Vietnam were. A few years before Alzheimer's had claimed her mind she had shown them to me. They'd been in a filing cabinet with letters from my uncles when they were in the service, favorite greeting cards, and newspaper clippings of the grandchildren.

I didn't get them then, probably because she was still of sound mind and didn't offer them to me. I knew they were in the filing cabinet, but after my grandparents died and my aunt moved out, the letters disappeared. My aunt went through all the boxes from the filing cabinet. She told me she'd thrown away a lot of things, like electricity- and water-bill receipts dating back to the 1960s, and she hoped she didn't accidentally throw them away, too.

The loss of the letters, combined with selling my grandparents' house, added to my grief. The next day, my sister Jennifer, her husband Allen, and two of my uncles met us at the house for a final walk-through.

Now that the house was empty, I didn't feel the same nostalgia for it. Suddenly, I was ready to go. Besides, it was late afternoon, there was no power on, and it was stifling and dark. Part of me wanted to just go outside, dig up Mamaw's irises and leave. My sister and I could make sure her flowers carried on; that was enough.

But I couldn't go. I needed to walk into each room and gather what memories it offered. The back bedroom is where the cat stole into an open drawer and had her kittens on the soft shirts inside. The middle room was where we kids would play when it was raining. This was also the room where my dream had taken place. I glanced into the hall where my grandmother's spirit had sat smiling, wishing she'd appear there again. I instinctively "looked up," as if to heaven, and stopped. *The attic.* I'd dreamt Mamaw was sitting right under the attic. I'd forgotten all about it.

"Hey, Jen. What about the attic? Do you think there's anything up there?" I asked with new energy.

Sure enough, my uncles confirmed that no one had been physically up to the task of looking in the attic. They figured there was mostly junk up there anyhow. My brother-in-law volunteered to check it out and was soon handing down bags of clothes and dusty decorations, followed by an old school bench, a twin bed, and iron barn hooks that my uncles thought came from my great-grandmother's farm. The furniture wasn't anything of value, except sentimentally, yet we were ecstatic to have it.

Then came the boxes. Most contained old files from my grandfather's auto-body repair shop. I opened another box and found the rubber-banded stack of white envelopes with red, white and blue edging that I recognized as military stationery.

They were my dad's letters! We couldn't believe it.

I longed to open them right then, but the sun was low, and there was barely enough light to see into the boxes, let alone read the letters. My sister and I hugged each other. The mood lightened. Even digging up irises in a light drizzle was bearable after that.

I spent that night with my sister. Like teenagers, we got snacks and sat around her kitchen table in our PJs, crying, laughing and connecting with our dad as a young G.I. Through his letters to his parents, we experienced his country-boy ache for home, his observations of a foreign country and a grueling war, and his joy at receiving the news and pictures of my birth.

My dad described his job, his life in the barracks, and his terror when the incoming mortars would drive them to shelter in the ditches. We were shocked at the raw honesty of his letters.

The letters affected me deeply, as I'd always felt like he wasn't ready to have a new baby when he came home. But that wasn't the case at all. Reading the waking nightmares he experienced, which created the PTSD that mad him sometimes difficult to live with, made me more compassionate and patient in dealing with his erratic moods.

Now that he has also passed away, those letters are invaluable to me. Some people might think it's a coincidence that I dreamed about my grandmother sitting underneath the opening to her attic where my dad's letters were. However, I'll always believe that Mamaw Elsie sent me a message to help me find those treasures in her attic.

If not for the dream, I might never have searched the attic. I would have missed out on the rare and wonderful experience of knowing my dad as a younger man facing the most difficult year of his life. I wouldn't have understood as much about how it affected him later in life. I know Mamaw would have wanted that for both of us. I believe they are both smiling down at me right now.

— Lorraine Furtner —

47

I'll Never Walk Alone

Love as powerful as your mother's for you leaves its
own mark... To have been loved so deeply... will give
us some protection forever.
~J.K. Rowling

It was April 6, 1996, my birthday. I had just gotten out of a miserable relationship and was also recuperating from hand surgery. Needless to say, I was in desperate need of some encouraging words. So, when Mama called to wish me a happy birthday, it really made my day.

We talked for a couple of hours that day, and I was thrilled to learn that she was planning to make the two-and-a-half-hour trek down from Washington to see me before the month was over. I had no idea that phone call would be the last time I would hear her voice.

The next call I got from home was to inform me that Mama had had a massive cerebral hemorrhage, and they were waiting for me to come and say goodbye before they turned off the machines. I rushed to her side and insisted on holding her hand when they turned them off. If she changed her mind at the last minute, she could give a little squeeze, and we would turn everything back on. But this, too, was not meant to be.

I came into a little money later that year and bought my first house. Moving ten years of accumulation in my pick-up truck was an indescribable experience. We must have made that thirty-five-mile round trip at least fifty times that day. I was exhausted by the time the move was over.

As I settled into my little house, I started to wonder what I had done. I had bought this house and moved everything I had into it, but I didn't even have a job. I had no idea how I was going to pay for it.

I collapsed into my recliner thinking that I would just take a breather, a little break to organize my thoughts before I got back to the task of finishing the move. Suddenly, I could no longer keep my eyes open. I never nap during the day, especially when there's so much to do.

I just remember wishing, as I dozed off, that I could find Mama's recipe for banana bread. I knew that it was in one of the hundreds of moving boxes that surrounded me and filled most of the rooms in my little house. A hot cup of tea and a warm slice of Mama's banana bread would be just perfect right now, I thought, as I drifted off to sleep. But judging by the sea of boxes, it would likely be quite a while before the aroma of banana bread would be wafting through my house.

The next thing I remember, I found myself entering a darkened room. I could see the soft glow of a light that seemed to be coming from one corner. I stepped from the alcove and started to move slowly toward the center of the room.

The first thing that came into view was a huge, ornately decorated porcelain flowerpot that held an enormous plant in full bloom. As I got closer, I could clearly see that the foliage of this plant looked exactly like a big bouquet of peacock feathers. They were shimmering softly in the hazy glow.

Then a movement in the far corner of the room caught my eye. The glow slowly started to get brighter and brighter, and then there she was. It was Mama!

She was dressed in a flowing white gown, and there were purple flowers in her hair. She was surrounded by a golden aura, and when I saw her face, an overwhelming feeling of calm swept over me. She was smiling, and I smiled back. I asked her, "Mama, what kind of plant is that? It's beautiful!"

She didn't say a word. She just smiled at me and reached out her hand. I took it in mine, and another wave of calm rushed through me.

When I woke up only minutes later, my arm was extended out

in front of me, and my hand was in the exact position it would have been if I had been holding someone's hand. Then, without the slightest hesitation, I got up, made my way through the endless stacks of boxes, and found myself in the back bedroom. I walked up to a stack of boxes in the back of the room and removed the top four boxes. Reaching into the fifth box, I lifted up about half of the contents, and there, in the middle of the box, was Mama's handwritten recipe for banana bread.

There is only one way that could've happened. Some might say it was an unexplained coincidence. I say it was no less than angelic guidance.

Since that day, I try to pay attention to all the little, everyday miracles that happen in my life — especially the ones that seem to give me a gentle nudge toward the discovery of some astounding epiphany. It gives me great comfort to know that Mama still seems to know exactly what I need. She is still in my life, pointing me in the right direction whenever necessary.

— Cheri Bunch —

Words of Love

*There are grandmothers out there who would move
heaven and earth for their grandchildren.*
~Janice Elliott-Howard

etting married is stressful for any bride, but when my grandmother became ill, it added another dimension to the circumstances. She wanted very much to see me walk down the aisle, but her condition made it impossible.

I promised to go to the hospital room after the wedding so she could see me in my veil and gown. But one week before my wedding, we got the call that she had passed away. That night, she came to me in a dream.

She said she had something very valuable she wanted me to have. She said the precious gift was hidden in the top drawer of her china cabinet.

The next morning, my parents and I opened the drawer she had instructed we look in. There was nothing obviously valuable, just some linens. We pulled them out and finally found a little greeting-card box.

We sat at the dining-room table and removed the lid to find all the letters and cards I had given her over the years. These were the cherished treasures she wanted me to have.

It has been fifty years, and I still open the box every year on the anniversary of the night that she visited me as I slept.

— Lorraine Moran —

A Heavenly Party

Death ends a life, not a relationship.
~Jack Lemmon

Rainbow-colored balloons and streamers filled a large hall. Jovial partygoers chatted around an enormous, three-tiered birthday cake. Some attendees sat at tables, while others stood, visible as black silhouettes. Everyone in attendance was dead except for my brother and me.

This dream wasn't my first trip to a party with the deceased. I'd been doing it regularly since 1991. The first one I attended was with my Aunt Suzanne, who died at fifty-two of a sudden heart attack. She happily informed me at the party that her daughter, my cousin, was pregnant. I learned later that day that my cousin was indeed pregnant with her first child.

Usually, I enjoyed these parties and hated to leave, but this particular dream occurred during the COVID-19 pandemic, and for some reason it made me uneasy.

In this dream, Aunt Joan Marie, Suzanne's sister, was the guest of honor, welcoming guests in a receiving line. She had died from lung cancer in 2015. Her white hair was now short, styled, and shiny like Marilyn Monroe's. She wore a satin gold dress, like the kind worn by Joan Collins during her Dynasty days, which she paired with four-inch heels. When it was my turn, I leaned in to greet her with a hug. She smelled like flowery perfume.

"I hope you can stay." Aunt Joan spoke softly and in her usual breathy way. She stood with three other people, appearing only as black silhouettes.

I looked over my shoulder for my brother, who was engrossed in a conversation with Uncle Rich, Aunt Joan's brother. He had died of heart disease two weeks before his sister.

"Look, Jim even brought a professional athlete to my party," Aunt Joan said, pointing at my cousin Jim, who died of lung cancer in 2013. He walked across the dance floor alongside a muscular man. "He just showed up. A friend of Jim's. They used to play ball together."

Just showed up? Considering the United States was in the midst of the worst virus outbreak since the Spanish flu, I imagined a lot of people were newly arriving at this party.

Well, not me. Not yet. And not my brother. I rushed to my brother's side. "We've gotta go."

"But I don't want to leave. I haven't seen Uncle Rich in years," he said.

"We can't stay here." I didn't want to talk about death in front of my deceased uncle, so I wracked my brain thinking of something I could say to get my brother to agree to leave the afterlife. "We have... er... another party to go to."

Never wanting to disappoint, my brother finally stood up. I said a quick goodbye to Aunt Joan, and then we left.

That's when I woke up.

Later, I called my father and relayed the dream to him.

"Who'd you see?" he asked as if I had said I ran into someone at a store. He was used to my dreams.

"I was at a party for Aunt Joan Marie. Your brother was there, along with your sister and Jim."

"Did you say it was a party for Aunt Joan Marie?"

"Yup. Why?" I asked.

"Today is her birthday."

A chill ran up my back. I had no idea. As the youngest of the youngest, I was born a little too late to enjoy fun parties from the past. By the time I was born, get-togethers had been replaced by hurt feelings, too much pride, and busy schedules. I rarely saw Aunt Joan Marie as I got older, and I had no idea it was her birthday.

After I got over the initial shock that I attended Aunt Joan's heavenly birthday party, I meditated on the meaning. Was it a sign? If it was a sign, what was the significance? Was there even one? Or was this dream just a consequence of an overactive imagination?

Later, I learned that Aunt Joan's daughter had hired a psychic to get in touch with her mom. It didn't work, so she was grateful to hear about my dream and that her mom was okay.

She was more than okay. It was the happiest I'd seen her in years.

— Keri Kelly —

50

Some Things Never Change

A mother's love for her child is like nothing else in the world. It knows no law, no pity. It dares all things and crushes down remorselessly all that stands in its path.
~Agatha Christie

"I give up! You're both insane." That was my daughter-in-law's response when I told her that Larry was on the balcony in the rain, and I was going to the store. She had called to warn us that there was a severe-weather alert for Dallas County. I had already received the warning on my cell phone. Cindy meant well, but sometimes she worried about us — the "old folks" — too much.

We told each other, "I love you. Stay safe," and hung up.

I grabbed my purse and told Larry I was running to the store.

"Don't you see there's a serious storm coming?" my husband said.

"If it's so serious, why are you standing out on the balcony?" I countered.

I was going to Central Market — ten minutes away. What could go wrong?

As I left the house, I turned back to lock the door. *I was startled to see Mother staring at me through the window.*

I opened the umbrella we kept on the front porch and rushed the twenty feet to my car in the driveway. The wind and rain were stronger than I had expected, turning my umbrella inside out.

So what? I'm not a fragile woman who can't take a little rain.

Besides, they say, "If you don't like the weather in Texas, just wait five minutes."

I needed groceries for the next morning so I went. As I drove down Preston Road, however, I started hearing thunder and sirens in the distance.

The rain became more intense. Two blocks from my destination, I moved into the far-left lane, preparing to turn into the Central Market shopping center. By now, the winds were gusting, and the heavy rain was making driving extremely difficult. Debris was flying through the air, hitting the few vehicles still remaining in the street. On the radio, the word "tornado" was being thrown around.

It occurred to me that maybe I should have stayed home. The sirens no longer seemed so far away. The thunderstorm was getting worse.

"You're almost there. Almost there! Just turn left into the shopping center. Don't panic. You'll be fine." I found myself talking out loud.

At the corner, I stopped for a light. Maybe I lingered too long, mesmerized by the sight in front of me. *Through the rain on my windshield and the wipers, I saw my mother crossing the street in front of my car.*

"What the…?"

She turned to look at me. She made a gesture with her right hand like a circle, as if giving me a sign. What was she trying to tell me? The store was to the left. Was she pointing to the right? Or signaling me to turn around?

Of course, I knew it wasn't Mother — she had passed away ten years earlier — but she got my attention. I guess she still had influence over me. Some things never change.

Behind me, vehicles frantically blew their horns when, without warning, I abruptly changed direction and swerved two lanes to the right, away from Central Market and into a smaller shopping center.

"I hear you, Mom," I said to no one.

I found a spot next to a small grocery store and parked. I opened the car door, and it slammed closed. The wind had become fierce. I watched in horror as shopping carts zoomed through the parking area, crashing into the surrounding businesses and vehicles. Suddenly, the grocery store turned dark, and all the lights in the shopping center parking lot went out. It was impossible to believe what was happening around me.

Through the noise of sirens, wind and rain, a deafening sound like a freight train began somewhere in a distance and kept coming closer. I had to get out of there.

In the intense darkness, I took my shot. I drove out of the shopping center, turning away from the havoc. All the streetlights were out. All I had was my car lights and those of other vehicles attempting to escape anywhere they could. As quickly but as carefully as I could, I turned away from Central Market and headed in the direction and safety of my home. On the way, the rumble became increasingly louder.

A few minutes later, I pulled into my driveway. That's when the loudest noise of all hit. I never looked back. I was safe.

Larry met me at the door.

"I've been worried sick!"

An EF3 tornado ripped through Dallas that night in October 2019, destroying approximately fifteen miles. The Central Market shopping center was just one area affected.

Had I arrived at Central Market a few minutes earlier, I would have ended up in the cooler when the tornado struck. A store manager with smart thinking and common sense quickly gathered the remaining customers in the store and guided them into the only safe place on the premises — the cooler.

Had I arrived a minute or two later, I might have been trapped outside, right smack in the midst of the tornado.

The next day, I returned to the Central Market. Driving down the streets that had been as familiar as my own, I wondered, "Is this my town?" It was unrecognizable.

The Market shopping center was devastated. Restaurants, clothing stores, bakeries and the beautiful food supermarket that I had frequented a couple of times a week had been demolished. Broken glass, shattered trees, food and rainwater covered the grounds. Vehicles were overturned, one on top of another. Some were poking out of the buildings they had been hurled into by the storm. Collapsed rooftops and smashed-in windows were common sights.

In the neighborhood, modest to million-dollar homes were equally destroyed. Nature doesn't discriminate.

There were several tornadoes in Dallas that night. I only saw one. I hope I never see another.

That night in the aftermath, I stood outside on my balcony gazing at the disarray in our back yard. Our trees had broken limbs but did not get uprooted. On one side, I saw a neighbor's tree being supported by our fence. My other neighbor's tree, which had been knocked against her house, suddenly lost all support. Before my eyes, it slowly drifted to the ground, hurting nothing but some backyard furniture.

Standing on our balcony, staring at the damage, I was eternally grateful that — miraculously — there were no fatalities from that tornado. A few people got hurt but none critically.

Reflecting on the chaos the previous hours had brought, I thanked the Lord and my lucky stars for sparing us all that night. *Then, once again, I saw my mother's face. This time, she was smiling.*

— Eva Carter —

51

Honoring Love by Moving On

Our brothers and sisters are there with us from the
dawn of our personal stories to the inevitable dusk.
~Susan Scarf Merrell

My older brother Paul died on June 28, 2005, the day before he would have turned fifty-one years old. I found myself sitting with my aged mother in a funeral home, picking out a casket — on his birthday.

Paul had been my own personal Superman. After my divorce years prior, he flew me to his home in Syracuse, New York to give me respite from my single-mom stress.

He had helped me in my time of need, but I wasn't there in his darkest hour. He died alone. I couldn't bear it.

Cards and flowers with silky ribbons arrived — not to wish him well for his birthday, but to bid him adieu on his passage from this earth. I was angry with God. After a short hiatus where I traveled to my brother's out-of-state home to pack up his apartment and two cats, I returned to my job. It didn't seem right that the world should go on as if something horrible hadn't just happened. But each morning I awoke to a new day. The birds chirped. The mail arrived. People talked, worked and drove cars. Meanwhile, I moved through that summer in a fog. It took effort to smile. The first time I laughed was at work, and

I felt guilty. My brother was dead.

Since Paul had never married, I settled his affairs. Amid mailing death certificates to creditors, inventorying his comic collection that numbered in the thousands, and reading every shred of his writings in hopes of decoding his life in those last months, there was no escaping the grief. It consumed and drained me.

My husband worried. He knew I needed time, but it was not clear how much. Three months passed. Autumn approached — a time that held a glimmer in the form of an annual dance outing that I had organized each October for several years with family and friends. It was always a highlight of my year.

But my brother had just died. How could I possibly shimmy across the dance floor? I discussed the idea, thought about it, and rejected it. Then one night, I had a dream.

Paul came to me. I knew he was dead in my dream. He couldn't walk well; he was very weak and sort of limped. He held out his hand and asked me to dance. It's a feeling I will never forget — one of joy and realization, knowing that I would hold my brother in my heart forever. That joyous moment in my dream stood in stark contrast to the previous months.

When I awoke, the message crystalized. I needed to move on with my life. My brother would want me to move on. Specifically, I needed to move across the dance floor. I needed to do the thing that was good for my soul, which would pick up not just my spirits but those of my family as well.

The dance outing took place that year. My dream of dancing with Paul was a turning point in the miasma of grief that had been clouding out the light and laughter in my life.

Even after great sadness, when it's clear the world will never be the same again, we need to embrace the life we have. We honor the dead by finding joy in life.

I accept the possibility that my subconscious told me in a dream what my waking mind would not accept: To feel joy again would not dishonor my brother. Conversely, it would honor the family he loved so much.

That dream helped me recover sooner and allowed me to return to nurturing those still on earth — my husband, my children, my mother, and myself.

— Melanie Holmes —

Shared Comfort

There is always another layer of awareness,
understanding, and delight to be discovered
through synchronistic and serendipitous events.
~Hannelie Venucia

My father died on August 25, 1995. Throughout his whole life, he'd been riddled with illness the way an old oak tree is blighted by heart rot fungus. The diseases might lie dormant for a year or a season, but they were woven into his genes and would blossom forth with depressing regularity. He got epilepsy at fourteen and tuberculosis at sixteen. He developed arthritis at twenty and smashed his skull at forty. He broke his neck twice and was quadriplegic for the last twenty years of his life and more than half of mine.

Yet his fear of death was greater than his dread of pain. He died, waking from a coma to cry out, "I don't want to go yet."

I didn't mourn, though I'd loved him deeply. I was more than ready. Everyone was — except Daddy.

For more than a year, I had no dreams. My nights were empty as death.

Then, on August 25, 1997, exactly two years later, I began to dream:

A puppy was trapped upstairs on the wooden deck of our old house. The deck was so fragile and delicate that even cats feared it, but Daddy climbed up to it with confidence. Cradling the dog in his arms, he leapt into space and landed softly on the grass.

Messages from Heaven | 169

On October 25, 1997...

I dreamed he went diving sixty feet underwater clad only in swim trunks. He emerged from the sea like a geyser, hands dripping with rubies, pearls and golden coins.

And on December 25, 1997, I had the most amazing dream of all.

Daddy sat, back straight, legs folded as neatly as a basket woven into a lotus, framed by the arc of a huge cave. Its darkness was absolute, impenetrable, vast as a starless night. Before him, the earth fell away, dropping into a bottomless pit as round as a planet.

He saw me and smiled. "Come here," he said.

"I can't," I said, motioning to the hole. "I'll fall."

"It's not a real hole," he said. "It's just an illusion. You can walk across."

I reached out and touched the darkness with my toe. He was right. The hole was painted onto the earth — a clever deception, a mini masterwork, a delusion of depth. I crossed it in three steps.

"Daddy," I said. "Why is it that in life you were crippled — sometimes you couldn't even curl your fingers around a fork or raise your arm to feed yourself — but now you are always super agile, swimming underwater without tanks and climbing up to the deck that even our cats avoided?"

"When we die," he said, "all the pain and suffering — all the ills that are physical — fade. The body is only a surface, only skin. But the truth inside, that survives. This is my truth."

I never told anyone but my sister about those dreams.

Years later, Mom died. As far as death goes, one might say it was a good one, but no death is ever good.

She lay in bed, ready to go, young eyes peering from an old face. She smiled, wanting to be free from pain — free from the congestive heart failure that drowned her nightly.

After Mom passed, my sister began emptying drawers, tossing journals and photographs into the trash. I tried to stop her. I'd been living with my mother, caring for her as best I could. My sister had been grateful, but now she wanted to finalize things faster than I was ready for. After two days, she departed, leaving me alone in the empty house.

That night, I was awoken by the howling of my mother's cat. He was on her bed. I climbed in beside him. He purred and snuggled into me. We slept for a few hours and then awoke. The cat sat up on the bed, looking blankly into the dark, sniffing the night. His head turned from side to side. His eyes widened, glowing in the dark. Then, he leapt off the bed and cowered beneath it.

"What is it?" I asked. "What do you see, boy?" But there was no answer. I went back to sleep and awoke a while later with a thought in my mind. It wasn't deep or profound. It was simple, silly, and possibly not even original. Nevertheless, I wanted to save it.

I pulled open the drawer of my mother's bedside table, searching for paper. They had already been emptied by my sister. My hands moved in the empty drawer, hollow as a coffin. Then, trapped in the metal drawer slide, I felt a single piece of paper.

The moon had risen and shone in the window. By its light, I could see that the page was used on one side. On the blank side, I scribbled down my thoughts and fell back into a dreamless sleep.

The next day, I read what my mother had written on the paper I had found during the night. It was topped with a date: August 25, 1997.

I had the strangest dream. Jules climbed up the back trellis onto the terrace to rescue a dog. He took the puppy in his arms, and he leapt into the back yard. Very odd.

A few lines down, the paper was dated October 25, 1997.

Dreamt of Jules again tonight. He was diving in the ocean, deep as a scuba diver but without any equipment. Every time he rose from the sea, he brought treasure with him.

I rummaged in the drawer once more, searching, hoping but not daring to believe. And then I found it: a single page that had fallen under the drawer. It was dated December 25, 1997.

Dreamt of Jules again. He was sitting like a yogi in the entryway to a huge, dark cave. Before him lay a bottomless pit. He smiled when he saw me and motioned me toward him. "Come here," he said.

I pointed to the pit.

"It's not real," he said. "It's only an illusion. You can walk across."

He was right. The hole was painted onto the bare earth.

"Jules, why do I have these dreams?" I asked. "In life, you were crippled, but now you are almost superhuman."

"When we die," he said, "pain, suffering, all the ills of the physical fade. The body is only skin. But the truth inside, that survives. This is my truth."

That was all she wrote. It was enough.

I sat on the bed that still smelled of her. I looked over at the deck that Daddy had ascended so easily. It was covered by the twisted limbs of old roses and wisteria. A few lavender ringlets hung down like fragrant tears.

I called my sister and read her Mom's notes. We were silent for a while, remembering, forgiving, healing—taking comfort in each other and in our parents' last gift.

—E. E. King—

Prophetic Premonitions

53

Somebody's Miracle

Remember there's no such thing as
a small act of kindness. Every act
creates a ripple with no logical end.
~Scott Adam

I pretended not to notice the face in the window next door as I knelt beside the unkempt flowerbed that separated our properties. It was a glorious spring morning, the perfect day to get my garden in shape for summer, and though I liked Mrs. Webber very much, I simply did not have time for her. Still, last night's dream had unsettled me.

I tried to lose myself in the chirping of the birds and the sunshine on my face as I stuffed dried leaves and stubborn weeds into trash bags, but my joy was eclipsed by a nagging worry. There was no good reason for me to dream about Edna Webber. The dream hadn't even made sense: a wistful Mrs. Webber rocking a tiny baby. I told myself the dream stemmed from my recent lunch with my friend Claire. We'd brainstormed ideas for our upcoming fundraiser for Rachel's Heart, a local shelter for teenage mothers. The dream was a jumbled mess. But the sadness I'd seen on Edna Webber's dream-face was too real to ignore.

With the last weed pulled and the soil turned up for planting, I stood back and surveyed my work with satisfaction. The tulips and daffodils were already poking through the earth. My little patch of loveliness, like my drab neighborhood, was slowly coming back to life. My gaze drifted to the window again, where a slight fluttering of the curtains told me Edna had watched me the entire time. She was lonely, I supposed. Isolated. In the year I had been her neighbor, I'd never once seen her old Buick leave the driveway.

She'd lived in the little house on the corner of Edgewood Avenue for more than fifty years, she once told me. Back in the day, it had been a quiet, close-knit community of German immigrants. In the last twenty years, the loss of industry and the new super-plaza on the highway outside of town had caused the city to die. One by one, businesses were shuttered, houses were abandoned, and the crime rate soared. Recently, there'd been a home invasion two blocks away. At eighty years of age, I was sure she felt fearful. I rarely saw her outside, and the only company she seemed to have was her daily delivery of Meals on Wheels. I stopped in to visit when I could, but I had a busy life. I couldn't be expected to be her savior, could I? My gaze rested again on the empty window. But what if the dream was a premonition? What if Mrs. Webber were ill or in trouble?

I packed up my garden tools, hauled the trash bags to the curb, and went inside to wash up. I still had a mountain of laundry and a sink full of dishes to deal with. Even so, I put two blueberry muffins on a plate and headed next door.

The sheer happiness on Mrs. Webber's face made me feel ashamed.

"What a nice surprise. Please come in."

"I made these yesterday. I thought you might like some," I said, thrusting the plate of muffins into her hands.

"How lovely. I was just about to have some tea. Will you join me?"

Without waiting for an answer, she hobbled to the kitchen, where I could hear the teakettle whistling. Glancing around her small, tidy living room, I noticed a basket of yarn next to her chair. A half-completed blanket lay on top, looking so soft I could not resist touching it.

"May I?" I asked when Mrs. Webber returned.

"Of course."

The blanket was as soft as I'd imagined. "It's beautiful," I murmured.

"Thank you," she said, all at once shy. "Would you like to see the others?"

She led me to a hall closet, opening the door to expose a dozen or more baby blankets in mint green, pale lavender, and baby blue, each more beautiful than the last.

"What are all these?" I asked, incredulous.

"My work," she said with a small shrug.

"Who are they for?"

She smiled a bit sadly. "I don't know."

Back in the living room, I examined the half-finished blanket again, stroking its delicate ruffled edge. "You do beautiful work."

"I won't be able to finish it." The sadness returned to her face. "This is my last skein of yarn."

The statement took me back in time to my Great-Aunt Esther. An avid knitter, Esther was obsessed with yarn and lived in fear of running out. I well remembered Esther's frantic phone calls when a winter storm was in the forecast, followed by my mother's quick dashes to the store for milk, bread and yarn. It had seemed funny at the time, but now I began to understand. Aunt Esther's knitting, like Mrs. Webber's crocheting, filled many lonely hours. It gave her a purpose, even if she didn't exactly know what that purpose was. All at once, the jumbled pieces of my dream came together, and I knew why I was there.

Over tea, I told Mrs. Webber about Rachel's Heart and all the good the organization did for young, scared girls and their babies. "Would you be willing to donate one of your blankets for our raffle?" I asked hopefully.

The smile on her face was radiant. "Dear, I'd be willing to donate them all."

"Oh, I couldn't ask you to do that."

"But you didn't. I offered." Taking a sip of her tea, she sat back, a contented smile on her face. "I was meant to make the blankets. I felt it in my heart. I like to call it the still, small voice of God whispering to me. So, I made the blankets and trusted God to show me who they were for. And now he has."

A chill ran down my spine as all thoughts of dirty dishes and dusty windows slipped away.

"I have to pick up a few things at the grocery store," I heard myself saying. "It's in the same plaza as the Yarn Barn. Would you like to ride along?"

"Are you sure it wouldn't be too much trouble?"

"It would be a pleasure, Mrs. Webber."

A half-hour later, as Edna Webber's hands caressed the soft, colorful skeins — her gnarled, arthritic, beautiful hands that would fashion this yarn into something amazing — I was glad I had listened to my dream. The work I had planned for the day did not get done, but the greater work, the work of kindness, was so much more important. As I stood with Mrs. Webber in the checkout line, I felt like I could hear that still, small voice she was always talking about. It whispered that if you have the means to help someone, you should do it. What may be a slight inconvenience to you just might be somebody else's miracle.

— M. Jean Pike —

54

The Corridor

Not flesh of my flesh, nor bone of my bone,
But still miraculously my own.
Never forget for a single minute,
you didn't grow under my heart but in it.
~Fleur Conkling Heyliger

My parents waited at the end of the hospital corridor, beaming. My husband and I rushed to meet them, and I could hear the thundering sound of our steps. The baby in my arms wriggled as if she were plugged in to my own excitement. The disappointment of years of infertility treatments and unanswered prayers melted away.

Dad reached for the baby while we were still ten yards away. Triumphantly, I deposited her into his arms as his massive hug engulfed me. One arm held the baby, and the other clasped me so tightly I could barely breathe. Mom's arms encircled us all. Tears and laughter mingled as we exulted in our answered prayer.

Then I woke up. Though I was still laughing, reality encroached bit by bit. My smile faded, and I sat up. My husband's snores provided cover for my tears. I hugged myself and rocked. Though the dream had been intense and unforgettable, that's all it would ever be.

A fertility specialist had diagnosed polycystic ovary syndrome twelve years earlier, launching a monthly cycle of misery. Occasional surgeries were the only interruptions to rounds of tests, medications, and recurring disappointment.

Weariness settled in beside the grief. I finally said to my husband Dale, "I want to stop hoping. It hurts too much." He hugged me and encouraged me not to give up.

After more than a decade of treatments, no viable options remained. My doctor summoned us to his office. "I'm sorry," he said. "You'll never get pregnant."

Shortly thereafter, I dreamed about the corridor. Whenever the hope in that dream tried to surface in the ensuing months, I pushed it away. Facts were facts, and the dream did not change them. But hope refused to die, kept alive by the dream.

On New Year's Day 1990 the front page of our hometown newspaper featured a heartbreaking picture. A wide-eyed Romanian baby stared through the slats of a metal crib, his tiny hands gripping the bars as if he were in jail. The image seared itself into my soul. I thrust the paper under Dale's nose and said, "We have to do something about this!"

We formed an audacious plan. Dale's paternal grandparents were Romanian, having immigrated to the United States in the early 1900s. The Dragomir surname smoothed the way as we navigated a maze of regulations and paperwork. Seven months after first seeing that haunting photograph, we boarded a plane and crossed the Atlantic on a quest to rescue a child and fulfill our desires for parenthood.

A nasty surprise awaited us. For two miserable weeks, Dale and I trekked through the country visiting four orphanages, all with the same result. Communism had disintegrated, and along with it most semblance of legal order. No one seemed to know who was in charge. Obstinate orphanage directors claimed none of the hundreds of children in their facilities were available to adopt. Later, we learned a well-placed bribe would have swung the doors wide open.

Completely disheartened, we knelt to pray on a bare wooden floor beside our humble guest bed in a small apartment. Dale's eyes sparked with determination. He said, "What do you want, a boy or a girl?"

"A girl," I replied, a little shocked.

He peppered me with other questions. Then we prayed — asking God for a little girl, under a year old, with brown hair and brown eyes. Dale even embellished our request, lifting his gaze to heaven and saying,

"And just to make it fun, God, make her look a little like each of us!"

We agreed to search for ten more days, assisted by a cadre of Romanians touched by our plight. If we could not find a child, we would leave the country sadder but wiser. On the ninth day, the telephone rang. One of our new friends squealed, "We have a little girl for you!"

When we first glimpsed Jana a few days later, my heart nearly stopped. The child who slept in the crib was the spitting image of my brother. Wispy chestnut curls framed her placid face. When roused, she opened her luminous, dark-chocolate eyes and gave us such a big smile that it peeked out on both sides of her pacifier. Dale imagined her tiny voice saying, "Hiya, Dad! Where ya been?" She became his daughter that instant.

On the night before our adoption day, the weight of the past drove me to my knees. I needed to relinquish my hope of bearing a biological child so I could open my heart fully to our adopted baby. Through tears, I acknowledged that the hospital corridor had been only a dream. Our reality would be different but still joyous.

The Romanian government issued Jana's exit visa a week later, and we flew to the U.S. Our connecting flight would be a domestic one, and in those days, it was possible for family and friends to greet us as we exited the plane at the gate. I dressed her in a beautiful, hand-embroidered Romanian dress to meet the crowd of people gathered at the airport for our arrival. We waited for all the other passengers to disembark, and like celebrities, we stepped out of the plane and onto the jetway.

A familiar image swirled into my thoughts, and I got goose bumps on my arms. I had seen this before! A long corridor, bright lights… I lifted my eyes to the doorway, and there stood my beaming parents. Dad reached for the baby. We ran down the walkway as it thundered under our feet. Jana squirmed, and a cheer sounded from the onlookers as we dived into my father's embrace. Laughter and tears mingled with the realization my dream had come true! Although I had perceived the corridor as a hospital hallway, the jetway was God's plan all along.

A familiar hymn includes the prayer, "Let not my star of hope grow dim or disappear." If I'd been successful in making the hope of motherhood disappear, I might never have had the courage to embark on our journey to adoption. Though my dream caused pain for several years, it was not given to hurt or discourage me. It was sent so I would persevere until the day I carried my daughter down the corridor to our family's destiny.

—Rhonda Dragomir—

55

The Purple Gingham Shirt

Always laugh when you can. It is cheap medicine.
~Lord Byron

y husband, seated in the hard, plastic chair reserved for the patient's companion, watched as I paced the small exam room. We waited for the oncologist to enter and tell us what we already knew. It was cancer. When the doctor came in, I recognized him immediately from a dream a few months before. All my life, I've had premonition dreams. I know they're premonitions when the future part of the dreams doesn't fit with my current reality.

In the dream, I was in a hospital bed. Chip and I were talking when that doctor walked into the hospital room wearing a purple gingham shirt. The dream stuck out because I thought that the shirt looked odd on him. That was the entire dream.

Chip had been with me long enough to see many of my premonitions come to fruition. He no longer questioned their validity. He tried to reassure me when I told him about that dream, though, telling me not to worry. "For right now, let's just believe that everything will be okay."

Now that dream was our reality—leukemia. The doctor said he'd do the bone-marrow biopsy that day in the office. In a few days, he would have the results and see how far the disease had progressed. I would start taking an oral chemotherapy pill daily. I would take the medication for the rest of my life, but my quality of life should remain the same. "It's not curable, but it is very treatable," he reassured us.

After he performed the biopsy, Chip cautiously helped my aching body into the car and proceeded to drive home. On the way, he was upbeat and positive, relieved by the doctor's report. I was sore from the procedure and lay on my side in the reclined front seat. My mind was back on what now seemed to be a troubling dream. I said, a bit irritated, "I know what he said sounded great, but I am not going to be okay."

I started the chemotherapy pills the next week, and the side effects hit me hard. My body was wasted by exhaustion, bone pain, and raging headaches. I was freezing all the time. It was the end of August in Florida, and I was walking around in jeans, a long-sleeve shirt, and a hoodie but still shivering.

I wondered why the doctor told me that nothing in my life would change. After three weeks of treatment, I developed a fever. I had been warned that if I developed a fever over 100 degrees, I was to call the office. I did and was instructed to go to the emergency room.

When I arrived, I learned that by telling the triage nurse that I had leukemia and a fever, things would become very serious. I was whisked to an enclosed room, and the medical staff took multiple blood samples. My fever was rising, but I was still freezing, and my pulse was extremely low. They ran several tests, but nothing other than the cancer was immediately obvious. After several hours, they took more blood for cultures to try to find out what was going on with me.

Naively, I asked when they would be releasing me. Since they could not find anything obviously wrong with me, I assumed I would be sent home. The nurse looked at me, surprised that I thought I was leaving. She told me that since I still had an uncontrolled fever, a low heart rate, and an unknown infection and cancer, the only place I was going was upstairs to a bed. I asked how long I would have to be in the hospital, and she told me at least three days since the cultures needed seventy-two hours. I accepted my fate and waited for a room to become available.

Later, I was settled in, and my husband went home for the night with a plan to bring me everything I would need for the next few days. Three days turned into five, and doctors and nurses came and went from my room. I was pumped full of IV antibiotics and taken for multiple tests, but still my high fever remained, and no known infections were found.

The sixth day was Saturday, and my husband arrived with a large cup of coffee and a breakfast of non-hospital food. We chatted about my night and were about to set up the Scrabble board to kill some time when my oncologist walked in wearing the purple gingham shirt. Laughing, I said, "See! I told you." My confused doctor walked over to my bed to shake my hand and asked what was so funny.

My husband chimed in, "Oh, she had a dream about this exact moment months ago."

"Hmm. That's odd," he replied absently as he looked at my chart. He told me that he was releasing me. They still could not find what was causing the fever, but I was not worsening, so I would be able to go home later that day.

When the doctor left, Chip looked at me and said chuckling, "You're right. That shirt does look weird on him."

— Amy Michels Cantley —

56

Hush

It takes a lot of courage to show your dreams
to someone else.
~Erma Bombeck

I was only five years old in 1958 when I had my first prophetic dream. The next morning, at breakfast, I asked my mother when I would be able to use my swing at our new summer cabin.

"How did you know we bought a cabin?" Mama asked.

"I dreamed it," I told her. "There was a swing for me, but you didn't see it."

"She must have heard us discussing it last night," she told my father, shrugging. "Now eat your oatmeal and stop asking so many questions." She added, "Maybe we'll put up a swing once we clean up the land a little."

"But there's already one there!" I exclaimed. "It's in the middle of two white trees. You can see the other three little houses from it and..."

"Eat!" Mama repeated in a startled voice, scaring me into abruptly ending the conversation.

Several weeks later, in mid-spring, our family climbed into our car and went to see the overgrown property for the first time. The main house that we would use stood on an unkempt acre of land. We could barely see the other tiny three-room cottage or the one-room cabin next to it that my parents would rent out. Farther down, a small shed in the same peeling paint color as the other three buildings was barely visible amid brush and trees — mirroring my dream to the last detail.

I trudged over to two birch trees. Sure enough, right in the middle, tangled in raspberry bushes and vines, hung an old rope swing with a wooden plank for a seat.

"Mama, look!" I screamed with excitement. "Here's the swing I told you I saw!"

Her face paled, and she hesitated before speaking.

"Come help carry some bags into the house. We have to start cleaning," she told me brusquely, and then quickly walked away.

As I struggled to keep up with her through thicket taller than me, I smiled, knowing I'd get to swing soon. After all, I saw myself doing it in my sleep.

We all worked hard that weekend. My brothers weren't much older than I was, but Papa had all three of them dragging branches, twigs and brush to a fire he built as he scythed and mowed. I helped Mama clean inside that musty house as well as I could for a small child.

Eventually, my mother, brothers, and I spent the rest of our summer vacations there, while Papa worked in the city and joined us every weekend.

Vast fields and forest surrounded our house. A tributary ran close to our cottage — a series of rivers, falls and lakes. We had access to them all, spending our days swimming, fishing, boating and canoeing. A bridge suspended on massive concrete pylons spanned the river, and we would cross it to go berry picking.

A local tourist attraction called Dorwin Falls was located a quarter-mile from us. It was a part of that waterway. Almost every year, tragic drownings occurred there despite posted warnings. People would either try to swim in or would accidentally fall into its deep plunge pool sixty feet below when the swirling cascade of water would dizzily mesmerize them. Strong currents swiftly washed them away, making rescue impossible. Others tried to get too close to the slippery rocky edge for a better look at a legendary stone head jutting out of the face of the waterfall.

I was seven the summer when I had my second prophetic dream. I ran into my parents' room crying and shook my father awake.

"You have to help him, Papa. He's stuck behind the big post at the end of the bridge and under a rock. No one will find him. Everyone is looking, but they keep passing him," I wailed.

"What are you talking about?" my father demanded groggily.

"The man who drowned. He came to me in my dream and said he needs help!"

By that time, my mother was awake. My brothers, hearing me screaming, also came rushing into the room.

"Everybody, back to bed!" Mama ordered. "I don't want to hear any more talk of silly dreams!"

I swiped at my tears and followed my brothers back to bed, but the memory of the horrific nightmare kept me awake the rest of the night.

Our walls were thin, so I could hear my mother telling Papa that, again, I must have overheard talk regarding a man who drowned two days earlier but wasn't found yet.

"I'll go check where she said, but it's probably nothing," my father mumbled wearily.

At dawn, I heard him get up and leave. About twenty minutes later, I heard sirens coming from the direction of the small village near us.

Papa came back much later, avoiding my gaze. He jerked his head at my mother, indicating she should follow him outside. I heard them murmuring in low voices.

"Listen to me, all of you. What Marya dreamed last night stays here, understood?" Papa ordered, pinning us each with a stern glare. "You don't tell anyone about it. People won't understand, and they'll make fun of her!"

"Did you find him where she said?" my older brother asked.

"Yes," he replied curtly. "And we won't discuss it anymore!"

"You're a witch," my younger brother teased. "Creepy, creepy witch!"

"I am not!" I protested.

"Enough!" my mother shouted, and I cringed at the fearful look she gave me before adding, "What your brother said — that's exactly how people will react, maybe worse, if you mention your crazy dreams. They'll think there's something wrong with you because you see things you shouldn't see. You hush about this. All of you!"

I've had many prophetic dreams, precognitive episodes, and

premonitions since then. Some were simply minor ones—locating lost objects, predicting events, etc. Others were more vivid and frightening. Remembering my parents' protective reactions, I kept them all to myself during that less tolerant, superstitious era.

It wasn't until my husband Don and I went camping in a national park shortly after we met that I finally spoke again. I dreamed his car had a blowout that sent us tumbling into a ravine. I awoke, surprisingly composed.

The next morning, we left to return home. I remained focused and vigilant while he drove.

"What's wrong?" Don asked. "You're so quiet."

Before I could answer, I spotted an oddly shaped tree, its trunk protruding at a sharp angle. It was the one in my dream!

"Stop the car!" I yelled.

The second he braked, our front passenger side tire exploded, sending us swerving harmlessly onto the soft shoulder.

We changed the tire and continued on our way. As we passed that tree, we both saw the guardrail separating the road from an eighty-foot drop.

"How did you know?" he asked me finally.

I told him about that dream and so many others I'd had. He expressed no fear or distaste—only relief for saving our lives and sympathy for the many omens I'd never disclosed to anyone.

He's supported and encouraged me to share them with him ever since that day.

—Marya Morin—

57

Christmas Vacation

*Good instincts usually tell you what to do long before
your head has figured it out.*
~Michael Burke

hatever they had slipped in my ginger ale had taken its toll. I couldn't believe someone would invite me to a party and do something so cruel — even dangerous. My insides burned, and my head was spinning. I could hardly see, let alone think.

"What's the matter?" he asked. I didn't think I could feel any colder, but his tone chilled my blood. "Think you're too good for me? You thought you'd be with my friend tonight, didn't you?" I staggered to the side of the road and vomited over a snowbank.

University had let out for Christmas vacation. The holiday break had left my boss shorthanded, so I'd offered to stay in town and work at the bank until the day before Christmas Eve.

Only a few students remained in the dorms, none of them on my floor. When I had volunteered to work, I had no idea that I'd spend my nights with no front-desk security and the main entrance unlocked. Anyone could come and go, and no one would ever know. So far, I'd spent several nervous nights locked in my room with my dresser pushed against it for added protection.

Hours before the party, my mother had called. I lied and told her my girlfriend and I had dinner plans and might go see a movie after that. Mom would not have approved of me going to a party with men

I didn't know, and I didn't want her to worry about me.

Ever since accepting the party invitation, I'd had a powerful feeling I shouldn't go, but I didn't want to appear rude. After all, they were new customers of the bank. How dangerous could they be? As I stood there shivering in the night air, I kept thinking of my mother and desperately wished I'd heeded my disquiet.

After leaving the party, I'd asked my so-called date to take me back to my dorm. Instead, he'd headed to a desolate area in the countryside and driven the car into a snowbank. Sick as I felt, I'd had to help push the car back on the road. Now, I had no choice but to get back in the car or freeze. Again, I pleaded with him to take me to my dorm, which made him so angry he floored the gas pedal, causing the car to slide back and forth over the snowy road, scaring me to death. At least we were going the right way. During the drive, my mother weighed heavy on my mind.

When we pulled into the dorm parking lot, I thought about screaming but knew no one would hear me. I slid out of the car and staggered inside, hoping he might stay behind. Instead, he followed me up to my room.

Unable to see clearly, I fumbled with the lock, which ticked him off. The second the door opened, he followed behind me, shut the door, and blocked it. I asked him to leave, but he refused. At that moment, I wished I'd been honest with my mother in case the worst now happened.

Then the phone rang.

"Don't answer it!" he said, but I'd already picked it up.

"Jill?"

"Mom?" It was 1:30 a.m. My parents had always gone to bed after the ten o'clock news. A fresh wave of panic swept through me. "What's wrong?" I asked, suddenly aware that I'd thought about my mother all night because I'd probably sensed that something horrific had happened back home. What if a family member had died? As I waited for her answer, my date's threatening eyes remained glued to me.

"I couldn't sleep," she said. "I had an urgent feeling you needed me to call you. Let's talk."

I could hear it in her voice. Mom knew something had gone awry and that I wasn't alone. Throughout the early hours of that morning, my mother stayed on the phone with me. We talked about cooking, sewing, vacations, relatives, and everything under the sun until my intruder became so enraged that he finally left, slamming my door behind him. Once I locked my door, I peeked out my window to make sure he'd driven away. After that, my mother hung on while I left to use the restroom. Once I returned, Mom waited until I'd secured and barricaded my door before hanging up.

I'd been foolish to ignore my uneasiness about attending that party. Thankfully, my mother acted on hers, most likely saving me from harm. It's possible that nothing would have happened to me, but I'm grateful I never had to find out.

—Jill Burns—

58

Danger Danger

Out of this nettle, danger, we pluck this flower, safety.
~William Shakespeare

For many years, my dreams and premonitions ended with positive or miraculous results. I didn't have an unhappy ending until the first week of November 2009, when I woke up from a dream in which a large log, about ten-feet long and two-feet in diameter, rammed the front door of my house. As I got ready for work that morning, I dismissed the unsettling dream. It was probably just something I remembered from a movie or book about armies ramming the gates of castles to get in.

A week later, I dreamed a second time about the log ramming the front door. I wondered what it meant, but work and the upcoming holidays kept me too busy to spend much time thinking about it. It wasn't until I had the same dream a third and fourth time that I guessed something big must be coming into my life.

After the long Thanksgiving weekend, I took the first Wednesday in December off from work to thoroughly clean the house and put up Christmas decorations. It turned out to be a relaxing and productive day with no interruptions. As I finished a late lunch, the buzzer on the dryer let me know that the last load of laundry was done. Placing my husband's shirts and my blouses on hangers, I folded the remaining items and took everything to the bedroom to put away. Walking into the closet, my inner voice unexpectedly said, "You should take all your jewelry and put it in a box in the back of your car."

Shocked by this unusual suggestion, I looked over at my necklaces hanging on multiple hooks and my four-drawer wooden chest containing bracelets, earrings, and a few rings. None of it was really expensive except a pair of diamond earrings and a matching pendant that my husband had given me on our anniversary. But all of it was unique and special to me. One of my favorites was a silver, gold, and bronze heart-shaped locket that my daughter had given me on Mother's Day. The word "Mother" was written in gold script across the front of it and on the inside was a picture of her and my granddaughter. As I touched each necklace, I recalled when and where I bought it or who had given it to me.

Trusting my premonition, I went and retrieved one of the empty storage containers that had held some decorations. Carefully, I put the necklaces and the wooden chest in it. As I carried it to the garage and put it in the back of my station wagon under a gray vinyl cover, my sensible mind silently countered, "A car sitting in a public parking lot is not safer than your locked house."

Feeling a little foolish, I had to agree with the logic that a locked house is safer than a car and half-heartedly carried the container back to the closet. Not quite sure why I was debating the safety of my jewelry, I decided to wear my diamond earrings and pendant for the next week or so. They would definitely be secure that way. Confident that I had satisfied both suggestions, I turned off the closet light and got busy finishing a few more projects before the day was over.

The next day, I was busy nonstop at work. In order to complete an important report, I skipped lunch and stayed at my desk. However, my efforts were frequently interrupted because the telephone kept ringing. A few times, the caller hung up, which was unusual. It was around quitting time that my daughter called and said, "Mom, the police are on their way to your house."

Since she lived two blocks from me, my granddaughter had decided to go to my house to do her homework on my new laptop. As she went to put the key in the lock, the door swung open, and she could see our flat-screen TV was missing. She knew immediately that we had been burglarized. As she ran up the street to a girlfriend's house, she called her mother on her cell phone. My daughter then called the police.

Upon arriving home, I saw two patrol cars in front of our house and two policemen taking pictures of footprints in the snow. Some of our neighbors were standing on the sidewalk wanting to know what happened. One of the officers asked my husband and me to walk with him through each room, the basement, and garage in order to make a list of the items stolen. The burglars had taken our large flat-screen TV and two smaller ones, a video camera, two laptops, a color printer, and two suitcases. In order to help the police find our items, I got out the file folders with receipts, manufacturers, and serial numbers. They were going to fax the list of stolen items with this information to all the surrounding city and county police departments and pawnshops.

The only irreplaceable items, which also happened to be the least expensive, were my jewelry. In disbelief, I asked the police several times, "Why would anyone steal jewelry that is not worth hundreds or thousands of dollars? It can't be sold or pawned."

They didn't have an answer. I felt extremely violated that strangers had been walking around in our home ransacking every room and closet and emptying the contents of every drawer and shelf onto the floor. Our next-door neighbor came over and told us she had seen a white van backed into our garage and figured we were having some work done in the house. Wondering how they had closed the garage door when they left, we discovered a garage wall remote had been taken, too.

Now I know the four dreams and the premonition in the past month had been a warning. To me, it is amazing that occasionally my intuition is capable of knowing in advance when something is going to happen. Fortunately, I have my anniversary diamond earrings and pendant to prove it does.

— Brenda Cathcart-Kloke —

59

An Unexpected Friendship

You know that feeling in the pit of your stomach?
Listen to it.
~Sally Kathryn

I don't know why I didn't want to go. I just had this feeling that I shouldn't. I couldn't pinpoint why I was dreading it. Normally, I was a pretty social person. I loved mingling and road trips.

My good friend was celebrating her "big 4-0." She was having a huge shindig in her back yard with close to seventy-five guests. The event was going to be catered, complete with a band. Many of my longtime friends who I hadn't seen in years would be attending as well. I was very excited about the party at first. I was looking forward to the six-hour road trip and an overnight stay in a hotel with my husband. But now as the date neared, I didn't want to go. I couldn't shake the feeling that something bad was going to happen if we went.

I expressed my concern to my husband. He assured me I probably had a case of the jitters about leaving our four young children home with a friend who would babysit. Thinking he was probably right, I tried to push my fear aside. After all, my friend has three children of her own, close to my kids' ages. The kids often played together and got along great. If anything, my kids would have lots of fun and make fond memories.

It was the day before the party. We would be leaving the next morning at 5 a.m. to bring our children to my friend's house before we hit the road. No matter my logic, I couldn't help but feel that we shouldn't go on the trip.

I was packing our suitcases when my husband walked in. He must have seen my worried expression when he asked softly, "Are you still having doubts about going? The children will be just fine."

I had thought about it. I wasn't having reservations about leaving our children. I knew in my heart they would be fine. It was something else, but I didn't know what. "Maybe something will happen to us on our road trip," I blurted. Harold shook his head sympathetically and once again assured me everything would be fine.

Reluctantly, I agreed. I was working myself up. That night as I drifted off to sleep, I heard a voice whisper one single word: "Stay." I turned to my husband and poked him, "Harold, did you just say something?" His snore confirmed he was sound asleep. I realized I must have had a dream. The word "stay" lay heavy on my heart. I decided then that we shouldn't go away for the weekend. "Are you positive?" my husband asked, bleary-eyed, when our alarm went off at 4:30 a.m. I couldn't be surer. After I made calls to both friends about our change of plans, I felt a sense of relief.

We had a nice, laid-back Saturday. We took the kids to the park and ordered pizza for dinner. After I tucked the kids into bed, a wave of dread washed over me again. I got a sick feeling that something was wrong.

Something made me look out my kitchen window to our neighbor's house across the street. It was completely dark. Mrs. Biddle was an older woman who kept to herself. She lived in a big house by herself and rarely left except to go grocery shopping. Her son would visit from time to time. All my efforts to be neighborly toward her had failed. I tried to strike up conversations, but she would cut me short. Oftentimes, if she saw me walking to her house, it was obvious from the scowl on her face that she didn't want to be bothered. She would scurry inside to avoid me.

I thought it was odd that all her lights were off. Mrs. Biddle never went out at night. As a matter of fact, she was a night owl like me, with her lights usually burning way past midnight. That's when it hit me: I had to go over to her house. I knew something was wrong.

I walked across the street and rang her doorbell several times. There was no answer. I tried peeking through her window, but her curtains were drawn. I went back to her door to ring the bell again when I heard something stir inside. "Mrs. Biddle?" I called out loudly. Then I heard a small voice. I couldn't make out what she was saying, but I knew it was Mrs. Biddle, and she needed help. Running back to my house, I told Harold what had happened. I called 911.

Minutes later, the police arrived and broke down Mrs. Biddle's door. Soon after, the ambulance arrived. As she was wheeled away on a stretcher, she looked over at me.

The next day, we went to the hospital to visit Mrs. Biddle. She had fallen down the last few steps in her house, hit her head as she fell, and broke her ankle. She was unable get up. She told us she was going in and out of consciousness. "Thank you for helping me. I will forever be grateful," she said.

That's when I saw her smile for the first time.

That evening, I realized we were meant to stay home and be there for Mrs. Biddle. All the fear of something bad happening finally lifted. I felt at peace. She could have been lying there the entire weekend if we had gone away. And something special came from that weekend — we became good friends with Mrs. Biddle. Her attitude changed, and she smiled often. She joined us for many family dinners and holidays and became an honorary grandmother to our children.

— Dorann Weber —

Heavy Dreams, Light Sleep

Childhood should be carefree, playing in the sun;
not living a nightmare in the darkness of the soul.
~Dave Pelzer, A Child Called "It"

I was nine years old and in the fourth grade, living on a compound in Saudi Arabia. My friend Joel and I had been hanging out together since first grade, as our parents worked for the same oil company. Naturally, everyone knew everyone. It was a very small-town, folksy kind of vibe. It was a fun childhood. We lived by the beach, and Joel and I would spend hours riding our bikes along the coast and exploring the parks in town.

One night, I had a very disturbing dream, and it involved my friend Joel and his family. I told my dad about it because I didn't know what to do. *The dream felt like a premonition, and what I saw was two planes in mid-air with their front ends about to touch. I didn't remember seeing any faces. I just remembered that one of the flights was from India.* Here was the problem. I knew that Joel's mom was visiting her friend in India for a wedding.

I explained the whole thing to my dad. He listened carefully and tried to make me feel better. "It was just a dream, son," I recall him saying. Although I found some solace in his encouragement, I still felt the urge to tell my friend Joel.

Joel was one of the smartest kids in the class. Concepts came to him easily whenever the teacher instructed us. I thought if I told him what I was feeling, he'd figure out a logical way to interpret it. I called Joel and told him to meet me in the park across the street from my house. About ten minutes later, we were riding our bikes nearby the sandpit full of monkey bars, slides, and swings. We were circling the pavement slowly. I remember the sound of our rubber tires crushing the grains of sand lightly spread across the pavement. A couple of kids were in the park, but it was empty for the most part.

I didn't want to look him in the eye when I told him. I kept looking down at the pavement, watching my tires turn as I steered in circles. Joel was talking to me about his day, telling me how excited he was to see his mom again. That's when I had to clear the meteorite-sized lump in my throat and speak my piece:

"Joel, I need to tell you something," I said as I stopped pedaling my bike.

He stopped his bike. "What's up?" he asked. I looked at his bright blue eyes and the blond hair perfectly arranged on his head, and then I started my story.

"I, uh, I had a dream last night."

"About what, Steven?"

I circumvented the question. I told him he should consider asking his mom to reschedule her flight, but he just laughed a little. I pressed harder. I told him I saw two planes in my dream and they were about to run into each other.

Joel didn't believe it. He was excited to see his mom again. It had been two weeks since he'd seen her last.

A few days or a week later, my father called me downstairs. I rushed into the living room not knowing what he had called me for, but then I saw his face. He was distraught. He pointed to the television and said, "Look at the news."

The reporter was discussing a fatal accident that occurred somewhere in India.

My eyes widened. "What about Joel's mom?"

"Let's wait until we get more information," Dad said.

The next morning, my dad was reading the *Arab News*. It's considered to be *The New York Times* of Saudi Arabia. He found the article. Two airplanes had a head-on collision in mid-air, killing 349 people — one of those being Carol Stern, Joel's mother. She was one of three Americans who had boarded the flight from India to Saudi Arabia. She was a brilliant woman, with the same bright blue eyes and blond hair as Joel. She was always nice to me whenever I visited their house.

My heart sank. I had no words, just utter sadness. My dad offered some words of encouragement:

"We should reach out to Joel's family," he said as he rested his palm on my head.

Eventually, when I found the words, we began talking about what to do. My father helped me write a letter to Joel. We started the note out with empathy — my father had lost his mom at a young age and had a hard time dealing with it. He wanted me to show compassion for Joel losing his mom and to tell him that if he needed a shoulder to lean on, we'd be there.

After we finished the letter, I put it in an envelope and rode my bike to his house to drop it off. I rang the doorbell — no answer. I knocked a couple of times — still no answer. So, I left the letter and rode back home in time for dinner.

Joel was never the same again. His family repatriated back to Utah, where his mother's family was. He didn't finish the fourth grade with us, but I remember seeing him once or twice after the event. We never talked about it or even the fact that I dreamt about it before it happened. About a year later, my dad got a promotion, and we moved to another town. I never saw Joel again, but we reconnected on Facebook eight or nine years later. While we're friends on Facebook, he hasn't responded to any of my messages.

I've never again had a dream as vivid as the one that preceded the 1996 Charkhi Dadri mid-air collision. And I hope I never do.

— Stevie Shield —

Choosing Our Destiny

Give yourself permission to immediately walk away
from anything that gives you bad vibes.
~Author Unknown

I was beyond ecstatic. My chance had come! I'd even gotten up at 5 a.m. to hide pancake mix and syrup in the bottom of the large picnic basket. Now I was panicked that my husband was going to ruin my carefully thought-out plan!

"Honey, I have no idea why you packed breakfast items in this basket," he declared with a look of confusion on his normally smiling face. "Let's just stick with coffee, juice, and snacks for the kids. The plan is to be there for just a few hours."

"Well, hon," I began nonchalantly, "I was thinking that I'd spend the night. You and the kids can come home this evening, and I'll catch a ride with Bob and Beverly tomorrow."

"You know the authorities are not going to allow you to spend the night, so I suggest you get that idea out of your head right now," he chided. "Besides, Bob has told you repeatedly that it's way too dangerous!"

My husband knew how desperately I'd been trying to get to the mountain for this once-in-a-lifetime opportunity to observe and photograph the phenomenal volcanic activity. However, he did not share or understand my adrenaline-charged enthusiasm to spend the night.

Knowing I was not going to win this argument easily, I decided to change the subject and figure out something when it was time to return home.

It was early Saturday morning, May 17, 1980, the day before the devastating eruption of Mount St. Helens. Authorities had given the few property owners permission to enter the restricted danger area near Spirit Lake for a few hours to retrieve their possessions. My parents and brother had cabins within the danger zone.

My husband, the kids and I were driving the fifty miles from Portland to the mountain in southwestern Washington to help my parents gather some belongings, and to visit with my brother and his girlfriend who were already at their cabin.

Bob and Beverly were amateur volcanologists who had been granted permission to stay at his cabin and monitor the volcanic activity. Bob was a research scientist by trade, but without credentials in this particular field. He loved learning and jumped at the opportunity to study an active volcano quite literally in his own back yard.

I had begged my brother continually to take me along on his weekend visits. He refused, arguing that he would be compromising his own authorization to be there by infringing on the agreement. He was also well aware of the danger, and I'm sure he felt a need to protect me.

But I needed to be there! It was difficult to explain. It was as though the mountain was a powerful magnet pulling me.

We were the first ones to arrive at the huge gate that blockaded the "red zone." This gave us a chance to observe the surrounding area. Everything was oddly quiet and eerie. My brother's car was parked just off the road where he had left it to bicycle the final five miles to the cabin.

The deer and elk stood motionless along the roadway. They seemed to sense that danger was looming.

Once in a while, we could feel a little tremor under our feet, a reminder that the mountain was not motionless. I embraced the thrill of it and felt even more compelled to stay the night.

After signing liability releases, we were escorted by state troopers to the cabin area. While the rest of the family checked out my parents' cabin, I hiked down the gravel road to check in with my brother. Bob and Beverly were on their deck surrounded by telescopes and cameras with powerful zoom lenses. News reporters were already there interviewing them about their volcano-monitoring experience.

"Hi, sis," he beamed, obviously happy to see that we'd made it. "Do you guys want to run up to the base of the mountain in a bit?"

"Try to stop me," I laughed.

An hour later, as we sat on the ash-covered asphalt where hitherto snowmobilers and mountain climbers had parked, the ground trembled gently beneath us. Although it was a bit eerie knowing we were the only people sitting that close to the mountain, in a sense it was also very peaceful, and my mind wandered back through the years of picking huckleberries, swimming in Spirit Lake, and snowmobiling with family and friends on this mountain.

While staring at the mountain from this vantage point, a feeling of finality engulfed me, and I knew things were never going to be the same. My desire to spend the night suddenly vanished. It had nothing to do with fear; rather, something spoke to me. "Go home with your family," it said, as clearly as if the words were uttered aloud.

After gathering a few irreplaceable items from my parents' cabin, we visited with Bob and Beverly for a short time at his place. When we said goodbye, an uncanny feeling came over me as I beheld my brother's smiling face. It was the happiest I'd ever seen him. I will never forget that smile!

The next morning at 8:32, a huge earthquake caused the entire north face of the mountain to slide away, creating the largest landslide ever recorded. Bob and Beverly were in the direct path of the blast. They were among the fifty-seven people who lost their lives — two of the three who were within the declared danger zone; the other being the infamous Harry R. Truman. Their bodies were never recovered.

Although I found solace in knowing that Bob was well aware of the risk he was taking, I still wished I had tried to persuade him to leave with us — but I knew without a doubt that he wouldn't have gone. He was far too captivated by his study of the volcano, and he loved spending every moment possible at his cabin. I completely understood.

I had listened to my premonition and made the choice to go home; in like manner, Bob chose the mountain as his final resting place with the girl he loved. I am completely at peace with our decisions — and I believe Bob and Beverly are as well.

— Connie Kaseweter Pullen —

62

A Spooky
Forest Day

Don't go against your inner knowing.
Just don't. Trust yourself.
~Maria Erving

Armed with animal repellent, I headed to the far end of our property to spray it on the trees that my husband had planted along our gravel road. While mixing the spray, I'd felt anxious and rushed, but I couldn't come up with a good reason to postpone this chore, especially since the forecast called for a sunny day with no chance of rain—perfect weather for spraying.

The high humidity made it sticky and suffocating. For a day that had zero-percent chance of rain, the sky overhead had grown darker by the minute. Yet, while the sky looked wicked, the forest seemed extra spooky and still. Any other morning, the sounds of birds singing and animals chattering would have filled the air. I tried to brush off my unease, knowing it could simply mean a hawk, bear, or even a hiker was close by. Yet my need to hurry escalated.

Even though I was moving as quickly as I could, I still had half the road to do when the sprayer quit working. By then, I felt so nervous and terrified that I wanted to call it quits anyway. I reminded myself how ridiculous I was acting. After all, it wasn't raining, so why not finish the job? The sprayer often clogged, so I'd come prepared with a pocket full of toothpicks to push the clog through. Normally, the toothpicks did their job, but each one I tried broke to pieces.

The silence grew deafening, and even though it seemed silly, I was feeling more frightened by the minute. All at once, my blood ran cold, and I knew that someone or some creature was watching me. Something horrific was about to happen. My insides screamed, "Run!" I grabbed the sprayer and bolted through the shortcut that led through the woods to our cabin, tripping several times. Racing up the stairs, I turned to see what was chasing me. I saw it all right. I slammed and bolted the door.

"Grab the cats and get downstairs now!" I hollered to my sons.

Tons of debris smashed the door and our windows as the entire forest bent and twisted in a wicked whirlwind of darkness. It was terrifying. Later, we learned that a small twister had dipped out of the sky and skipped along our property through the forest, downing trees in its path and uprooting many of our huge, healthy oak trees as it moved along. The damage was unbelievable! Thankfully, our cabin escaped unharmed.

The scene before me made me shudder. If I had fixed the sprayer and continued to work along the road or had walked back to the cabin instead of running, I would have been seriously injured or possibly killed.

Usually before a storm hits, we get some sort of warning. That day, we had no wind or rain, no lightning or thunder, not even the greenish glow that I'd grown accustomed to in the violent Midwestern storms. When I see the damage that still lingers in our woods and remember that day, I am forever grateful that I trusted my gut feelings at the last minute and took off running for my life. It's a race I'll never forget!

— Jill Burns —

Chapter 7

Comfort & Closure

63

Final Departure

Deeply, I know this, that love triumphs over death.
My father continues to be loved,
and therefore he remains by my side.
~Jennifer Williamson

O
ur father had remarried ten years after Mom passed from cancer. His new wife, Nerene, was someone he had known all his life, and she was the most beautiful, caring soul this side of heaven.

After her husband left her, she had raised her children by working in factories and sitting with the elderly. She had eventually remarried but then became a widow. At that point, she wasn't interested in finding anyone else. However, after a matchmaking effort by her family, she reluctantly went on "just one date" with my quiet dad. They were married just three weeks later! From then on, they were hardly ever apart.

We kids absolutely adored her, and she loved us right back. We became her kids, all six of us, along with her own five. She was our Mother Hen, fussing over all of us, Daddy included.

Our father was an auto mechanic for many years before retiring. He loved Crown Victoria cars and owned many of them before we finally had to take the keys away from him when his health and reflexes declined. His diabetes and heart problems had gotten the better of him.

In fact, it was his heart that finally failed. He was having trouble breathing and the cardiologist had bad news for him. "I'm sorry, Mr. Miller. Your mechanical heart valve is failing. Due to your age, valve replacement isn't an option at this point."

There was nothing more that could be done. The congestive heart failure was closing in on him.

We were in total shock. It wasn't the news we were expecting. "What do you mean?" my stepmom answered for him, as she often did. We could hear the concern in her voice.

"You are eighty-eight years old." The doctor spoke loudly due to Daddy being hard of hearing. "There is nothing more that can be done. If it were me, I would go home and spend the rest of the time I had left with my family. Do you understand what I am saying to you?" he asked. Daddy simply shook his head.

The curtain on my father's life was rapidly closing. He was placed in hospice, and the last few weeks of his life were spent at home in bed, with family gathered near. He held on until Nerene reassured him she would be okay, and then he passed quietly.

Six months later, due to health issues, she moved in with a daughter almost an hour away. We were all crushed because we had lived near her for twenty years. It felt like we lost both parents at this point.

Due to work, I didn't get to visit as often as I would have liked. A year later, before Mother's Day, she spent a few days with me, visiting our family and going to church.

One night, while everyone else was in bed, we stayed up late crying and discussing how much we missed Daddy. She related waking up the past few nights, hearing Daddy calling her. That's when I remembered a dream I had experienced a couple of weeks earlier when I had a restless night.

In my dream, I was standing in the living room looking out a big picture window. My sister and niece were talking. I noticed Daddy was slowly passing by the driveway.

"Look, it's Daddy!" I pointed.

He was in an old Crown Victoria. I could clearly see Nerene in the passenger seat. Both had their eyes fixed on the road ahead as they drove into the sunset. In the dream, I was aware that Dad was still deceased.

I could not explain it, but the dream made me know that Nerene would not be with us much longer. I could not shake the feeling and told my sister.

I almost didn't tell Nerene but I finally did, thinking it would give her some comfort. The look in her eyes told me that she knew her time was up. We cried together, but it wasn't all bad, because she was ready to go be with the love of her life.

A few months later, she was admitted to the hospital with abdominal pain. Something told me not to wait until the next day to visit her. My husband, daughter and I went.

We found her in good spirits, with her familiar laughter filling the room. We reminisced about past family gatherings and meals. Reaching for my hand, she thanked me for all the errands I had run for them and all the rides to church.

The next day, she left us.

I still chuckle at the thought of Daddy slipping the keys back into his old Crown Victoria! I can see them both giggling again while he quietly opens the door for his sweetheart for one last spin — sneaking off into the sunset.

— Renee Greene —

I'm Home, Mom

*The relationship between parents and children, but
especially between mothers and daughters,
is tremendously powerful, scarcely to be
comprehended in any rational way.*
~Joyce Carol Oates

S
ome people report that they dream nightly and can often recall tidbits or entire dreams the next morning. I am in the minority. I rarely dream, but when I do, I normally remember the dream as vividly as if I were actually living in the moment.

One such dream started with my grown daughter Danielle stepping through the front door of our home and calling out, "I'm home, Mom." There was nothing unusual or odd about this; this had happened hundreds of times. Then she said, "Come on, I need to show you something."

After I slipped on my shoes, we stepped onto the front porch. The sun had begun its nightly descent from the indigo blue sky. The stars had yet to make an appearance, but the moon hovered in silhouette, and the night critters had started to stir.

We walked over to where Danielle's small car was parked, and I watched her climb in and buckle up. I hesitated for a moment. I hate small cars, mainly because I hate the claustrophobic feeling of having my knees shoved almost into my nose once I am buckled in. I offered to drive my larger car, but my daughter waved aside my suggestion, so I had no choice but to take a seat.

Comort & Closure |

Comfort & Closure | 211

A peaceful silence settled between us as she started the car and pulled out onto the main street. We had traveled only a short distance when I became aware of the sound of beautiful music floating from her radio. I could not make out the words of the song, but the chords were mesmerizing. When I closed my eyes, it felt as if the music had entered my bloodstream and was traveling deep into my soul. I opened my eyes and asked Danielle what she was listening to, but she never answered me. By the light from the control panels, I could make out her peaceful smile. Taking a cue from her, I quieted my mind and focused on the music.

The music continued to play as the two of us enjoyed our drive. I was at peace, and I could tell my daughter was as well. There was nothing but companionship and music. Neither of us had any fears or cares; we were just living in the moment.

After a few miles, the road began to curve, and I could make out a set of corkscrew curves just ahead. I became fearful as we drew closer to the curves. By the time we entered the first curve, I was grasping the edge of the seat like a lifeline.

We navigated the first turn perfectly, but as we entered the second curve, our back wheels lost traction and we began to swerve in the wet leaves that covered the roadway. The car continued its sideways trajectory, and the steering wheel seemed to be twisting on its own as we swerved into the next curve, rounded the sharpest bend, and slammed into a pair of bright lights.

My heart pounded in my chest. Temporarily blinded by the light, I desperately reached over to grab Danielle's hand. As our fingers entwined, I was struck by how warm her hand was in mine. I gave it a quick squeeze just as we were thrown forward. I tensed for the impact of flesh against glass, but it never came. In seconds, we were floating outside the car, and then we began to rise upward as if some invisible vacuum were pulling us. We were not flying; we were just rising. The higher we got, the brighter the sky became.

I looked down to where the car sat twisted with smoke pouring out of the engine. I could see people scurrying around, yanking the doors open. There was no sound at all, and I felt no pain or fear. It was peaceful and, as odd as it sounds, it felt normal to be floating in the night sky with my daughter.

Glancing over, I caught and held Danielle's gaze. Her face radiated joy, and her eyes danced with laughter. She was singing, but I could not make out her words; I just knew she was singing. My fingers were still entwined with hers, and I wanted to stay this way forever. And then, as if she heard my thoughts, she gave me a reassuring smile and released my hand.

As I began to fall back into the darkness, I didn't feel any fear, only sadness. I watched my daughter continue her upward climb, as I slowly sank back to the darkness below. I tried to reach out and grab her, but all I got was empty air.

As she began to fade from sight, I screamed her name. I continued falling toward the hard ground. Just as I slammed into it, I awoke in my own bed, surrounded by my familiar pillows and our old down comforter.

My husband's soft snores were the only sound in the still, dark room. I could see the red glowing numbers on the alarm clock.

I looked around, hoping to catch a glimpse of my daughter, but I knew she was not there. You see, my daughter died in a car accident in November 2008, and it was in the summer of 2012 that I had this dream.

After her wreck, I prayed so hard. I pleaded with God to let me know that my daughter was okay, and that her last moments had not been filled with fear. He answered my prayer when he sent me this dream. I feel he allowed me a glimpse of what Danielle experienced on the night she left this earthly realm. And the words she spoke to me in that dream were, "I'm home, Mom." Those are the same words she always called out to me when she got home from school or work, but now they hold such a profound meaning for me.

— Sharon Rosenbaum Earls —

Stone of Hope

We all have a guardian angel, sent down from above.
To keep us safe from harm and surround
us with their love.
~Author Unknown

Despite the warm sunshine, the chill of an early April breeze hung in the air. My daughter Juliana had come to visit but stood across the sidewalk while I sat just outside my front door. She remained more than six feet away, as we conscientiously observed the social-distancing rule ordered during the coronavirus pandemic of 2020.

"I'm really worried about Dad," Jules said.

My husband still traveled to and from the office daily, while other non-essential businesses were ordered to shut down. His accounting office, ruled as essential, was mostly under a work-from-home code. However, with tax season in full swing, he needed to perform certain tasks securely and confidentially from the main office.

"He's being careful," I assured her.

"It's just so scary." Jules scraped a bit of mud from the sole of her running shoe. "And now, with the stay-at-home order being stretched from fourteen days to thirty…" She kept her head down.

"It's going to be difficult." I kicked a small stone, and it rolled into the mulch. "We can do this," I said.

"Do you have enough food?" Her expression couldn't conceal her worry. "I'm going to the grocery store one more time."

Juliana had been shopping for us over the past two weeks and delivered items to her in-laws, as well. As a graduate student in molecular genetics and developmental biology, she juggled classes that had been recently shifted to webinars and teleconferences because of the pandemic. And even though her research lab had been essentially closed, she worked on writing experimental results and analyzing data, while still finding time to spend with her new husband.

"I don't know if I can do this for four more weeks." She sniffled a bit and stopped herself short before touching her nose.

Watching the tears well in her eyes, I fought the urge to rush over and wrap my arms around her.

"We'll get through," I assured her again.

That night, my daughter had a dream.

Juliana found herself in my husband's childhood home. Grandma sat in her favorite spot in the corner of the couch, legs propped up, with Jules nestled up beside her.

"I miss you," Jules told her grandmother, who had passed away more than ten years ago.

"I miss you, too," Grandma answered. She looked like she did before she grew ill, with her hair perfectly coiffed, nails painted, and peach-colored lipstick brightening her smile.

"I love you." Jules leaned her head on Grandma's shoulder.

"I always love you," Grandma said.

Jules rose and began looking around the room. "I have to find Dan," she explained. Jules wanted to introduce her new husband to Grandma. She struggled and searched, but she couldn't find him.

Feeling desperate, she looked to Grandma for help. "I want you to meet him. You have to meet Dan."

But Grandma remained still in her spot. "Oh, I know him." She smiled. "Don't you worry, dear. I know who Dan is."

Feeling a sense of relief, Jules sat again, facing Grandma this time. "I have to ask y⸱⸱⸱ Jules t⸱⸱ ⸱⸱ ⸱⸱dma's hand. "I'm just so worried. Will any of us contract COVID-19?"

Grandma placed her free hand on Jules's arm. "Don't you worry about that either, dear."

Juliana woke abruptly and sat straight up, feeling an overwhelming sense of relief.

The next day, she visited me again, taking her place on the far side of the sidewalk. That's when she told me about the dream. "It felt so real, Mom. I had to convince myself it hadn't actually happened."

I could almost see the wonder in her eyes. And I undoubtedly shared her sense of relief.

Jules continued, "I have never conversed back and forth with any of the grandparents in a dream."

Sadly, all four of her grandparents had died within five difficult years while my children were pre-teens and teens.

"Each of the grandparents has appeared in my dreams," Jules said, "but they usually don't speak any words to me. And I have never been able to ask questions of them."

"Do you feel better?" I asked.

I knew I did.

Even though Juliana said she felt extremely close to all four of her grandparents, she told me she believed this grandmother had appeared in her dream because Jules was most concerned about her dad. It was as though his mom had come to say, "Everything will be okay."

"Do you want to know what else Grandma said?"

"There's more?" I asked.

The sun brightened one side of Jules's face as the wind blew her curls in the other direction. "Grandma said to me, 'I want you to know that Grandpa is having the time of his life here.'"

We shared a laugh saying how typical that was of her gregarious Grandpa.

I eyed the stone I had kicked into the mulch during our melancholy exchange just one day ago.

"When this chaos is over," I scooped up the rock and brushed it off, "this stone of hope is coming your way." I reached my hand toward hers.

She pantomimed taking the rock from my hand. "I know exactly where I'm going to put it." Jules balled up her hand and placed it securely over her heart.

We said our love-yous, and she drove off.

I squeezed the rock tight and tucked it in my pocket, lingering in the spot on the sidewalk that had become our makeshift family gathering place. Closing my eyes, I let the sun warm my face. "Thank you for this stone of hope," I whispered.

Then, the cool breeze kicked up and I ducked inside.

—Judith Burnett Schneider—

A Tale of Two Dreams

Those whom we have loved never really leave us.
They live on forever in our hearts and cast
their radiant light onto our every shadow.
~Sylvana Rossetti

"I can't stay here," my mother exclaimed. I had driven five hours so that Mom could stay with my sister after my dad's funeral. But, for some reason, she didn't want to stay there.

"What's wrong, Mom? I thought you wanted to stay with Theresa for a while."

"It's not Theresa," she said with an edge of panic in her voice. "It's those white pillars. They weren't there before."

"Yes, I know. Theresa said they were put up last fall to keep the roof from sagging, but they're not really pillars. They're just beams painted white to match the house and add a little support. Do you want to go back home?"

"No, I guess I'll stay," she replied.

"What's wrong with the pillars anyway?" I asked. "I think they're secure."

"It's not that. It's just that I have this recurring dream with white pillars. Oh, never mind, I don't want to talk about it."

"Okay, Mom, are you sure you want to stay? I can take you to my house if you want."

"I'm fine," she said a little nervously. "It's just been a lot to take in with the funeral and all."

Later, I asked my sisters privately about the pillars. They both said that Mom refused to talk about the dream.

Coleen voiced her concern. "Mom talked about a dream but wouldn't say anything except that there were pillars in her dream."

So, the mystery remained. We had all asked, but Mom steadfastly refused to talk about it.

In the meantime, I continued having a dream about a door, one in which I went upstairs and found a door I'd never seen. I always stood at the threshold deciding whether to open it, and then I would wake up.

I had often wondered what it meant and had even looked up the meaning once or twice, but I had never felt satisfied with the interpretation offered in the dream book — something about a door symbolizing the future.

If only I could open the door before I woke up, I would at least know what was behind it. Truthfully, the dream was starting to feel creepy. What if it was like a horror movie, and there was something terrible behind that door? Maybe it was a good thing that I woke up before I opened it.

Somehow, my concern about dreams faded as real life took over. My mom was without her husband of fifty-five years and living by herself in a town that was two to three hours from her closest family. We waited patiently as she tried to sort out her affairs, and then we helped her get the house ready for sale. Three years later, she moved downstate to be near two of her children who could offer her support. She spent twelve years in her lovely apartment enjoying her children and grandchildren, when her health began to fail. Then, she got the diagnosis. It was throat cancer, devastating news that took our breath away.

At the age of eighty-five, Mom was battling one of the hardest things in her life. We did everything we could to help her and spent many long nights in the hospital when she needed extra support and monitoring.

One month after her eighty-sixth birthday, during one of those long nights, my sister finally learned the rest of the dream story. She told me the next day after we had made hospice arrangements for Mom in Ann Arbor, Michigan.

"So, Theresa, tell me about the dream with the pillars," I said. "Coleen said Mom told you."

"Yes, she did," she said, shaking her head sadly. "Mom said the place with the white pillars is the place where she dies."

"That's why she didn't want to stay at your house," I added in shock, "because of the white support beams. She thought those were pillars."

Theresa teared up a bit and said softly, "Yes, that's it."

One wish Mom had after staying at a care facility was to return to her tidy apartment that was filled with her own pretty things. However, a flood at her apartment complex made it impossible for her to go home.

Instead, Mom was admitted to the hospice facility in Ann Arbor, and I had agreed to drive her there. My sisters would meet me to help her get settled. It was such a bright day in June that Mom complained about how the brilliant sunlight, combined with her macular degeneration, limited her vision.

I didn't know if she could see much of the place, but I was awestruck when we arrived at the hospice. The front of the building looked like the White House, with four huge white pillars gleaming in the dazzling sun. I silently prayed that Mom could not see these, and she never said a word about those columns.

Exactly fifteen years to the day after my dad's death, our mother quietly passed in the hospice facility. She had only been there four days. It was a peaceful death but tragically sad for all of us.

Strangely enough, although her dream had fulfilled itself, my dream did not return for several months. It was as if it were buried in my subconscious, which I believed was trying to heal from the trauma of Mom's battle with cancer.

Finally, one night in a dream, I headed up the staircase, stood at the threshold and opened the door! I walked through it to find a room in my house that was not there previously. It was filled with antiques, and in the middle of the room stood a stately, old mahogany table and chairs. The table was set with lovely translucent china. The blue-and-white dishes stood out against the white lace tablecloth with the cobalt blue glasses glittering in the light that filtered in from the lacy curtained window. My first thought was that Mom would have loved this room. She had always loved antiques and pretty dishes. As my eyes took in the scene, I realized there were just enough place settings for our family.

I smiled then, knowing in my heart that my mother was truly where she belonged and eternally home.

— Nancy Campbell Renko —

Between Here and There

Just a thin veil between this world and that world
of beauty and love. Just a thin veil that hides
the view of our Spirit loved ones above.
~Gertrude Tooley Buckingham

I saw him standing at the side of my bed, watching me. He was surrounded in light and looked as handsome as I remembered him from years ago. He was so close, yet I couldn't touch him. He looked radiant, with his singular smile and penetrating dark eyes. He was dressed in his favorite beige suit with the brown tie I had given him as a surprise gift.

I awakened from my dream at 4 a.m. believing this love from my past was right beside me.

When we first met, I was a performer who had just closed one production and was auditioning for another. To make ends meet, I took a temporary secretarial job at a local hospital that was rich in community history. My office was a throwback to the twenties, with furnishings and décor to match, including a Double Dutch door. I felt so comfortable in that environment, as though I belonged.

On the day we met there, I heard his deep voice from the hallway as he greeted other employees. It was familiar and comforting, as though I had heard it before. I remember my back was to him when he spoke. "Good morning! What's your name?"

I turned, and time froze. He and I talked about that first meeting many times because we both felt a passionate connection that could not be explained. We just knew that somewhere between here and there, our paths had crossed. I replied, "My name is Elaine." He quickly responded with one of his memorable smiles. "Oh, you don't look like an Elaine. Hope you don't mind, but I need to call you Lainie!" From that moment, I chose to be called Lainie by everyone.

That was an intense year. We were inseparable! Words didn't have to be spoken; we just knew what the other needed to say. We felt complete, like old souls who found each other again, and we were the only two who existed. We couldn't wait to be together.

He was nearing the end of a very messy divorce before I came along. He shared his reasons as to why he had left his wife. He was sorry to have caused her heartache, but he knew it was the best decision for all.

He proposed to me while we walked along the boardwalk at the ocean. An incurable romantic, he pointed to a few stars in the sky that November night, wondering if there were two souls on the brightest one who were in love with each other as we were. We talked for hours about what made us happy and sad. He shared that he never found happiness with his established career and longed to pursue another. I told him he must listen to his heart and follow his dream to be happy.

Then he asked me, "What would make you happy?" Without having to think about it, I answered, "Being with you forever!"

Our plan was to marry as soon as his divorce was finalized. He would leave his career, and I would leave mine. We would build a new life and family together and live happily ever after. But sometimes our life stories have different endings.

The next day, his soon-to-be ex-wife and their little children visited my office. She sat across from me and asked for his schedule, knowing I kept his calendar. She looked tired and distraught and then began crying uncontrollable tears. While catching her breath, she shared their plans to divorce. Then she said, "He's found peace and love, and I am heartbroken to let him go."

That, too, was a moment that moved my heart. She and the children left my office, and I followed a few minutes later, leaving my job and him behind. He tried many times to reach out to me, but I never responded. Ever since, there's been a little empty place in my heart where I knew he belonged, but still, I moved on.

I hadn't thought of him until a song I heard years later brought back intense memories. I played that song, "My Favorite Year," over and over again. Its melody and lyrics brought us back together in my dreams, my music, my writing, and my thoughts. I tried finding him, but to no avail. Yet, somehow, I felt he was thinking of me, too.

And then, like a miracle, my dream brought him to me. He whispered that he loved me, and he knew I loved him. His vision gave me peace but frightened me, too. I felt he had died and wasn't able to move on without sharing that he knew how much I loved him. A few weeks later, I discovered what I feared most. His obituary was long and fulfilling. He divorced, but never re-married, dedicating his life to his children and the career I encouraged him to pursue. He had an incredible life! But more incredible, he died on the day I dreamt of him.

I know this was not just my dream, but *our* dream! I believe when I pass, he'll be waiting for me. Between here and there, love never dies.

— Lainie Belcastro —

68

Chicken Soup for the Soul

No Need for Goodbye

More and more, when I single out the person who
inspired me most, I go back to my grandfather.
~James Earl Jones

I t had been a year since my grandfather passed away, and I was bothered by the fact that I never got to say goodbye to him. My parents had tried calling and texting me, but I was taking a nap, and my phone was in the other room. By the time I read my parents' messages and drove to the hospital, my grandfather had already passed away.

Although a year had passed since his death and I had a plethora of things to look forward to (senior prom, high-school graduation, the start of college, etc.), the fact that I never got to say goodbye to my role model weighed heavy on me.

I blamed myself for being asleep that day when I knew darn well that I should've gone with my parents to visit him. Of course, nobody knew that day was going to be his last. But if I had only gone with my parents to visit my grandfather, I would have been able to say goodbye.

One night before I went to bed, I was thinking about my grandfather and was overcome by sadness. I decided to close my eyes and pray to God. I asked God to allow me to dream of my grandfather; I just wanted to see him one more time. I didn't know if my prayer would be answered, but it was worth a shot. I cleared my thoughts and fell asleep.

Later that night, I felt a tap on my shoulder and jumped up. Darkness surrounded me, but that quickly ended when my lamp was turned on. The person who turned on the lamp in my room was a tall man, wearing pants and a shirt that were blindingly white. I tried to speak, but I couldn't; it felt as if my vocal cords had disappeared. The man in the white clothing softly took me by the hand and led me out of my bed. I was not hesitant at all, for his presence gave me a sense of comfort. The man walked me to the door of my room and slowly opened it.

On the other side of the door was an entirely white room. And there was my grandfather, sitting in his favorite chair. I stared at him motionless, not knowing what was going on. As I stood in shock, my grandfather began to sing his favorite song: "The Party's Over" by Willie Nelson. I ran toward him and hugged him while he sat singing in his chair. I cried on his shoulder. I didn't want to let go.

My grandfather then placed his hands on my shoulders and maneuvered me so we were face to face. He then said, "Everything is going to be alright. There was no need for you to say goodbye because I'm not going anywhere. I'll always be with you. I am so proud of the man you are becoming and look forward to watching you live your life. I love you."

I still couldn't speak, so I smiled and hugged him once more.

I arose to the sound of my neighbor mowing his lawn at eight in the morning. My eyes were still watery, but I couldn't help smiling, for I knew that everything was going to be all right.

—Arturo Guajardo IV—

69

Give Me Back My Mother

Mother, the ribbons of your love
are woven around my heart.
~Author Unknown

My mother pointed a shaky finger my way. "Get out of my room now!"

"You don't mean that, Mom," I said. "You're upset, that's all."

"I do mean it. Now, go… Don't come back, and shut the door on your way out!"

In my entire life, my mother had never looked at me with such hatred on her face or kicked me out of her room. Before I closed her door, I took one last look at her and felt like screaming, "Give me back my mother!"

Dementia is no stranger to me. Over the years, our family has watched many of our loved ones suffer this fate. I had read loads on the subject and done tons of research. I knew what I should and shouldn't do. So far, with each loving person we'd lost, I'd handled it well—until dementia took away my mother.

While I felt grateful Mom could act civil to friends and acquaintances, she bashed my sweet sister (Mom's amazing caretaker) and me while our brother—the eternal golden boy—could do no wrong. And since my children and husband are mine, she punished them, too.

The change in Mom astounded us. The sweetest woman our family had ever known had become a cruel monster.

I found it extra-tough each time Mom attacked my sister — day and night. Of course, I knew Mom couldn't help herself, but her behavior still horrified me. It also made me feel ashamed and guilt-ridden for not accepting what had happened to Mom with grace and understanding.

While we hadn't always agreed on everything, Mom and I had always shared a close, loving relationship. Now she made it clear those days had ended, and I missed her.

One night, I tossed and turned, unable to sleep. I could see the rosy hue coming from the window shades and figured I might as well get up and get my morning going. I closed my eyes for a minute to meditate on the day ahead, but I fell asleep and had a vivid dream.

I stood before an old-fashioned television set. On the screen, I saw my mother. I couldn't believe how great it felt to see her again. Mom was wearing a colorful print blouse she had sewn, one of my favorites, along with her dangling yellow earrings. She looked much younger and wore her hair longer and softer than usual, the way I'd always loved it.

My sister and I stood behind Mom with tears coursing down our cheeks. We looked younger, too.

My mother looked out at me, stared deep into my eyes, and said, "If you are seeing this now, then it means something has happened to me. I'm not here anymore."

Her words shattered the darkness that had weighed me down, leaving my heart and soul so light and free. I felt as if I might float away. A feeling of peace enveloped me, and I knew whatever happened in the future, I'd be okay.

In a flash, memories of the three of us together faded in and out on the TV screen. They were wonderful moments, happier times with Mom and my sister. I wanted to keep watching, but the alarm sounded, and I woke up.

According to the clock, I had only slept minutes. Dream or reality, I could still feel Mom's presence as I wiped the tears from my eyes and told my husband what had happened. Loved ones have often come to me in my dreams. And I knew wherever the mother I knew had gone, she'd found a way to visit and send her much-needed message.

My mother continues to make it clear that I no longer fit into her life. I miss our numerous phone calls. I miss talking to her on our visits and the closeness we once shared. Perhaps that will change, but maybe not.

The loving mother in my dream made it clear that even though she's not here anymore, she will always live in my heart and memories. No one, including Mom's new reality, can take those away. And if I'm lucky, my loving mom, wherever she is, will continue to visit me in my dreams.

— Vera Frances —

70

Elsa's Story

Love and kindness are never wasted.
They always make a difference. They bless the one
who receives them, and they bless you, the giver.
~Barbara de Angelis

"I had the strangest dream last night," I said.

Dave, my fiancé, replied, "So, what's new?"

I was slowly learning how to embrace my gift as a psychic medium. I always seemed to have strange dreams, but this one was different. I just couldn't put my finger on it. I didn't recognize any of the people, and it didn't make sense.

He snuggled up to me and said, "So, are you gonna tell me about it?"

I took a deep breath, trying to put it together in my mind as I described it.

"*I was walking through this grassy field, tall grass, like waist-high. I was carrying a little blond girl, probably about four or five, in my left arm and a dark-haired baby boy in my right arm. I stepped across this wire fence, and a tan-skinned man in a long-sleeved denim shirt was walking toward me. When he got to me, he took the little girl and said, 'I've got her now. Thank you.' Then he turned, and they walked away. I turned to the right with the baby boy, and we walked off. Then I woke up. It was very strange.*"

Dave said, "I don't know, darlin'. I'm sure it will reveal itself if it's supposed to." He got up to go to the shower and get ready to leave for his early morning bartending job. The bar opened at 7:30 a.m. for the people who got off work on third shift, and Dave was always there to greet them with a smile and their "nightcap" before they went home to sleep.

The phone rang at 8:30. It was Dave. I thought he must have forgotten something when he left for work.

Dave said, "Hey, baby. You know Missy, the one who bartends, right?"

"Yes. Why?"

He said, "Her little girl was killed last night in a wreck. Sad deal. We will want to make sure we put the visitation down on the calendar."

I said, "Okay. Oh, gosh, how awful! I never met her daughter. Was she a teenager?"

Dave said, "I don't know. I think she was young, like a little kid. She was riding with her dad, and he went off the road."

I said, "Oh, my! Okay, let me know when you find out more, and I'll put it on the calendar."

The visitation was a few days later. Dave and I went to the funeral home. The line was so long that it stretched outside. As we got inside, we could see there was a big TV with a slideshow presentation that people were watching. As the line moved, we got close enough to watch it. When I saw the little girl's picture, my knees buckled. It was the little blond girl in my dream! Her name was Elsa. She was five years old. I grabbed Dave's arm and squeezed it tight, trying not to make a scene. I choked back the tears. He looked at me like I was crazy, and I pulled him down to my level so I could whisper in his ear.

"Dave! *That* is the little girl who was in my dream!"

He looked at me and whispered, "Are you sure?"

I said, "*Yes!* I am positive! Oh, my gosh, Dave, what am I supposed to do?"

He looked away, as if thinking, "Keep it to yourself."

We walked on through the line. It was all I could do to choke back the tears. I thought to myself, *If it were my child, I would want to know. But how on earth do you tell someone something like this?* Dave and I both gave Missy a hug and walked past her little girl, dressed like a fairy princess in her coffin.

Months passed, and I never said a word. In fact, I tried to put it out of my mind. Missy had begun bartending in the evenings at the bar where Dave worked, so our paths were now crossing constantly because he played in the band there one or two nights a week. She would always bring me a Mountain Dew while I watched Dave play.

One night, after the bar was closed and Dave was packing up his music equipment, Missy came up and asked me about helping her with some healing work. She was having a really tough time. I told her that a friend of mine, a shaman, was coming down in a few weeks to host a healing circle, and she was welcome to come. She said she would.

On the day of the healing circle, there were just four of us: Missy, another lady, the shaman, and myself. At the end of the day, the shaman asked if we wanted to share anything with each other, reminding us that we were in a sacred, safe place to speak.

I took a deep breath and said, "Missy, I know we don't know each other very well. You have always been kind to me. There is something I need to tell you that I hope will give you some peace and healing." Then I told her the story of my dream and how I had it the night her daughter had passed. I told her I couldn't make any sense out of it until I saw Elsa's picture at the funeral home and realized it was her little girl's spirit that I was carrying. When I told her that I handed Elsa to a man in a long-sleeved denim shirt with tanned skin, her eyes filled up with tears.

I reached out to comfort her and said I was sorry to have upset her, and she said, "No, you didn't. It's fine! That was my dad! He always wore long-sleeved denim shirts and worked outside, so he was always tan. Now I know they are together, and he is taking care of her! Thank you so very much. You have no idea how much this means to me to know this."

I said, "I was so afraid. I didn't want to hurt you, and I didn't know how to tell you. Do you have any idea about the baby boy? Who he was or belonged to?"

She smiled and said, "Well, I found out a few months ago that I am pregnant, and I haven't told many people because of everything that has happened. But I just found out the other day it is a boy!"

After that day, I began to embrace my gift. Even if I don't always understand what I am being shown, I always trust there is a greater reason behind it.

— Pamela Freeland —

71

Dreams that Bear a Message

The brave man is not he who does not feel afraid,
but he who conquers that fear.
~Nelson Mandela

I pushed hard against the writhing serpentine bodies that were thick in the roiling, muddy water. I had to keep them out of my small boat. I had to! Like worms in a fisherman's can, their bodies were wound together so that it was impossible to see where one began and another ended. I was surrounded, but I pushed them all away from my little craft with my hands. Some of the muddy water had splashed in, but no snakes.

I woke up in terror, gasping for air, aching at the intense battle for survival in my dream. It became one among many that carried a message for me in that troubled season.

In the early years of my adult life, one individual was bent on destroying me and taking all that I held dear. A court battle loomed before me. I was alone, without financial resources to support a long, drawn-out legal conflict. I was unsure of the future and unsure of myself.

The serpents of my dreams represented the fear that was encroaching from every side. I had always been terrified of snakes in real life, after having been face to face with a venomous one on a construction site where there seemed no way out. Several of my cousins and I had been playing there. When the snake crawled out of its hole, they all scurried up the excavated wall while I stood frozen in time and space, unable to move or speak. One of the older cousins dropped a huge rock from outside the pit that landed squarely on top of the snake, and they pulled me to safety.

That paralyzing fear remains with me to this day if I see a snake unexpectedly. I certainly didn't want them showing up in my dreams.

In another dream during this court-battle period, a boa constrictor was coming for me. It was the hugest serpent I'd ever seen! Its head was the size of a horse's head. In the dream, as the constrictor's giant face and mouth loomed over me, I grabbed it around the massive neck and began to squeeze. I prayed while I squeezed and put every bit of strength I had into my hands around the creature's neck and continued to pray. The head began to shrink. The more I squeezed, the smaller the head became and the body with it. In the end, it was a harmless, small, nonvenomous species that I tossed aside and watched crawl away.

I took this dream to mean that my fears were inflated. I was struggling with something so much bigger than myself, which seemed to have the power to absolutely crush the life out of me, but it was an illusion. The person involved on the other end of the court battle ranted and raved at me. He tried to instill fear, made threats, and regularly harassed me. I had no peace from day to day. He was relentless in his strategy to wear me down.

Sometimes, I would realize in the dream that I was only dreaming. I would search for the meaning and the thing I needed to learn while the dream continued. I dreamed of two snakes biting me on the arm, but when I checked my arm, there were bruises but no puncture wounds. Whatever was going on would not be successful. It might hurt me, but it would not destroy me.

In the final dream from this period of my life, I dreamed I was surrounded by cobras. They had their heads raised, staring toward me, swaying back and forth, and I could see the brilliant colors and patterns on top of their heads as their tongues flicked in and out in my direction. As I searched for the meaning (even though I was asleep), something urged me to look closer at the markings and the coloring on top of the snakes' heads. I began to realize that something didn't look right. I reached out a hand and rubbed the coloring with a fingertip. It began to rub away like chalk dust. It wasn't real. The snakes were real enough, but they were not the deadly cobras they were pretending to be. They were not venomous. They had no power over me. Once I realized the truth, they stopped hissing, lowered themselves to the ground, and slithered away as I woke up.

As the court battle played out, I remembered each dream. I knew the greatest weapon that could harm me was my own fear. In the end, the struggle ended in my favor. I was relieved when it was over, but I had already seen the outcome in my dreams. I would be okay.

In the following years, I've learned that some dreams are only that — reflections of our imaginations, without significance to our daily lives. I've been a dreamer since I was a child. I usually dream in full color but sometimes in black and white. I dream of flying and time traveling. I have adventures like a movie plot in my sleep. These are usually forgotten by noon the next day if I don't write them down.

Dreams can, however, carry a message. If the same theme or same dream repeats several times, there is a lesson or warning for which we need to search. We are designed to be aware of the world around us, past, present, and even future. Our dreams are often the avenue through which our spirit and unknown circumstances join with our mind to bring revelation out of hidden situations of which we need to be aware and prepared.

Before the COVID-19 pandemic, my dreams had begun to warn me that something troubling was coming. I couldn't imagine what the dreams meant. *In one dream, I saw my grandchildren leaving my house with their suitcases after an extended stay, being picked up by their other grandparents who live far away.* This was totally out of the normal routine of our lives.

When the children came to stay with me for several days of "home learning" while their parents both worked in the medical field hours away from me, the dream of their extended stay and their suitcases reminded me that I had already seen the situation unfolding. Because of another dream I had experienced where the children were wearing masks while they were laughing and running about in the yard, I was relieved to know that at the end of this challenging time in our world's history, even though the children were wearing masks, we were all happy and doing well.

Time and experience have taught me that the dreams that repeat or have strong emotions are opportunities for me to face my fears, learn valuable lessons, or prepare for upcoming events that I may not understand at the time. I've come to value dreams as legitimate parts of our existence that have great value if we learn to listen to them.

—Judith Victoria Hensley—

72

Finally Free

A mother's arms are more comforting
than anyone else's.
~Diana, Princess of Wales

This was yet another hospital bed, like so many before. Institutional blankets that tried to offer comfort to a frail and beaten body. Beepers and buzzers monitoring a heart that had hung on far past its life expectancy, and a table holding a small white teddy bear with a card saying, "Mom, I love you."

My mother lay in the bed. She had suffered from a rare and fast-progressing form of rheumatoid arthritis that afflicted her in her twenties and ravaged her body. She was still a relatively young woman but had been through so much. Even while being painfully sick, she had raised two young children on her own after my father died at forty-four from cancer.

Her bones jutted through her fragile, pale skin as her face twitched from her severe pain even in sleep. She had hung on as long as she could without being able to walk, reliant on so many pills and medications to make sure that she could be there for her children. My mom was so proud to see us grow into successful adults... my brother — a financial planner, who lived out of state, and me — a teacher.

But as I sat at this particular hospital bed, something was different. This was to be her last. On top of her many afflictions, due to a compromised immune system she had become stricken with pneumonia and a high fever.

I thought that she would make it past this stay, like she had so many times before. With each hospital stay, she fought to hang on, knowing that I needed her so very much. To outsiders, it would seem that this sickly, feeble woman needed me, but that was not the case. What she couldn't provide for me physically, she provided emotionally — in spades.

Even as sick as she was, she dealt with my depression, my moods and my worries. And when people would tell me how much I did for her, I thought that to be so ironic because it was she who did for me. She was my safe place, my haven, my rock.

She was now in a hospice facility, but the hope was that the new complications brought on by her arthritis would be managed, her pneumonia would subside, and she would return to the nursing home where she had spent the last five years.

However, during one of my visits to her hospice facility, something compelled me — I was ready to tell her that I would be fine; I could make it on my own. I had always been sad that I wasn't married, and my life thus far wasn't what I had hoped it would be. But for some reason, I knew on that night what I needed to say, and it spilled out of me like a calm, steady river. I leaned into my mother and whispered gingerly in her ear, "I'll be okay. I'll get married someday. You can go."

The next day, as I was getting ready to go see her, I got a call from the hospice facility that my mom's temperature had gone up even further, into a zone of no turning back, and she was in a coma-like state.

What had I done? Why did I say these things to her? I was going to lose her, and I would be all alone.

It slowly dawned on me… She had been waiting to hear the words that I had breathed into her ear. She could be free at last. I had been selfish for so long, and now it was time to let her go.

After a couple of days, she passed with me in the room by her side. She waited until I slept, though. Even in death, she was more concerned with my comfort.

The next weeks and months were grueling. Emptiness filled me. I ached and yearned for her. Then one night, as I was finally able to get a somewhat decent night's sleep, she came to me in a dream.

My mom was walking toward me from the emergency-room entrance of a hospital. She looked different. I had never seen her walk without using a walker or cane, and for many years she was bound to her bed or a wheelchair.

Now, in my dream, there was no walker, cane or wheelchair. Her legs and arms were smooth — no twisted joints and jutting bones. She glided along without a care in the world, heading out into the fresh air and bright sunshine, her blond hair bouncing along in the breeze. Being as ill as she was, so much of her life had been spent indoors. Now, I could see the rays of sun enveloping her.

The outfit she wore was one she would have donned in her younger days — a short skirt and short-sleeve blouse covered in splashes of pastel greens and pinks. And she was smiling. Her daily suffering was over. As she strode with ease away from the hospital, she beamed with delight, her hair and make-up done just as she would have wanted. She seemed so calm.

As I dreamt, some of my emptiness began to fill up with relief and tranquility. Instead of twisting and turning as I slept, my body began to settle. My mom had suffered constant pain, but my dream told me she had been released from the body that brought her so much misery.

As the years pass, I still have those moments when I long to feel my mother's arms around me like a safe cocoon. Then, I think back to my dream, and how my beautiful mother emerged from the hospital with her arms wide open, able to embrace me like she never could before.

— Debbie Cohen —

Chapter 8

Love Come True

73

The Date

Love recognizes no barriers. It jumps hurdles,
leaps fences, penetrates walls to arrive at its
destination full of hope.
~Maya Angelou

Our mother was the one who taught us the technique. Cut a hard-boiled egg in two, salt it, eat only the white part, and then somersault into bed and sleep with your head at the foot of the bed. "Do that," she told us, "and you'll dream about the man you're going to marry."

The first time I tried the technique, I was twelve years old, and a stranger did show up in my dreams that night.

A long, dark car pulled up in front of the house, and a man stepped out of the driver's side and approached me. He didn't say anything—he just stood there gazing at me, which enabled me to get a good, long look at him. He had black hair cut neatly above the ears, and a handsome face with sharp, angular features. I could tell he was an intelligent man; I could see it in his eyes.

I don't remember how the dream ended, but I know that the stranger and I never spoke to each other. He probably just got back into the car and drove off. But even though I'd forgotten the ending, my mind never let go of the central part of the dream. I'd replay it in my thoughts every now and then. The car. The black-haired stranger. That face. Those intelligent eyes.

One winter day, some five years later, my good friend Jean called me to ask a favor. "Jane, I need you to go on a double date with Ralph and me."

I'd never been on a double date before. And this would be a blind double date. I asked Jean for more details.

"Ralph's buddy from the Navy is in town," she informed me. "He's nice. His name is Joe. I think you'll like him."

"And what if I don't?" I asked.

"If you don't like him, we'll all say goodbye at the end of the night and go our separate ways. Come on, Jane. It's just one date."

I agreed to do my friend a favor and go on the double date. That evening, after getting myself ready, I sat in the living room and waited for the three of them to come and pick me up.

Seven o'clock came and went, and my friends didn't show up. At 7:30, I called Jean's house. When I learned she wasn't home, I figured she'd be arriving with the guys any moment.

Eight o'clock came and went, and still there was no sign of my friend.

By 9 p.m., I was beginning to get agitated. Of course, I worried that maybe something had happened to them, but only for a few fleeting minutes. Somehow, I knew that they hadn't gotten into an accident, and nothing bad had happened to them. They were simply being irresponsible and had lost track of time.

By 9:30, I'd decided that I definitely was not going on a date that evening. It was too late for me to leave the house. I was only seventeen, and my mother would worry about me if I went out after 9:30, accompanied by a stranger no less! I sat there in the living room and fumed. How could my friend be so rude?

It was just before ten when a knock came at the front door.

I marched to the door, prepared to tell Jean and the guys that they'd have to do their double date minus one. I wasn't leaving the house this late, and if they had any sense, they'd have known better than to show up now!

But when I opened the door, my attitude immediately softened.

Jean and Ralph were there on the front porch, but I didn't pay any attention to them. Standing right in front of me was a stranger... a stranger I had encountered five years earlier. Same black hair. Same handsome, angular face. Same intelligent eyes. How could I ever forget those eyes?

"I'm Joe," he said, smiling as he shuffled forward. "Nice to meet you."

He put his hand out and waited for me to shake it. But instead of shaking his hand, I pointed at him and said in a voice brimming with certainty, "You're the man I'm going to marry."

"I am?" Joe replied, visibly taken aback by my bold remark.

I held his gaze as I allowed the moment to settle in. Then I glanced over at Jean. "Let me get my coat."

Joe and I had a wonderful time that evening. In the weeks that followed, we shared many other wonderful days and evenings together. That double date was in December. By March, less than four months later, Joe and I were married.

My sweetheart passed away a number of years ago, but prior to his passing, Joe and I enjoyed forty-four years of wedded bliss. We built a life together — and a legacy. Five children. Ten grandchildren. And now so many greats and great-greats, I practically need a spreadsheet to keep track of them.

Sometimes, at family gatherings, I look around the room at my children, my grandchildren, my greats and great-greats, and I think about that December night in 1950. One thing I know for sure: I wouldn't have accompanied Joe on that date if he hadn't appeared in my dream some years earlier. I would have gone to bed and missed out on sharing a life with the black-haired Navy man.

If I hadn't experienced that dream, it's often occurred to me, none of these beautiful people around me would exist. None of them would have been born. There would perhaps be other people in my life, other children and grandchildren, but not these specific people — the wonderful, talented individuals I've come to think of as the jewels in my crown.

It's amazing what a dream can lead to if you listen to it and act on it. You can build a life on one dream, as I did. If you're fortunate — as I was — you might even create a legacy that lasts for generations to come.

— Jane Clark —

74

A Wanderer in My Dream

Dogs are miracles with paws.
~Susan Ariel Rainbow Kennedy

"How did you sleep?" my husband asked, as he poured me a cup of piping-hot coffee.

"I had a weird dream," I said, blowing soft ripples into the sweet, light-brown liquid. *"I was standing in the yard, and a light-haired dog was running toward me. I stretched my arms wide and called her Lily."*

"Hmm," he said, not looking up from his paper, "wonder what it means."

We didn't have a dog and had not discussed owning one. We also didn't interpret my dream as a sign that we should go out and get one.

A week or so later, I noticed a dog curled up in the corner of our yard. I assumed it belonged to one of our neighbors and thought nothing more of it.

A few nights after that, we came home from a party and saw a dog lying on our porch. It was winter, and we frequently found a cat or two sleeping in the cushions of the wicker furniture. It was comforting to know we were a haven for animals that were out in those cold temperatures. We kept food and water on the porch for those passing through. So, it was no surprise that a dog might take shelter under the cover of our welcoming front porch. We had motion-sensing lights, so I could see how a wanderer might take that as a signal to come up the steps and rest her weary bones.

While my husband parked the car and unlocked the front door, I approached the strange animal slowly. She had chosen our welcome mat for her bed and had her back against the front door. The dog lifted her head and looked at me. She was a beautiful blond husky. Her tail wagged. I reached out to pet her, and she tried to stand. My husband opened the door from inside, and the dog quietly limped down the brick steps and off into the darkness.

"Did she have a collar?" he asked.

"I didn't see one," I said. "She's hurt, though. Should we go look for her?"

"Not at this hour of the night," he said. "Maybe she's going home." I wanted to believe that because I couldn't stand the thought of that sweet dog suffering in pain from an injury.

"I wonder who she belongs to," my husband said, still holding the open door with one hand.

"I don't know," I said, looking out into the darkness, "but I've seen her before."

"Where?"

"In my dream." I looked at him with tears beginning to pool and shivered in the cool night air. "It's Lily."

Days later, she was on the porch again. She let me pet her. I noted that she had hairless spots rubbed down to the bone at her joints. She was covered in fleas, and there were some infected places behind her ears. This poor dog had not been cared for by anyone in a long time.

My husband wrangled her into the truck and took her to a local veterinarian. Unfortunately, her injury had happened some time ago and had already healed. The limp would be permanent. We provided her with everything she needed to recuperate from her other problems — a trip to a groomer, medication, and constant love and attention — and decided to let her stay inside at least until the infections cleared up. We tried to find her owner, but no one claimed her.

She loved baths but was afraid of lightning. She never barked; she talked. She tried to sit in our laps as if she were a small dog. She understood simple commands. She was eager to please. Someone had loved her before; that was easy to see. And having only three good legs did not hinder her ability to run. We found that out the first time we took her for a walk.

Lily decided to keep us.

Even though we hadn't planned on getting a dog, she had sent me a sign in my dream that she was on her way. Call it fate or whatever you want, but Lily would never have to find a place to sleep again. She had found her home, no longer a wanderer in my dream.

—Vickie McEntire—

75

Meant to Be

Miracles, in the sense of phenomena we cannot
explain, surround us on every hand:
life itself is the miracle of miracles.
~George Bernard Shaw

In the spring of 1992, I was eighteen years old, a senior in high school, and deep in a dark, suicidal depression. I was taking medication and going to therapy, but I didn't seem to be able to find my way out of the abyss that had a hold of me.

One night during that time, I had a dream that I couldn't shake afterward.

I was walking down the middle of a dark street with my parents and brother at night. I didn't know the area we were in or why we were there. Suddenly, a dark truck turned the corner and headed down the street toward us. We all moved to the side of the road. As the truck drew nearer, my brother suddenly exclaimed: "Hey, it's Corbin!" I no longer felt anxious and afraid. Instead, I felt joyful and light when we realized it was Corbin. When he got out of the truck, we saw he was a big man — over six feet tall with a stocky build and brown hair. I just couldn't make out the features of his face.

The dream ended then, but the joyful feelings stayed with me.

At that time in my life, I dreamed every night, but the details never stayed with me, and I never bothered to write them down. This one lingered, however. I had no idea why seeing the mystery man named Corbin brought such joy to my day, but it buoyed me in ways that nothing else did at that time.

Fast forward eight years, and I was married and trying to start a family. We went through cycle after cycle of infertility treatments with no success. Once again, I fell into a deep depression. In the spring of 2000, we decided that we would try one last infertility treatment and move on to pursuing adoption if it didn't work.

The night before the last treatment, I dreamed once again that I was walking down the street with my family. We all grew very happy and excited when a man named Corbin arrived in his truck.

I didn't know why, but the dream reassured me. Somehow, things were going to be all right. Even when the pregnancy test was negative and I was devastated, I still felt optimistic in a small corner of my heart.

In 2002, we finished our home study for the adoption process and were informed that a child had been selected for us. We would hear about him and his history before deciding if we wanted to meet him. My husband decided that, to be impartial, we would hold off on knowing the child's name or seeing pictures until after initial disclosure. Our adoption worker shared all the information she had with us, and my husband and I looked at each other and both exclaimed, "He's for us." Then she took out some pictures and handed them to us. A three-year-old with an impish grin, wearing one hat and holding another, smiled at us in the picture. I had thought I would feel an automatic connection with the picture, but while he was a cute kid, I found myself flipping through the pictures searching for a spark. Then our social worker asked if we wanted to know his name. When we said yes, she shared, "His name is Corbin."

There and then, I knew I was meant to be his mom, and it would all work out okay. Today, Corbin is over six feet tall with a stocky build.

— Tina Szymczak —

76

The Right Man

If two people are meant for each other,
it doesn't mean they have to be together right now
or as soon as possible, but they will... eventually.
~Nina Ardianti

"**W**ait. This is wrong. Why is it you? You're not supposed to be here!" I woke up just after he smiled and shrugged. Then I realized I was smiling, too. What a silly dream!

I was newly married and forging a life with my husband Andy in New York City. I was slowly getting used to the fast pace, strong language, and absence of personal space. I landed a job in a gift shop to help pay bills between theater auditions, and I was starting to feel like I fit in. But all the hustle and bustle, even at my young age, took its toll. I was exhausted when I returned to our apartment on Staten Island every evening, and I slept like a baby every night.

My slumbers were so sound, in fact, that I rarely dreamt, which is why that particular night was so peculiar. Not only did I have a dream, but it was vivid, the kind where I had to look around when I awoke, making sure it wasn't real.

I was walking down the aisle at my wedding on the arm of my father, except this didn't look anything like the actual church wedding I'd celebrated just a few months earlier. This wedding was outside in a beautiful garden in front of a white gazebo. Still, there Dad and I walked, nodding to family members seated around us, smiling and happy.

Then I reached the clergyman standing in front and turned to my handsome groom. It wasn't Andy. It was my high-school boyfriend, Alan, whom I hadn't seen since graduation over five years earlier. We had parted friends, wished each other luck, and went our separate ways. But now here he was, about to marry me in my dream. I gasped and exclaimed, "Wait. This is wrong. Why is it you? You're not supposed to be here!" He smiled and shrugged. He never spoke. My goodness, he looked handsome!

I woke up, laughed, and told Andy about the bizarreness of it all. He laughed too, and we agreed my brain was probably overtired. We never gave it another thought.

Nearly four years later, Andy came home one day and asked if we could talk. He announced that he no longer loved me and he didn't want to be married anymore. He packed a bag and left, leaving me sitting frozen in a chair, too shocked to speak. The months that followed were bleak as I struggled to get on with my life. There were good days and bad, and I was fortunate to have amazing family and friends to support me. But I was broken.

Then one day there was a message on my answering machine. I listened to it once and then hit "Repeat" because it was too surreal to believe. "Hi. My name is Alan. I'm looking for a girl I used to date in high school named Joan. Is this you? If so, I'd love to catch up. Call me back." I rewound it again. It had been eight years. How had he found me? *Why* had he found me?

I called him back, and we talked for hours. Then he called again the next day. And the next. He listened while I told him about my failed marriage, and he told me about his own. He understood all the pain and shame, and we helped each other heal. We also reminisced about high school, all the marching-band trips and homecoming dances, and the years melted away. By the time we finally reunited in person, I already knew I had fallen in love with him. It took a few years because we were both so gun-shy after our previous failures, but one evening he asked me to marry him, and I replied "Yes!" without hesitation.

We started looking for venues and found a lovely resort that specialized in weddings. As they walked us around to the back of the hotel to show us the grounds, I stopped dead in my tracks. I hadn't thought of that dream in years, but here it was in front of me. There was the garden. There was the white gazebo, exactly as it had appeared in my dream. "This is the one," I simply told Alan.

The day of our wedding was glorious. Surrounded by the family who had so lovingly supported me through all the dark days, I walked down the aisle holding onto my father's arm. I reached the clergyman and turned to my smiling, handsome groom. He was definitely supposed to be there.

Today, a lovely framed photo of my groom and me standing in front of that gazebo, overlooking that garden, hangs on our wall. I study it every day. I'm still not sure what that dream meant. Was God trying to warn me that things were going to get a little rough, but there was a greater plan down the road? Who knows? I just tell people that it took me a while, but I finally married the man of my dreams and I wouldn't change a thing.

— Joan Donnelly-Emery —

77

Dull Dreams

Dreams are today's answers to tomorrow's questions.
~Edgar Cayce

My dreams have always been unimaginative, bland, and downright dull. I've had dreams of sitting on my couch and scrolling through Instagram. I've had dreams of standing in line. Once, I had a dream where I was eating Cheerios — and not even the honey nut kind.

I could probably bore even the most devoted psychologists with my tedious dreams of shopping for towels on Amazon. But I've never really minded.

I wasn't envious of my college roommate, who would wake up in the morning and recount wild and vivid dreams of going back in time. I didn't feel like I was missing out when my mom told me about exciting dreams where she found herself in a new land, in someone else's body. And I certainly have never envied my husband's night terrors.

I always liked that my dreams were boring and practical. My mind's unexciting, unimaginative images were appreciated in a life that can, too often, be stressful.

Perhaps I appreciated this most when I was a little girl. Maybe most kids dream of Santa and unicorns and candy, but for me a monotonous dream world was refreshing in a childhood filled with extremes.

Back then, I was always traveling between my divorced parents' houses. I spent most of my time with a doting, loving mother who liked to take me out for ice cream. Then I threw my parental expectations out the window when, every other weekend, I spent time with my angry, aggressive, gun-toting dad. A bland dreamland helped me wipe the slate clean.

And I still appreciated my dull, sleeping subconscious as I got older.

Between the sudden death of a close friend from work, a busy and taxing time in grad school, and the even more stressful experience trying to pay down loans for those grad-school classes, all I wanted to do in my mid-twenties was escape. I wanted to throw myself into a simple dream of brushing my teeth. Or folding laundry. Or cleaning the stove.

I could always depend on a safe, boring dream to give my mind a break — that is, until last year.

It was November, and my husband and I had just packed up our whole life and moved from California to New York. He'd gotten a job offer he couldn't pass up, with a start date just weeks away. It meant a quick move, frenzied packing, and lots of short goodbyes to our friends, family, and home.

When my husband and I arrived in New York on a cold winter night with our four tightly packed suitcases, we both felt a little lost. We didn't know our way around or where we could find something to eat. We didn't even have an apartment, just a two-week reservation for a small Airbnb in Brooklyn.

We were able to find our way to our temporary address, and we unpacked and settled in. But those first few days, we missed our family, friends, and the warm weather back home much more than we thought we would.

Then, more than ever, I wanted a nice, boring dream to ground me. Maybe a short one about washing my hands, followed by another dream where I could find myself sitting on the couch, watching something uninspiring on TV, like a commercial.

But instead, just a few days after moving, I dreamed I was pregnant. In the dream, I was holding a big belly, waiting to feel the baby kick.

I woke up from my dream unlike how I'd ever woken before: sweating, anxious, and exhausted. Maybe I shouldn't have had such an extreme reaction — it wasn't as if I'd had a nightmare filled with monsters. But after a week of stressful moving, a weird pregnancy dream was too much. I went into the bathroom and washed my face. I thought that running some cool water would help, but it didn't.

I'd always depended on my dreams to give me time to relax, not to imagine possibilities. My dreams were supposed to be small, boring moments of my real life, nothing else.

But as I stood there scrubbing my cheeks with the apricot face wash I'd brought from California, I realized that there was something familiar about the dream. It had the same dull feel I was used to.

The vision of me holding my belly had been such a small, quiet moment, just like the dreams of brushing my teeth or curling my hair. Maybe this wasn't such a wild or fanciful image after all. Maybe, in the madness of the move, I simply hadn't noticed the first signs of pregnancy. Maybe the dream was just showing me my new normal.

It was a big, exciting moment when, the next evening, my husband and I peeked at my pregnancy test after three long minutes of waiting. We had another big moment a week later when we went into a doctor's office for a check-up, just to be sure. But that first test, and the dream, were right from the beginning. We were going to have a baby.

My husband and I were so excited for the pregnancy, even though we knew we had some stress ahead of us. We had to worry about finding an apartment, settling into new jobs, and now the health of our growing baby.

In the months that followed, I was especially thankful for my dull dreams, which helped keep me grounded in such a crazy time. But I was even more grateful for that not-so-boring dream that helped me see a new life.

—Jillian Pretzel—

78

Man of My Dreams

The love game is never called off
on account of darkness.
~Tom Masson

Regina, Saskatchewan, autumn 1992. My job as a communications specialist at Farm Credit Canada had been transferred from Ottawa, the capital of Canada, to this small city on the Canadian prairie. My marriage had broken up several years before, so my son and I were on our own in a new city.

Shortly after the move, I had a particularly vivid dream. I don't remember most dreams more than a few seconds after waking, but this one was different.

In this dream, I saw a smiling, large man in a buff-colored jacket. His mouth was smeared with lipstick. He was standing on top of a berm beside Wascana Lake. It was a bright, sunny day in winter.

I've always been a hiker and had already explored the shores of the lake. The western half features expanses of tree-lined lawn, with paved paths for cycling and walking. The eastern part of the lake is a bird refuge, with some paths paved, others only dirt and narrow and overgrown in spots. One was a bit tricky as it bit into the side of a berm. In my dream, we were on top of that berm, with a neighborhood to one side and the lake on the other. We had been kissing passionately, and his lipstick-smeared face was glowing with happiness. I felt that I had finally found "the one," although I did not recognize the man as anyone I knew at the time.

Throughout the months and years to come, I looked for that man. My boss was a friendly man who seemed attracted to me, but nothing much happened. I tried to imagine him with his face smeared with lipstick, but as he was bearded, I couldn't quite bring up the image. And I wasn't really attracted to him. I put ads in the personals column — that was what we did before online dating. If I felt attracted to a colleague, church member, or someone I met at a social event, I would gaze at him intently, wondering if he could be the man in my dream. But no one sparked more than a passing interest. If he did, he wasn't interested in me.

I joined the Unitarian Fellowship of Regina and was given the task of promoting a series of lectures we were offering in hopes of attracting more members. I created posters and took them around to community bulletin boards, including the kiosks in Wascana Park. By this time, I had pretty much forgotten about my dream.

One evening, a large, heavyset man with curly brown hair, a gentle manner, a kind face and, yes, a buff-colored jacket, came to one of these events. He had seen my poster in the park. My first thought was that it would be comforting to hug him. He stayed afterward for coffee, and we talked. After a few such meetings, he suggested we go for a walk. For several weeks, we walked together every Sunday, often stopping for tea or a meal at a restaurant. One day, he took my hand and held it. We proceeded from there to kissing, and soon we were lovers.

One day, when we were walking around Wascana Lake on a bright, cold winter day, we stopped to kiss. As we pulled apart, I looked into his face, glowing with joy and smeared with my lipstick. I realized with a jolt that this was the precise moment, at the precise spot, that I had seen in my dream. I didn't tell him; he would have scoffed. Robert was a scientist who was quick to categorize anything like this as silly nonsense.

In time, my son grew up and moved out. Robert moved in.

One morning, Robert woke up seeing flashing lights and jagged edges to his vision. We went to the emergency room and were told that he should see an ophthalmologist without delay. After further tests, they discovered a tumor in his left eye. He underwent radiation treatment, which seemed at first to be working.

During this time, I had another dream that we were lined up for a bus tour. Robert got on the bus, and it left without me.

When I told him about my dream, he said I was probably thinking I might be left behind if he didn't get well.

At the next appointment with his oncologist, it looked like there might be some regrowth of the tumor. He began having pains in his side, which didn't go away. His doctor ordered more tests, which revealed cancer in his liver, probably metastasized from the tumor in his eye. Six weeks later, he died.

I fell into a deep depression and had another vivid dream in which I searched for him everywhere.

I found him in a high-ceilinged room lined floor-to-ceiling with mahogany bookcases. He and a few other men sat facing each other on leather couches. Some were leaning back, nodding. Others sat forward on their seats in animated discussion.

Robert turned to face me. "I'm with Albert Einstein, the great mathematician Hermann Weyl, and all the beautiful angels," he said. "If I had stayed with you…" He gestured toward tall windows framed in rich brocade curtains.

The windows expanded, and I found myself looking down on a swimming pool flanked on all sides by a decrepit concrete building. Several elderly people were parked in wheelchairs around the pool. Then I was on the pool deck, where I found Robert slumped in one of the chairs, his legs swollen, his head drooped to one side, moaning in pain. "Do you want me to live this way? If you do, I'll return," I heard his voice saying.

Then we were back in the room. "Galileo, Copernicus, and Newton are here, too, and all the great minds whose work I lived to study and try to build on. They're impressed with my ideas. I'm happy," he said.

Then I woke up.

I have often seen Robert in dreams since then. "Conjugal visits," I call them. I have dreamt that we're together, happy as before, and then become separated in a crowd, and I can't find him anywhere. I panic and wake up crying.

At some point, I realized that it wasn't healthy for me to brood so much about Robert. I tried looking for the kind of intimacy we shared but have not found it. My grandchildren started arriving, growing, and thriving. I threw myself into several activities and stopped looking for romantic love. I even stopped wanting it. Eighteen years have passed since Robert died. It's been twelve years since my last relationship fizzled. I had no wish to date, believing all that was behind me.

Recently, I learned that a hiking buddy whom I have known and liked for some time — a scientist who reminds me of Robert — is now a widower. We go sometimes for walks together. And, once more, I have begun to dream.

— Florentia Scott —

Shooting Star

For my part, I know nothing with any certainty,
but the sight of the stars makes me dream.
~Vincent van Gogh

I was driving down the highway one night in early spring when I saw the most amazing shooting star fly across almost a third of the sky right in front of me, ending in a brilliant burst of glittering light. It was a spectacular yet fleeting cosmic display. Even though I've been known to set my alarm for the early hours of the morning to watch the Perseids or other predictable meteor showers, I had never seen a meteor so bright and beautiful as that one.

That night, I had a dream where a small lake appeared in front of my house. From the far shore, a puppy swam toward me. His eyes locked on mine, and he made his way to me as if he knew me, with a purposeful stroke and a canine grin of joy.

He leapt into my arms, and the next thing I knew I was holding his squirming, solid body and laughing as he licked me.

Suddenly, in the surreal timeline of dreams, we were snuggling on my couch, and that was when I noticed his short fur was scattered with mocha-colored splotches, including his round puppy belly, which he let me rub while he wiggled into a corner. A feeling of completion expanded within me, like a missing piece was settling into place. This dog was meant to be mine.

The combination of the shooting star and the powerful, vivid dream felt like a portent. Maybe the universe was trying to tell me something. Perhaps there was a dog out there looking for me, and I just had to open my heart to find him.

At the time, I wasn't looking for a dog. I had already rescued two: Jasper, a seventy-four-pound Hound with a touch of Catahoula and maybe Lab, and Lilah, who had Border Collie roots, along with a few other breeds mixed in. I also had rescued two cats — Dawn and Athena — a perfect balance in my interspecies home.

I didn't need another dog. That's what I kept telling myself the next day as I sat in my cubicle at the consulting firm where I worked. But I couldn't shake the feeling that there was a puppy out there who was destined to find me.

So, instead of creating yet another PowerPoint presentation for one of our corporate clients, I went to Petfinder.com, searching for this theoretical dog. I looked at dozens of photos, but none of them seemed like the dog I had dreamt about. Then I remembered another pet-adoption website: Adoptapet.com. I scrolled the pages, reviewing each adorable puppy and sweet dog.

Feeling a bit foolish — and also aware of the pile of work I had to do — I was just about to give up when I saw a face that made my heart skip a beat. I gasped, and my pulse began racing. It was him. I knew it. It *felt* like he was that dog.

He was a scruffy Terrier, and he didn't look exactly like the dog in my dream, but he was staring at me through the picture as if he knew me.

I sent an e-mail inquiry, wanting to know all about him. But the response I received was, "Fill out the application. Then we'll talk." I understood. Rescue groups are run by volunteers who don't have time to answer e-mail from someone who isn't serious about adopting.

Was I serious? Yes, I realized, I was.

So I filled out the application. Coursing through my body and my mind was this feeling of rightness, as if this were a path I needed to follow.

A few e-mails went back and forth between the rescue group and me, and I learned that the puppy was being fostered with — and got along well with — kids, dogs, and cats, which was very important in order for him to fit in with my gang.

I asked if the rescue group had all the information they needed from me so I could meet him. At that point, I thought he was local, but the puppy had been pulled from a kill shelter in South Carolina hundreds of miles away and was being fostered there.

I heard back: "I have no problem if you adopt him." So, while I thought I was arranging a "meet and greet," the rescue group assumed it was a "pick him up and take him home." Things were happening awfully fast. Yet the dream still seemed to be guiding me, so I kept going along with the process.

Several additional e-mails, a set of photos, and a few weeks later, the puppy was on his way to New Jersey.

I couldn't believe I was adopting a dog based on a meteor, a dream, a few pictures and some e-mails. I would never recommend that someone do this, and even today I have no idea why my family went along with the plan.

The woman who set up the adoption didn't want to meet in her home or a park, so we agreed on a Chili's parking lot in a nearby town. I was to bring $250 in cash. It felt like a drug deal, and I told my family that if things seemed weird, we'd get back in the car and drive home without the dog.

But we all fell in love the minute a sweet, wiry-haired puppy greeted each of us individually with a snuggle, kiss, and wag. The woman said, "I love it when they pick their families."

At home, we introduced the dog to Lilah and Jasper. They got along instantly, although it took a little longer with the cats. As a family, we discussed names, and one of my daughters suggested Tucker. Why? "Because he looks like a Tucker." It was true then, and throughout his life he looked like a Tucker.

A few days later, I was rubbing his sweet Terrier belly, and I saw those spots — the ones I had dreamt about.

It was in the stars: Tucker was my dream dog.

He was a ball-obsessed, scruffy Terrier who lived his life to the fullest. He loved to play, and his joy was contagious as he chased balls, squirrels and chipmunks, and barked at deer and the UPS guy. He often slept upside down, with his legs stretched out in multiple directions and his head hanging over the side of his dog bed. He loved to roll around on his back just for the fun of it, serenading us with moans of delight. And even though he was a goofy, silly dog, he was always tuned into the needs of the people around him, offering snuggles, a paw of sympathy, or his signature hugs, leaning into anyone he knew needed comforting. He became good friends with one of my cats, and I often found the two of them hanging out together.

Tucker was only with us for eight years. Like a shooting star, he came streaking into our lives, lit up our home and everyone he touched, and was gone. He was my heart dog, the dog of my dreams.

— Susan C. Willett —

80

Feels Like Home

In dreams and in love, there are no impossibilities.
~Janos Arany

I boarded the plane and hoisted my carry-on luggage into the overhead compartment. I sat down in seat 32-A and gazed out the window. I was leaving South Africa, the country that had been my home for the last three months.

I closed my eyes. I could still taste the spicy curry samosas on my tongue. I could still feel the warm water of the Indian Ocean. The scenic views from the top of Table Mountain were forever etched into my mind. As the plane began to ascend, I looked out the window and said goodbye to this beautiful country. I was unsure if I would ever return, but I knew that the people, culture, and landscapes had forever changed my heart.

The flight attendants closed the shades and dimmed the lights. I put on my headphones, listened to some of my favorite Adele hits, closed my eyes, and drifted off to sleep.

In my dream, my boyfriend Chris was standing just outside of security, wearing his white T-shirt, blue jeans, and white Nikes. I ran into his arms and almost immediately began crying. The last three months apart had felt like an eternity. He grabbed all my bags and loaded them into the trunk of his old Toyota Celica. I hopped in the passenger seat, and it felt like home.

I held his hand while he drove. I could see a picnic basket in the back seat. I couldn't stop talking about the miraculous things I had seen and experienced over the last few months. I hardly noticed where we were going until he pulled into the parking lot at the Huntington Library and Botanical Gardens, where we had one of our first dates.

He carried the picnic basket and a blanket under one arm, and I wrapped my arms around the other. He led me to the Camellia Garden, and I was enveloped in the rich smell of those beautiful flowers. We ate together, and then he grabbed a stack of letters.

"I wrote you every day that you were gone. I missed you every single one, but I knew that you would be coming home soon."

I opened one and began to read when he stopped me. "Would you dance with me?"

We danced to "Unchained Melody" by The Righteous Brothers and to a few more of our favorites from Sam Cooke. He then knelt down, pulled a little black box from the basket and opened it to display a beautiful engagement ring.

"Our friendship is the best thing that ever happened to me. Every day that I am with you, I fall more in love with you. I know now that I can't imagine my life without you. I want to spend the rest of my life loving you. Will you marry me?"

The plane hit some turbulence, and I awoke with a jolt. I pulled my headphones off and sat in utter disbelief. It felt so real. Was that seriously all a dream?

One layover and thirteen more hours later, I got off the plane at LAX. I couldn't seem to get that dream out of my head. My heart raced as I tried to wrap my head around saying "Yes" to someone. I didn't say "Yes" in the dream, but I had a feeling that I was about to. If I was going to say "Yes" to anyone, Chris was the only one I would ever want to spend the rest of my life with. I knew in that moment that I wanted to marry him. I was just hoping that he would refrain from proposing in the middle of the airport.

I got through customs as quickly as possible and ran to the arrivals terminal. There he was, wearing a white T-shirt, blue jeans, and white Nikes. I ran into his arms and immediately began crying. The last three months apart had felt like an eternity. He grabbed my bags and loaded them into the trunk of his old Toyota Celica. I hopped into the passenger seat and looked into his eyes. I was home.

"Where do you want to eat?" he asked. "I've been waiting for you to get back, so I haven't eaten sushi in three months."

"Sushi it is," I replied. "I loved the food in South Africa, but I definitely could go for a caterpillar roll!"

And just like that, all memory of my dream vanished from my mind.

After lunch, Chris drove us to a park near my college. He put on his backpack, and we began to walk around. A few families were playing in the park, and little kids were laughing on the swings.

"Remember the first time we came here, when we finally decided that we were ready to start dating?" he asked.

"I remember. I was so nervous that dating would ruin our friendship. I'm so thankful that I was wrong."

Chris pulled his backpack off his back and pulled out a small blanket. He spread it out over the grass, and we sat down facing each other. He then grabbed a journal and handed it to me.

"I wrote to you every day you were gone..."

His words began to fade out as I opened the journal to see letters spelling out his love for me.

"You don't have to read it all now. Would you dance with me?"

Chris pulled out his laptop and began to play some of our favorite songs. As we danced in the park, we laughed and talked. It just felt so natural and carefree. It was as if the world had stopped just for us.

Then I could sense a shift. He seemed a little nervous and on edge. As Chris knelt on one knee, he pulled a beautiful wooden box out of his backpack. Then, as he began to speak, he looked up at me.

"I am so thankful to have you in my life. You are my best friend, and I can't imagine my life without you. I will always love you and would be the luckiest man to have you always by my side." He opened the box to reveal the most beautiful engagement ring and asked, "Melissa, will you marry me?"

For a few seconds, I stood there in utter disbelief. My dream came rushing back to me. I told him about every detail, how it was so real and exactly like what he had just done.

He looked like he was in shock and finally cut me off. "Wait, was that a yes?"

"Absolutely! Absolutely, I will marry you!"

Four months later, we got married.

Nine years have gone by since that day. We have walked together through some of the most wonderful and some of the most difficult experiences. He will always be the man of my dreams, and as long as we are together, it will always feel like home.

— Melissa Moore —

81

The Wake-Up Call

We must be willing to let go of the life we've planned,
so as to have the life that is waiting for us.
~Joseph Campbell

The house was unusually quiet. All four kids were out. The younger ones were playing with their friends. The older two were up to whatever unsupervised teens are usually up to on a hot summer afternoon. I was taking advantage of the time alone to hide inside a book. Reading a good mystery always took me away from my fear as I waited for my husband to come home from work.

What would he find fault with this time? How had I failed to anticipate his ever-changing expectations? Why was he so impossible to please?

Would this be one of the days I was too ugly to look at? "Why don't you even try to fix yourself up? Do something with that rat's nest you call hair. And put on some make-up. No wonder I take my time coming home after work."

I tried to look my best, but with four kids, housework, a nervous dog who peed when stressed, and a job, there were days when pulling on a clean pair of jeans and a fresh T-shirt, arranging my hair in a ponytail, and washing my face before he arrived was the best I could do. And, frankly, it was all I wanted to do.

But when I made the effort, it was worse.

"What's with all the make-up and the dress? Who are you trying to impress? You're a wife and mother, for God's sake. Are you running around on me? Who is he? Tell me, or I'll beat it out of you!"

So far, he hadn't done it, but the threats were coming more often. The rage in his eyes was becoming more intense, and then there were the clenched fists, no longer trembling at his sides but raised and brandished at me.

I'm trapped, I thought. With only a high-school education, I was trained for nothing that would pay enough money to support the kids and me.

I'd done well at the job I did have. Starting as a waitress at a new restaurant in the mall nearby, I watched and learned. I filled in for every job in the place. A few years later, when an opening came up for a new manager, I applied. I was thrilled to get it.

Although he tried to hide it at first, he was very angry. The verbal abuse intensified. When I wouldn't react, he'd hone in on one of the kids so I would have to step in and bear the consequences of disrespecting him. I knew it was only a matter of time before he went too far, but I saw no way out.

I tried to distract myself with my book, but I must have drifted off to sleep.

I heard the sound of knocking and the rattle of the flimsy screen door repeatedly hitting the doorjamb.

"Just a minute. I'm coming!" I called as I did my best to smooth my wrinkled shirt. "Oh, God, what's happened? Are my kids okay?" The sight of a cop standing on my porch sent my heart racing, fear of what he would say next buckling my knees.

"I'm not here about a child. It's your husband. There's been an accident. I'm so sorry. The paramedics did all they could, but he didn't survive."

"I need to sit down," I gasped. The words were barely out of my mouth when my butt hit the floor.

"May I come in?" the officer asked. "I'll help you to a chair and get you some water. Is there someone I can call to be with you?"

What happened next was a blur of neighbors taking over. "You go up and rest. We've got this. We'll get the little ones fed and into bed and stay with the older ones while you take some time to yourself," they insisted.

Somehow, everything got done.

Next, I stood at the gravesite surrounded by my children and a huge crowd of friends and neighbors I hadn't seen in months. When it was finally over and we were alone at home, I gathered my kids around me and assured them they would be okay.

That night, alone in my bed, I cried. I mourned for what might have been. I cried for what the future would hold as I struggled to hold my family together. Mostly, I cried tears of relief. I didn't need to be afraid anymore.

When I woke up, I flipped through the phone book for the name of a divorce lawyer. The dream was a wake-up call. I didn't want him to die, but I did want the pain and fear to end, and I was ready to make it happen.

Going it alone was every bit as hard as I feared it would be. Many months, a bill or two went unpaid. I learned how to stretch my grocery budget as far as possible and skipped dinner often to make sure there was enough for the kids to eat. A cup of tea with an extra spoonful of sugar would get me through to the next morning. It was all worth it. Even the loneliness was better than what had been my life before.

I thought when I made the decision to walk away from my marriage that I would be alone forever. Who would want to become involved with a woman like me?

I never suspected he was close by.

One night, as I was leaving work, I stopped at the bank to deposit the day's receipts, and there he was: the handsome guy with the warm smile and beautiful brown eyes who sometimes came into the restaurant for lunch. After chatting for a while, he invited me out for ice cream the next night.

A date to go for ice cream. I couldn't resist.

Five years later, I married this special man. And now, every day, I wake up to the love of my life — a man who does all he can to be the best husband and father possible.

— Bobbi Carducci —

Chapter 9

Miraculous Bonds

82

The Favorite

She did not stand alone, but what stood behind her,
the most potent moral force in her life,
was the love of her father.
~Harper Lee, Go Set a Watchman

Growing up, I always believed I was nothing like my father. I was blond and blue-eyed like my mother, her carbon copy everyone said. I was certainly never under any illusion that I was Dad's favorite. That position was reserved for my older sister, born in Hawaii during the first year of my parents' marriage, or maybe my brother, the only son, who would carry on the Remick name and take over the family business.

I was the one whose birth Dad had missed, the one who stopped living with him at age three when my parents divorced. So, when he died, I almost felt like I had no claim on him, nor even the right to thoroughly grieve the loss. By my own admission, we were never really close.

Yet somehow our relationship would unfold and grow after his passing, and most of that development would take place within the vivid dreams I had of him in the weeks following his death. I would come to think of them as visits, snatches of time when I could have him all to myself, saying things meant for only me to hear.

The first one occurred right after his funeral. The setting for it was the living room of the Bickley House, where I'd spent my adolescence. Oddly enough, I'd never lived there with my father. He'd never even been inside. But the Bickley House was the first place I could truly call a home, the first place where I had my own room and felt I belonged. It was natural that my father would visit me there in his spiritual state, in the place where I had always felt safe and at peace.

We both knew he was dead, but that fact seemed a mere inconvenience, just another hurdle to jump in our obstacle course of a relationship. There was no question as to why we were in this house where I no longer lived, where he had never been. Both of us accepted that while this meeting was unpleasant, it was necessary — and ultimately inevitable.

"I don't know how I'm going to do this," I told him.

"Oh, you'll be fine," he said. "You've always been fine. You always find a way to work through things. You don't need me. You never did."

I started to cry. How could he think that? Why did he think that? Of course, I needed him. It was he who didn't need — or want — me. Could I tell him that now? Would he be open to hearing it?

So, I let him have it. I told him how I felt he'd always favored my older brother and sister. How he bought her a house and then let my brother have the family home when he moved to Baltimore to be with his new wife. How he went to dinners at my sister's place and spent weekends working on old cars with my brother but somehow always seemed too busy for me.

"I know I'm not the favorite," I sobbed. "And I'll never carry on the Remick name for generations to come. But can't I have something? Aren't I special to you for any reason at all?"

He stared at me for a moment, processing my words. I feared I'd said too much, that he would walk away from me and decide to be permanently dead.

But then he said, "Rachel, did you ever think that maybe you were the favorite? That you are the one I believed would carry the Remick name? That you are my hope?"

Upon waking, I remembered nothing after those words. But as I lay there clinging to this fleeting dream, my life with my father came at me in flashes: his enrolling me in a private high school, writing a check for the expensive tuition without hesitation because my getting into a good college was so important to him, a high-school drop-out.

His smile when he announced to his family at his fiftieth birthday celebration, "We just may have a writer in the family."

His driving my friends and me to a local, live televised dance show and waiting for hours in the parking lot for us to come out. That was so unbelievable at the time to my fourteen-year-old self, a girl who grew up under the assumption he'd never been there for me. The pride on his face when he told me he watched me dancing on the old black-and-white television he plugged into the cigarette lighter.

The time my car broke down in Cape May, and he drove down in his tow truck to pick me up, and we stopped to have chowder in the Lobster House cafeteria. Three days later, the car was parked in front of the Bickley House, running like new.

Shortly after his funeral, I was going through the things in his old bedroom in my brother's house and found dozens of notebooks, scrapbooks, picture albums, and school composition books. They were all meticulously maintained, written in brightly colored pens and pencils, mementos taped to the pages like the wrapper he saved from the stick of gum offered to him by a school crush. There were photos from road trips he'd taken in the fifties, including one of the Devils Tower in Wyoming that was eerily similar to the shot I'd taken on my own trip some forty years later. I saw myself in those pages: the writer, the dreamer, the planner, the wanderer, the explorer, the documenter, the romantic. I'd inherited it all.

The last time I saw my father was at the Cape May house. He was waving to me in the driveway as I backed out my car. My eyes teared up as I drove away, and I resisted the urge to turn the car around and go back, throw my arms around him and tell him I loved him. Of course, I didn't and have regretted the decision ever since. But years later, I had a dream that would give me my chance to make it right.

It was a continuation of that day, yet this time I knew my father was dead. I knew for certain when I drove away that I would not see him again.

This time, before climbing into the car, I told him that I loved him. I told him that he didn't need to worry about me. He was right when he told me I was going to be fine, that I was capable, that I knew what to do. That even if I couldn't see him, I would know he was still with me, always watching over me. That I would be the one to tell our story. That I was the hope. The legacy. And, like his other two children, the favorite.

—Rachel Remick—

83

Kisses from Lady

If there is a heaven, it's certain our animals are
to be there. Their lives become so interwoven
with our own, it would take more than
an archangel to detangle them.
~Pam Brown

I was diagnosed with the first of my three cancers almost twenty years ago—a cancer which I was deemed "too young" to have. It was a cancer for which I was completely unprepared as I never knew it ran in my family—a colon cancer that required surgery, chemotherapy, radiation and years of recovery.

Of course, I had wonderful doctors. I had dedicated technicians and advisors. I had great friends and family members cheering me on. I had the best care in one of the best medical facilities in the world. But, most of all, I had Lady.

Lady was my love—a big, strong, yellow Labrador Retriever. And, although my family always had dogs when I was a kid growing up, Lady was my first dog as an adult. My charge. My constant companion.

Throughout my cancer experience, she never left my side. Through the long days of pain, trips to the hospital, and continuous IVs of cancer-fighting drugs. Through the never-ending nights of nausea and diarrhea. We slept in the bathroom together, with me on her doggie bed placed next to the toilet. She lay on the tile floor next to me, with her head on my chest, kissing my chin with her tongue whenever I moaned or cried. I would sometimes wake up and see her watching me—listening to my breathing and making sure I was all right.

Months went by. And months turned into years. Suffering mostly from radiation poisoning, I slowly began to regain my health. I got stronger. I began to eat. I began to walk. And Lady was by my side, encouraging me, wagging her tail for me and kissing my chin at every opportunity.

Yet as I grew stronger, I began to notice she was growing weaker. As I began to eat more, she began to eat less. As I began to walk faster, she began to walk slower. Then she was diagnosed with cancer.

I took her in for surgery one cloudy Saturday in January. I told her everything was going to be okay, and I said goodbye. With her nose next to mine, she kissed my chin with her wet tongue, turned and walked away with the technician. That was the last time I saw her. I lost her on the operating table that day—one week before she was to turn thirteen.

Death was no stranger to me. I'd lost loved ones before, but it's different when we lose an animal. Perhaps it's because there is no ego involved. There is no history of disagreement or anger. There are no unresolved issues that often remain stuck between human beings. There are no feelings of betrayal or guilt or remorse. An animal—a beloved pet—is only there to love us. Unconditionally. Without question. No matter what. That is what we receive, and that is what we remember. There's nothing more to it.

When I lost Lady, I wasn't sure I could continue with my recovery. My support system unraveled. My strength disappeared. I felt alone. Lost. Inconsolable. For heartbreak is real. The physical tissue or muscle or nerve endings of the heart are damaged. They're broken. They hurt. And the pain can be excruciating. I became unsure of my ability to recover my health, and I began to slide into doubt and despair.

Then two events occurred that changed my life.

The first occurred on a rainy night in May. Having returned to my bed, I cried myself to sleep, due to the physical pain I still experienced and the heartbreak that consumed me. Yet, this night a peace began to envelop me. An embracing comfort.

As I surrendered to it, I became aware of a person — or, rather, a Being. Male, I think. I could not distinguish the face as it was obscured by a cape or coat or garment of some kind. This Being was holding a small cloth bundle in his hands.

He approached and held it out to me. I could see there was a tiny creature wrapped in the cloth. It wasn't human nor was it any animal with which I was familiar. Not a dog or cat. It was clearly an infant of some kind — a baby. Small and fragile.

I received the small creature and held it to my chest. To my heart. And in doing so, I could feel the tiny creature's life force enter my body. A soothing warmth encompassed me and permeated my chest. Penetrating deeper and deeper, it burrowed into my heart. And we remained in that state for hours — the tiny creature and me — until I became aware of a growing light around me, the light of sunrise. And with that awareness, the Being returned, holding out his arms to indicate it was time to give the baby back. So, I did.

That morning, I opened my eyes to a new world. I was completely aware that something extraordinary had happened. For the first time in a long time, my heart didn't hurt. I could breathe again. The crushing pain was gone. The enormous burden had been lifted. I went through my day and into the night with relief, renewed hope and gratitude. Then the second event occurred.

Falling asleep that night, I became aware of another light. As I watched, the light began to move toward me. It clearly was another Being — vibrating with energy. As it got closer, it took shape. It was a shape with which I was all too familiar — four legs, thick beaver tail, floppy ears, and deep, soulful eyes. It was Lady.

She was shimmering. Shining. Surrounded with light. Indeed, she was the light. My gorgeous girl glowed with health and vitality. And as she glided toward me, I knelt to greet her. Her beautiful face met mine. Her eyes shone into mine. And she lifted her head and kissed me on the chin — in her familiar way. I smelled her thick fur coat. I felt her breath on my face. And in that instant — with that gesture — she told me everything would be okay. She was okay. And I, too, would be okay. And then she retreated into the light and faded away — leaving me with love, hope and all good things that life and the universe have to offer.

I don't pretend for a second to understand the inner workings of our physical world, our spiritual world, or any other world that makes up the vast reality of which we are a part. Were these events dreams? Premonitions? Fantasies? Figments of my imagination? The result of loose neural wiring brought on by grief and illness? I don't know. I'm an academic. An attorney. I believe in evidence, hard facts and things I can see and touch. Yet, something happened to me that I cannot deny. And these two events changed me forever. The first healed my heart. The second healed my soul.

I know that Lady orchestrated both events. Love in all its forms is a powerful thing. I see no reason why it can't punch a hole between the worlds of life and death. Or any world in between. And with her love — her kiss — she imparted to me the knowledge that I would recover and go on without her.

Love is the force that unites us all — of that, I'm sure. I know in my heart she will always be with me — and there will always be kisses from Lady.

— Susan Wilking Horan —

84

The Old Army Trunk

*And above all, watch with glittering eyes the whole
world around you because the greatest secrets are
always hidden in the most unlikely places.*
~Roald Dahl

My husband kissed the nape of my neck before pulling back the quilt and slipping out of bed. I smiled, half asleep, mumbling a faint acknowledgement. It was 5 a.m., and he had a long drive ahead of him on this cold November morning. His Aunt Jan had died weeks before and, being her sole surviving relative, he was left with the task of cleaning out her house. But it wasn't just Jan's house. This was Chris's childhood home. He had grown up there with his mother and grandparents, all of whom had since passed.

I heard his car backing out of the driveway and tucked myself further under the blanket. With two hours before my alarm went off, I closed my eyes and drifted into a quiet slumber.

Chris's mother, Nadine, led me through a back door and down a dark, narrow staircase to a basement filled with furniture, boxes, and household wares. I had no idea where I was or why I was there, only that I had a connection to this place. Somehow, these items now belonged to me, even though I had no attachment to them and didn't want them. I turned to leave, but she grabbed my hand and insisted I follow her. We walked through a maze of garbage bags stuffed full of broken, discarded objects. At the rear of the basement, next to a wooden bar cluttered with blenders and cocktail glasses, she stopped and turned to me.

"I want that," she said, pointing at a green army trunk sitting against the wall alongside the bar.

"You want that?" I repeated.

"I want that!" It was a command.

"Okay," I said, giving her permission to take it.

I walked out of the basement and up the stairs, leaving Nadine behind, happy to get away from all that clutter.

The alarm jolted me awake. My eyes shot open, and I lay in bed recounting every detail of my dream — the basement, the bar, the cocktail glasses, and the army trunk. This was no ordinary dream. It had been so vivid. So real. This was a message. As I pieced together the images, I knew the basement had to be Aunt Jan's. I had only visited the house once or twice years before and had never ventured beyond the kitchen, but where else could it be if not Chris's family home?

It was odd that Nadine had come to me instead of to my husband. But it made sense. This wasn't the first time I had received and acted on messages from those who had passed. My father had come to me in dreams offering guidance during troubled times, and even my recently deceased dog had shown up with an image of the puppy she wanted us to adopt. Chris, on the other hand, did not believe in communications from the Great Beyond. If his mother came to him, he would think it was his grief talking and promptly dismiss it.

When Nadine was alive, we would chat on the phone, make plans and even, on occasion, conspire together. Chris and I missed her, and now with Aunt Jan gone, the last of that generation, the gaping hole in our hearts was even deeper. Perhaps Nadine was telling me to hold on to what little was left.

I wanted to tell my husband about my dream, but I worried that it would make him feel his loss more keenly. He was in mourning and had a huge task ahead of him, and I didn't want to complicate matters. I would have to be careful how I approached him, but until I figured it out, I would keep the dream to myself.

I slid on my fluffy red slippers and made my way to the shower. As the warm water washed over me and the grogginess of the morning faded, I began to plan my work outfit and go over my to-do list, the dream all but forgotten.

At 10 a.m., Chris texted to update me on his progress; he was getting a big Dumpster and throwing out everything. The image of the green army trunk and my mother-in-law pointing at it popped into my head. She was not going to let this go. "Okay," I whispered out loud. "I'll tell him." But still, I was hesitant. Would Chris be open to receiving the message? Would he think I had lost my mind? Honestly, it could go either way.

It was now or never. I texted back: "I wasn't going to mention this, but your mother came to me in a dream. She led me through a basement to a bar, and on the floor was a green army trunk. She pointed and said, 'I want that.' She was adamant."

I held my breath and waited.

"Is this a joke?" he responded.

I knew it. He didn't believe me. I was wrong to tell him.

"Why?"

"You're joking, right?"

"I'm not joking. I hope I didn't upset you."

He didn't text again. A few minutes passed, and then he sent a picture. It was a green army trunk. The trunk was sitting on the floor next to a bar filled with cocktail glasses.

I gasped so loud that my co-workers looked up. Recovering my composure, I picked up the phone and called Chris.

"How is this possible?" I asked.

"When we moved out of the house over twenty years ago, my mother told me she regretted not taking that army trunk with her. She'd had a terrible fight with her parents and never spoke to them again. She told me that the trunk was the only thing of value in the house. Whatever is in there had to have meant something to her."

"Well, open it!" I said.

"I'll bring it home," he said.

That evening, Chris and I sat on the living-room floor sorting through the trunk. Inside were neatly packed handmade cloth and wooden figurines, cut glass, and Christmas ornaments, all from Germany where Chris's grandfather had served during World War II. When Nadine died, we had turned her house upside down searching for the Christmas ornaments from Chris's childhood. They were nowhere to be found. We assumed she had sold them or given them away. Were the items in the trunk valuable? We weren't sure, but to my husband, they were priceless.

—Aileen Weintraub—

85

From Halfway Around the World

Brothers and sisters separated
by distance joined by love.
~Chuck Danes

"Is everything alright?" my sister asked. This was back in the days before cell phones, before texting, before people stayed up all night on social media. This was back when our household had one phone, and it sat in the hallway for everyone to share.

My mother, who was always ready for unexpected news, was the first one to get to the phone. She was barely awake as she held the receiver to her ear. "What? Who?" Then she recognized my sister's voice on the other end of the line. "Do you know what time it is?" she asked with obvious annoyance.

My sister did know what time it was, but she was insistent. "Is everyone alright?"

"Who is it?" I asked as I stumbled out of my room. I'd also heard the phone, but having the farthest bedroom in the apartment, it took me the longest to get there. At the time, we lived in an old, five-story walkup. The apartment was enormous. The building had once been considered luxurious, but that time had passed, and the structure was showing its age.

"It's your sister," my mother said as she came fully awake. "She wants to know if everyone is alright."

"Isn't she in Italy?" I asked, as if being halfway across the world made the call even more annoying.

"Yes, she is," my mother assured me. Then, turning her attention back to the phone, she said, "Honey, it's 2 a.m. here. Why are you calling to ask if everyone is alright?"

There was a hesitation, a pause, and then I heard my sister say in a small voice, "I had a dream."

In some households, that might have resulted in an eye roll or look of disbelief. But in our household, dreams were never dismissed. Dreams were important. With careful coaxing, my mother got the story out of her.

She'd dreamt that I was hurt. My face was bleeding, and my nose was broken. She thought I looked like I'd been in a car accident, but that was impossible since I was too young to drive.

My mother calmed her down and assured her it was only a bad dream. There was nothing to worry about. The best thing we could all do was go back to sleep. My sister agreed only after I got on the phone and assured her everything was all right.

"Well, that was…" I was going to say something "clever" as I hung up the phone, but I was interrupted by a loud crash coming from my bedroom.

My mom and I rushed to my room to discover that a six-by-four-foot section of my bedroom ceiling had collapsed. The ancient plaster had come down in a single block and landed on my bed. My pillow, the spot where my head had lain only a few minutes earlier, was pinned beneath the crumbling building material. My mother and I looked at each other in stunned silence.

We found out later that the collapse was the result of heavy rains and an undiscovered leak that funneled water between the walls. The plaster above my bed had gotten soaked and slowly peeled away from the wooden boards in the ceiling. My mother made me swear not to say anything to my sister, but it was obvious to both of us that something incredible had happened.

Had my sister not had a dream; had she not called us in the middle of the night; had she not pulled me out of bed and into the hallway, I could have been seriously injured. That didn't happen because of a dream. Or was it a premonition? Either way, it taught me never to take a dream lightly — even if it comes to you at 2 a.m. from halfway around the world.

— Arthur Sanchez —

86

Addressing
a Dream

*Everything science has taught me—and continues to
teach me—strengthens my belief in the continuity
of our spiritual existence after death.
Nothing disappears without a trace.*
~Wernher Von Braun

When I got over to Mom's one day for our usual weekend visit, she seemed a little anxious.

"What's wrong?" I asked, and she sighed.

"I've had the same dream three nights in a row," she said, sinking into the kitchen chair. "And you know that's happened before."

Indeed, several times Mom had dreams one night after the next, only to have them come sort of true the very next week.

Once, she dreamt a plane crashed at the airport five miles from our house. In her dream, sixty-one people were injured. She transposed the numbers because, in reality, sixteen people were hurt in a crash at the airport a few weeks later.

Another time, she'd dreamt of being at a funeral, unable to see who had passed away. Three nights in a row, she'd walked up to the casket and looked in but couldn't make out the face of the deceased. And then Grampa Jerry died.

So, I could understand her anxiety now.

"Tell me the dream," I said, expecting a similar tale.

"That's just it. I only dreamt an address: 3636 South 39th Street. It's crazy!" she said.

Closing my eyes, I tried to picture the address. It would be close to my college, which was in the 3400 block of South 39th Street.

"Let's get the map and look it up," I said.

We unfolded the big county street map onto the kitchen table and stood, bending over the tiny letters and lines. I traced my finger along 39th Street, south past my college, into what would be the 3600 block.

Mom gave a gasp and sat back down. My finger had ended up in the middle of a cemetery.

"Oh, I don't like this," Mom said.

"Do we have any family buried there?" I asked.

It turned out there were several family members buried there, including Mom's maternal grandmother, known as Gramma Mac.

"Maybe she's trying to tell you something," I suggested, and we tried to think what that might be. Gramma Mac had been gone for decades.

Mom didn't have the dream again, but a week later her dear Uncle Lester died after a serious illness. He was to be buried in that very cemetery on a rainy spring morning.

Had Gramma Mac known her son would be joining her soon? Was that what she'd wanted to tell Mom?

After the internment, Mom directed me to Gramma Mac's grave in the older part of the cemetery. I drove slowly down the narrow road that wove through the grounds as Mom scanned the terrain.

"Here!" she said, pointing.

Looking at the headstone, we took a moment to pay our respects. Then, when we looked up, it was easy to see South 39th Street straight ahead of us, exactly in line with the old family plot. To the east, several blocks away, we could see the houses on 35th Street. Gramma Mac's grave was parallel to a little blue Cape Cod.

"Let's go drive by that house and see what number it is," I said, thinking, *Could it be?*

The blue house had shiny brass numbers we could read from

the street.

Of course, they were 3636.

Mom gave another gasp, and I got a chill up my spine. If a grave could have a street address, Gramma Mac's would be 3636 South 39th Street, the very address Mom had dreamt about three nights in a row. Now, Gramma Mac's son, Lester, had come home to her only a week later.

"That must have been what Gramma was trying to tell me," Mom said, but we could never really know.

Still, it was an amazing experience, another in a line of interesting dreams that hinted at premonition of some sort.

Mom summed it up best. "Well, I'm glad Gramma Mac picked me to share it with," she said. "It's nice to know she's still thinking of me after all these years."

— Kate Fellowes —

87

Flowers for Three

In the garden of memory, in the palace of dreams...
that is where you and I shall meet.
~Alice Through the Looking Glass

S he died at the age of seventeen without a goodbye. The hospital wouldn't allow visitors, so I stood outside her window and waved. But there was nothing there. Linda was gone. Lupus took her fast that April afternoon in 1969.

Linda was my best friend in high school. We went on double dates and volunteered together for the March of Dimes. She called herself "Little Mouse" and signed the notes we passed in class with a sketch of a tiny mouse sporting big eyes and a long tail. She nicknamed me "Tree" because I was tall.

After she died, I looked but never found her grave. I always wanted to say goodbye. Eventually, I stopped looking, but I never stopped missing her.

Death comes in threes, they say. But after Linda's death, it was many decades before I felt another loss as deeply. I was fifty when my eighty-year-old mother's mind began to slowly disappear. First, a word here and there got lost. Then the car keys. Then the car. Roaches replaced milk and eggs in the refrigerator. Finally, even the woman in her mirror became a stranger.

Then, one night I dreamt about her. I found her standing barefoot in mud at the edge of a river, her face as ravaged by dementia as her mind.

A rowboat waited in twilight. It was empty except for the grizzled man in a fisherman's cap manning the oars, beckoning her with a nod of his head. My mother's forehead creased in fear, her eyes half-shut, not wanting to see the journey ahead.

"Mother," I called. Her eyes opened. She looked directly at me.

"I don't want to go," she said.

I kissed her wrinkled lips. The bald spots on her scalp were the color of bruises. Her thinning white hair was as pale as the petals of the lilies she used to grow at Easter.

"I know, I know, but it'll be okay." I kissed her again, took her elbow and helped her into the boat. "It'll be okay."

She settled onto the plank seat with surprising agility. Then she turned back to look at me and smiled. She looked like her old self—lucid and fearless. Her boat moved west into the setting sun, crossing the river toward the far shore that darkness hid from my view.

That was the April night mother died.

Nine months later, she stood before me again in a dream. Her hair, still white, was now long, lush, and shiny. I watched each strand turn to starlight. Her wrinkles had melted. She cupped my chin in her hands and smiled deep into my eyes.

"Tell everyone I love them," she said, transfigured. "We start and end in love."

Her radiance enveloped me. I wanted to stay in that warm light forever.

When I woke up, it was Christmas Day. As the family gathered, I relayed her glad tidings of love.

My father, ninety-three, whispered, "She visits me, too. Her Alzheimer's is gone, all gone."

Soon after that, I was with Dad when he got his final cancer diagnosis. I cried. He grinned, eager for the adventure. "I have someplace to go, honey. Don't forget, I have to meet up with your mother."

A few years later, I dreamt I was hiking in the mountains with my sister and three brothers. We came upon a log cabin. While my brothers explored the cabin, I followed a dirt path to a grove thick with cypress and pine. My mother stood there framed by green, with my father beside her. She held out her hand to me. I placed my palm in hers. She smiled. Her hair turned the

*color of youth, chestnut streaked with honey. She became young. My sister
followed me down the path, reached out, and touched Dad's hand. His silver
hair turned lustrous black as he, too, grew young again.*

*There was no sound but the breathing of trees. The grove became a
garden of Easter lilies where everything that Alzheimer's and cancer had
taken away was given back tenfold. A small mouse with a long tail and big
eyes danced between my parents' feet and then scampered west into the
garden past a pine tree. My parents smiled, turned, and disappeared into
the flowers as the sun set behind them.*

I awoke in joy the next morning, the Easter following Dad's death.

On the Monday after Easter, I went to the cemetery where my
parents were buried. In the years following my mother's death, I had
visited her grave at least once a month. Now my father was lying next
to her in the garden setting with its rolling hills and abundant trees
where, decades earlier, they had chosen their burial site. After placing
flowers at their headstone, I wandered across the narrow lane running
beside their graves. The morning sun was at my back.

Across the lane, west of my parents, I came to a grave I'd never
noticed, although I later discovered it had been in that very spot for
thirty-nine years. There, steps from my parents' final resting places, I
finally got to say goodbye to Linda.

The grave of my friend, the "Little Mouse," was close enough to
my parents' graves that when the shadows were long at sunset, the
branches of one very tall tree touched all three. YOU ARE LOVE was
carved on a flat stone lying on Linda's grave, reminding me of my
mother's message on the Christmas after she died.

In that moment, I learned that, sometimes, when we don't see
what's right in front of us, those we love will lead the way in dreams.
"From now on," I told the tall tree, "when I come here, I'll always bring
flowers for three." And I have done so for many years, awed by the
mysteries of love and the guidance of long-ago dreams.

— Mary Alice Dixon —

Just in Time

A man's growth is seen in the successive choirs
of his friends.
~Ralph Waldo Emerson

ingo! I'd just hit the jackpot on the easiest part of my search. Now, the hard work would begin.

My ninety-year-old mother had just moved into our home during the pandemic. She would help us by taking care of our brood of rescue animals while doing plenty of cooking, cleaning and gardening around the house. That left my wife and me more time to concentrate on working from home without as many distractions.

The COVID-19 world situation was mind-boggling, quickly changing the way we worked and lived. As the situation became serious, our family members were all having haunting dreams at night. I began dreaming of people whom I hadn't seen in years. Specifically, a woman who had been like a second mother to me kept consistently showing up in my dreams.

Long ago, while a freshman at university, I worked at a car dealership to make extra cash. Gwendolyn was an office manager there. She immediately took me under her wing and showed me the ropes. Over the years that I spent there, a long-lasting friendship developed between us. She became my mom away from home. As I finished university, Gwen and her husband moved to a new city out west when the company her husband worked for transferred him there. I began working full-time, so our communication with each other became long-distance mail and then slowly petered out.

By now, years had passed, a lifetime really. Yet here was Gwen, suddenly popping up in my dreams. If she were still alive, she would be as old as my mother. Since we were working from home now, I decided to spend some spare time searching for her online.

Feeling like an Internet stalker, I Googled the procedure for locating a person and followed the instructions. Since I remembered her last name and the city she had moved to, I had a head start. It wasn't long before I found some meager information on Gwen, as well as her husband's obituary. Though saddened that her husband was no longer with her, I was encouraged by what I found and kept digging, hoping that she was still alive.

Soon afterward, I located her kids on Facebook and decided to take a chance and send them each a brief message, trying not to sound like a dangerous, deranged person. I formulated a note, took a deep breath, and hit the Send button.

Then I waited… And waited.

I cannot claim to be the most patient person in the world, so waiting for a response was difficult. I had plenty of work to keep me busy, but my mind kept wandering to my quest to reconnect with Gwen. My wife tried to talk me into staying calm, but it was to no avail. I was becoming increasingly fixated on my search.

Finally, after what seemed like forever, I got a response to my query. In reality, only a few days had passed, but staying home all the time during the pandemic had put us into a weird time warp. One of Gwen's daughters responded, confirming that Gwen was still alive and remembered me fondly. Furthermore, her daughter claimed that Gwen had recently been dreaming about me, too. How odd.

Because Gwen was in frail health, she was now living with her daughter. They relayed their phone number, and we set up a time to chat. When I called, her daughter filled me in with some background information about their family and then put Gwen on the phone.

I was immediately beamed back decades in time as I became reacquainted with my old friend and mentor. Through tears of joy, I managed to tell her how much she had meant to me back then, and how I had thought about her often throughout my life. We had a wonderful time catching up as we reminisced about years past before we finally, tearfully, said goodbye.

Days later, I received another call from her daughter saying that Gwen had quietly passed away in her sleep. She kindly said that it almost seemed that Gwen had hung on just to hear from me that last time. It was a beautiful thing for her to say, and it put my dreams about Gwen to rest.

I'm searching for others from my past now, making sure to connect while we still can. Everyone I've contacted so far seems pleasantly surprised to hear from me. COVID-19 may be uniting all of us in ways we have yet to understand. It's a pleasure to be a passenger on this journey through time with everyone.

— Sergio Del Bianco —

An Unexpected Visitor

A father is neither an anchor to hold us back
nor a sail to take us there, but a guiding light
whose love shows us the way.
~Author Unknown

When I was six weeks from having my third son, back in 1977, my husband Dan finished his job in Utah and wanted to return to Mexico so our baby would be born at home on the farm. I had a very uneasy feeling about going back to Mexico. But he was adamant about going, and after traveling day and night, we arrived home after a couple of days on the road. The old house seemed damp and cold, but I got busy and fixed it up as best I could. I couldn't shake the heavy feeling that something was going to happen.

Four days before Jared was due to be born, I had a remarkable dream.

I dreamt I was in labor with him, and I was having such a hard time that my spirit left my body. I was traveling at top speed toward a light down a long, round tunnel. I was soon within the light and saw family members, some familiar and some not, standing and waving at me. To my surprise, I saw my father standing next to an older man dressed in white.

I was shocked to see my dad because I knew I was in the spirit world, and I thought he was in Wales with my mum. We seemed to be able to read each other's minds, and he knew what I was thinking. We didn't need words. I took note of what he was wearing, even down to his Welsh Guards tie pin.

The man standing beside Dad told me he had left Earth a few days before. He mentioned that my brother David had sent me a telegram, though I hadn't received it. The man asked if I wanted to return to Earth or stay with my father. I thought about my two little boys, Adam and Steven, growing up without a mama, and I knew I had to return.

In a split second, we were hovering over La Mora, the small American community in Mexico where I was living. I was looking through the roof of the old house. I could see Dan kneeling by my bed, crying and telling my sister-in-law Diane that I had died. Still dreaming, suddenly I was back in my body. I asked Dan to say hello to my father, who was standing at the end of my bed, but Dan couldn't see him. Then my father waved goodbye, disappearing through the wall.

When I woke, I sat up quickly in bed and woke up my husband, too. I told him about the disturbing dream I had just had. I knew my father had died, and I couldn't help but think that maybe I was going to die, too. When I fell back to sleep I had the same dream again.

In the morning, I told my sisters-in-law about it. Throughout the day, I couldn't get the dream or my father out of my mind. That night, at 11:30, I heard a knock on my bedroom door. I knew before I opened it that there was a telegram for me. Dan's brother had just returned home from a trip to Douglas, Arizona, and his wife brought me my mail, knowing a telegram was important news.

I opened it and read: "Dad passed away. Call home."

I wanted to call home to England and talk to my mother, but the nearest phone was hours away as there was no electricity in our valley at the time. The next day, Dan drove me over the muddy mountain roads to his cousin's home in Casas Grandes. It was bitter cold, and we got stuck many times, doubling the normal travel time. We got stuck in a deep mud hole, and as we sat there, unable to get out of our predicament, a very old bus drove up. Six men got out and waded through the mud in their nice clothes to push us out. By the time they got us unstuck, their clothes were completely covered with mud, but they were all laughing as they climbed back onto the bus. I had fallen in love with the Mexican people who were always so kind and helpful, and I was grateful in this moment that these men were there to rescue us from a desperate situation.

We arrived in Casas Grandes that evening, and I tried calling my mother several times, to no avail. I said a silent prayer and dialed her number again. I was surprised to hear a familiar voice on the line. It was my brother's friend! I had dialed my mother's number, and some glitch in the telephone system connected me to him instead. He told me that my mother had gone to Germany with my brother, who was stationed there in the Army. I wouldn't have known where she was or any details of my father's heart attack and funeral had it not been for that connection.

The following day, I went into labor. We went to a hospital instead of having me deliver at home on the farm as originally planned. I delivered my son after a very hard and long labor and I hemorrhaged badly. I knew that my dream had been a warning. If I had tried to have the baby at home I probably wouldn't be here to tell this story.

Two years later, I went to Wales to visit my family and learned that my father had been buried in the exact same clothes that he wore in my dream, down to the Welsh Guards tie pin.

— Jenny Langford —

Vatican Calling

Trust that God will put the right people in your life
at the right time and for the right reasons.
~Author Unknown

This restlessness was unusual. I'm a pretty good sleeper, so I wasn't sure what was making me toss and turn. But my subconscious used that night's long and vivid dream to reveal my inner stress.

I was terrified to go to church the next day. It wasn't for the usual reasons most of us dread church, like a funeral. Although I was probably overdue, I wasn't planning on going to confession either.

No, the next day's vigil Mass was the first time I would be serving as a Eucharistic Minister, and I was sure I would mess it up. It should have been a silly fear. I'd been Catholic my whole life. Although I'd turned away from the church in my younger years, and I was far from an angel, I was now a faithful parishioner. I wanted to serve and had even taught religious education. When my priest told me he needed more Extraordinary Ministers of the Eucharist, I was eager to answer the call.

So, what was I distraught about? Oh, maybe just dropping the body of Christ in the form of the consecrated host — just a little thing like that. Or how about going up to the altar at the wrong time? I'd been to Mass hundreds of times. I knew when to approach the priest. But now, with less than twenty-four hours before the vigil Mass, I suddenly felt very unqualified for such a huge responsibility.

When I finally fell asleep, I found myself at my beloved church. I was screwing up in every way possible. I was dressed inappropriately, and having approached the altar too early, I decided just to sit and hang out until the priest got to the consecration. When it was time to offer the Eucharist to parishioners, I couldn't remember the words I was supposed to say.

At one point in the dream, I was running out of communion wafers. I knew that I should break up the pieces in order to have enough for everyone, but I decided that I needed a fork to break up the pieces. I left the line to walk over to the rectory where I borrowed one of Father's forks.

In the last part of the dream, the cell phone in my back pocket began to ring. I should have turned that off! How could I quiet my phone while I was holding the ciborium, which is holding the Most Holy Eucharist?

Suddenly, I realized my phone was ringing. It was my actual phone in my conscious life, not in the dream.

I jolted awake. It was 4 a.m. Calls that early can never be a good thing. I grew even more concerned when I saw that it was my friend Dora calling. Dora was in Europe with her family. What could she possibly be calling about? Frightened and confused, I somehow managed to answer my phone. Dora sensed my sleepiness.

"Oh, no! Is it four in the morning? I thought it was four in the afternoon! This time-change thing has me all messed up. I'm sorry I called. Go back to sleep."

"Dora, wait. I'm up. What's going on? Is everything okay?" I asked.

"Yes. I just had a silly question, and I totally didn't mean to wake you up. It's no big deal. We can talk later."

"Now I'm curious. What's the question?"

"You should go back to sleep."

"It's okay! What's the question?"

"Well," she responded, "I'm in the Vatican gift shop. I wanted to bring you rosary beads that are blessed by the Pope, but I didn't know if you would want rosary beads in a box with the Fátima, Portugal visitation on them or with Pope Francis on them."

I thanked her and said that I actually had rosary beads from Fátima, handed down from my Portuguese grandmother. But rosary beads blessed by Pope Francis in a box with his image on them would be awesome.

We said goodbye, and I lay back down. Sleep eluded me as I began to realize the enormity of this coincidence. I had never received a call from the Vatican before. I probably will never receive a call from the Vatican again. I knew Dora and her family were going to the Vatican, but I had no idea during what part of their two-week trip through Europe that visit was scheduled. Yet, she called while I was dreaming about Mass.

How could the timing of this call be anything but a divine message? It seemed very clear to me that Dora's call, while I was dreaming of failing in the service of God, was Jesus saying to me directly, "Hey, chill out. We got this!"

And we did. At the Mass later that day, I managed to offer the Eucharist to many of my fellow parishioners without incident.

I didn't even need a fork.

— Yvonne deSousa —

What I Knew
All Along

Dreams Don't Lie

Deep within, there is something profoundly known,
not consciously, but subconsciously. A quiet truth,
that is not a version of something,
but an original knowing.
~T.F. Hodge

I woke up breathing hard, my heart beating fast. It took me a moment to realize where I was — facedown in my bed. I tried to move my arms or legs, but nothing was possible. I was paralyzed, helpless, unable to rise up or push up.

A large woman was sprawled on top of me, holding me down, crushing me. As hard as I tried, her weight was too much to overcome.

Slowly, I transitioned to reality. In fact, I could move, and I was alone in bed. I tested my extremities and could move all of them, even push up. I rolled over, caught my breath, and thought about what had just happened. Was this a warning? Was my dream trying to tell me something?

My apartment had two smoke detectors but no carbon-monoxide alert. My earlier rapid breathing got me thinking that maybe there was carbon monoxide in the air and my dream was warning me. Perhaps my subconscious mind could detect the invisible threat.

I shut off the air conditioning. I didn't believe it was the source of carbon monoxide, but I wasn't thinking rationally. I opened the apartment door to the courtyard, listening for a motor that I thought I had heard earlier. Perhaps somebody was using some kind of equipment and it was creating a threat for my neighbors and me. But all was calm — except me.

I never got back to sleep that morning.

Six weeks later, I had another strange dream.

I was swimming beneath the surface of a mucky pond. I could see lily pads above me as I tried hard to reach them. I wasn't panicking that I would run out of air, but I knew I had to reach the surface. It was only a matter of time before it would become critical. No matter how hard I swam, I wasn't making progress, and I knew I was using up my air quickly. Fish and other creatures were swimming normally around me. But despite my efforts, I remained in place, a couple of feet underwater.

Once again, I awoke gasping for air, facedown in my pillow. I turned and was able to return to normal breathing quickly, disturbed, but relieved that I was recovering.

I often remember bits and snatches of dreams, but it's rare that I remember the entire thing. That night, when I happened to be talking to my daughter Alison on the phone, I described this latest dream to her. She laughed at how odd it was but was sympathetic.

She asked if I still snore, and I told her I'd been told I do. She said her husband snored regularly until he got tested for sleep apnea. She encouraged me to get evaluated, too. This wasn't the first time Alison suggested I get tested, but I had always downplayed the need. This time, it seemed more relevant. I figured it couldn't hurt.

During my appointment with my primary-care provider, I told him about my long history of snoring, and he arranged for me to be evaluated for sleep apnea. It took a while to obtain results, but I definitely suffered from it, so the specialist prescribed treatment.

That night, I let my daughter know the conclusion. She said she suspected as much. She also asked if I had told the doctor about my dreams. I said, "No, my history of snoring and restless nights was enough to convince him. Besides, I felt stupid for waiting for my subconscious to tell me what's going on with my body."

— Stephen Schwei —

Reclaiming a
Dream Deferred

*We cannot become what we want
to be by remaining what we are.*
~Max De Pree

I take my cap and sash from my mom before I kiss her and dad good-bye. The energy in the building is electric. Today is college gradua-tion, and we can feel the anxiety, joy, and excitement in the air. Each one of us is ready to take our first steps into adulthood. Our parents are awash in a mixture of joy and nostalgia.

I pass by my classmates as I try to make my way to the designated area for students whose last names begin with T. As I find my place in line, the dean of my department comes over and asks if he can speak to me. I step out of line, nervously walking behind him. We step inside an empty office. Facing the dean, I let out a huge sigh. He begins to compliment me and all the work I've accomplished, but I can tell that he has something major to tell me.

After his effusive praise, the dean tells me that I won't graduate. Stunned, I loudly yelp, "WHAT?" He goes on to explain that I'm short one class, and that the university did not catch it until now. I begin to hyperventilate and yell, "How did this happen? I was meticulous with everything regarding my education. How did all of us miss this?" I sob between gasps of air. My breath gets shallower and shallower, as if I'm being suffocated. Tears stream down my face like Niagara Falls, and then everything goes black. I wake up in a cold sweat.

That was my recurring dream during the spring of 2020 during the COVID-19 crisis. I had it multiple times a week. The dream always ended at the same spot, and then I awoke in a cold sweat. Sometimes, I ended up crying afterward, sobbing myself back to sleep. Sometimes, I was so disturbed that I couldn't go back to sleep for hours.

After the first two weeks of having this dream, I started seeing that a bigger issue was at hand. I began to reflect on what this dream meant. What could it be trying to tell me? I assessed my life. I spoke to my mom, who is my ultimate confidante, as well as my closest friends.

I discovered that this dream represented my fear of being stuck in my present situation and unable to realize my true dreams and move forward with my life. I graduated college in 2009 during the height of the great recession. I had a degree in journalism with student loans to pay. Given the precariousness of the economy, I chose to find something a bit more stable and higher paying. Since then, I've worked in the world of digital marketing.

Today, I earn a six-figure salary with one of the biggest companies in the United States, and I'm miserable. I didn't go to school wanting to work on SEO or website traffic plans. I wanted to make documentaries, tell stories, educate, entertain, and inform. I wanted to do something that I found fulfilling. I ended up burying that part of myself as each job became more financially lucrative.

And as the newness of each job wore off and unhappiness crept in, I felt I had no choice but to stick it out, as it was too late to make a change. I would come up with ideas on how to make a change from my current work and halfheartedly follow through with one goal but fail to get started on others. Each time I tried to make a move, a little voice would start singing "It's Too Late," followed by a rousing rendition of "This Is Your Life, So Deal." It was topped up by the ultimate torch song, "Suck It Up, Buttercup." That voice was so strong and my spirit so withered that they prompted me to give up before gaining any sort of traction.

The revelation of this dream has been mentally and emotionally liberating. It doesn't mean that I've completely overcome those negative thoughts and emotions, but I know now where they stem from and how to deal with them. I have to remind myself daily that where I am is not where I will always be. My feelings are not facts, and there are actions that I can take to find my way back to the road I want to be on. Prayer and positive affirmations also help me center and find peace.

I believe dreams, be they good or bad, have messages for us. They speak to us about our past, present, and future. They speak to us about our fears, needs, and desires. The revelations we get from them can act as a guiding light to lead us where we want to be and as a spark to reignite those fires within us that we thought were long smothered and dead.

—Jia Thomas—

93

Attitude of Gratitude

If you want to turn your life around, try thankfulness.
It will change your life mightily.
~Gerald Good

I slid into bed exhausted. I shook my head as I remembered something I had read a few days earlier: "If you don't go around barking all day, you won't go to bed dog-tired at night." Well, I wasn't one to go around barking all day, but I certainly did my share of whining and whimpering to myself. Maybe that was why I was so tired.

I had been teaching and brought home more music theory books to correct. It had been a long, hard day, and I was disgruntled with many things. As usual, near the top of my list were my husband and his lack of help. Why couldn't he help out more? Why couldn't he see what I was struggling to do and lend a hand? The children needed constant care and supervision. The yard and garden work were never-ending. The wash was piling up, and my kitchen floor needed to be washed — again! All these things had been eating away at me all day. I mumbled a quick prayer and was soon fast asleep.

Sometime later, I awoke with the words from my dream ringing in my ears. "I'll meet you over at the appreciation table."

In my dream, I seemed to be at a large conference where there was so much commotion that I almost walked right past someone whom I knew to be very important. Was it God? He told me to meet him at the appreciation table, whatever that was.

Now I lay there in the darkness pondering his words. Of course! He was trying to tell me to be appreciative of my husband, children and home instead of bemoaning all the little things I would like changed. How easy it was to get all tied up in what I would like to have, instead of being grateful for what I did have.

As a new morning dawned, I realized I also had to start a "new" day with a new way of thinking about my husband and our home. With God's help I would choose to turn each negative thought into a positive thought or prayer. As I folded the laundry and matched up the socks, I thanked God for the little feet that pitter-pattered around our house. I thanked God for a husband who chose to spend his evenings at home. I could also appreciate the fact that he worked hard all day to support us, and I could fathom why he felt he deserved a break. Over the next few weeks, I learned to look for the positive and found I was a much happier person for it.

"I'll meet you over at the appreciation table." These words from a dream turned my life around! They helped me adjust my attitude and brought me to a beautiful place of thankfulness and true contentment.

— Annie Riess —

94

It's Time

Accept yourself, love yourself, and keep moving
forward. If you want to fly, you have to give up
what weighs you down.
~Roy T. Bennett, The Light in the Heart

My husband and I traveled to Santa Barbara to attend a business conference. We arrived after barely speaking a word to each other during the long drive. Our marriage of ten years was falling apart, and sessions with a marriage counselor only made us realize how unhappy we were.

We were meeting my husband's business partners and their wives. We tried to put on a happy face as we mingled at the opening social. We were both good at it. No one suspected our marriage was in jeopardy.

We asked for two bedrooms; we hadn't slept together in years. My husband and I were always cordial and polite to one another. We were not a loud, angry couple, although the quiet politeness seemed worse. We said goodnight to one another and went to our rooms. It had been a long day of driving, and the couple of glasses of wine with dinner put me into a deep sleep. The dream I had that night is one I'll never forget.

I stood by a small lake. The water was filled with colorful koi fish that swam to the surface and made slurping noises with their mouths, wanting food. I stared down at them, mesmerized by their colors, when a large gold koi emerged and transformed into a woman who stood before me. She wore a long yellow gown. She smiled at me with a look of compassion, kindness and wisdom in her eyes. I stared in disbelief. She said, "It's time."

I woke up startled and walked around the room. Outside, the sun was rising, sending an orange glow into the sky. I wanted to return to my dream but couldn't fall back to sleep. What did it mean? I knew it had to mean something.

When we returned home, we made the decision to separate. He moved out. I felt lost. I went back to counseling. My therapist recommended I go away for a while. She suggested I go to a retreat located near the ocean.

The drive was long, but once I got off the freeway and into the city of Encinitas, I felt better. The ocean was sky blue, and the cascading sunlight made the water twinkle.

I found the retreat and checked in. A woman told me lunch would be served in an hour, and she encouraged me to walk to the meditation gardens. I climbed the steep brick steps, passing a beautifully manicured landscape of flowers and trees. It was quiet. I quickly felt at peace. When I reached the top, something told me to turn left. There it was — the lake I'd seen in my dream. The koi swam and made their noises. I stood there thinking it was only a coincidence until I saw her. She walked from another path to the other side of the small lake and stood there smiling at me. It was the same woman in my dream, wearing the same long yellow gown. "I'm so happy you're here," she said. "Come join us for lunch."

Afterward, I found her in the office and asked to speak to her. I told her about my dream. She wasn't surprised. "It was time for you to move forward in your life," she said. I saw the same compassion and kindness on her face. She made me feel safe and no longer lost. I had found the place to begin my healing.

— Margo Sanchez —

95

Waking Up

*Just don't give up trying to do what you really want
to do. Where there's love and inspiration,
I don't think you can go wrong.*
~Ella Fitzgerald

I met my husband Paul on an online dating site. When he first read my dating profile, he said it was hilarious, which was music to my ears. I had a lot of fun writing it, and I was glad to hear that he enjoyed it. But when he went so far as to encourage me to pursue a career as a writer, I emphatically told him that I was "not a writer." I definitely enjoyed penning my quirky little jokes for the dating profile, but I did not think of myself as a creative person. Therefore, pursuing a writing career was a whole other animal I never even considered. Well, at least, not in the last two decades…

In high school, I fell in love with the written word, and the desire to be a professional writer was certainly inside me. But I quickly squashed that idea after countless people convinced me that I would end up as the stereotypical "starving writer." Given the economic challenges that my family faced as refugees when I was growing up, the thought of becoming poor terrified me.

So, after I graduated from high school, I said goodbye to the possibility of pursuing a life as a professional writer and earned a bachelor's degree in business. After college, I started a career in the healthcare industry, eventually becoming a project manager. I didn't think about writing again, even after Paul consistently encouraged me to do so. He said I had a knack for it, but I didn't listen to him. Long ago, I had already convinced myself that this wasn't my path in life.

But one night, I had a vivid dream that would change everything. This dream involved rebirth, kindness, the joys of life, and rediscovering love. The next morning, I awoke to remember that it was Valentine's Day. *What an apropos moment to have a vision of love,* I thought to myself. Was this a coincidence? Was it divine intervention or fate? At the time, I honestly had no idea.

I told Paul about the dream, and he just smiled, saying, "You need to write a screenplay about it." This time, I listened to him.

I began to write about my dream with furious determination. The words seemed to pour out of me like a river whose waters were overflowing. My words turned into a love story, and the love story turned into a full-length screenplay. By the time I finished, I had crafted a love story about a man who is figuratively "reborn" when he discovers his true calling in life. He goes on to create a new, meaningful life for himself and begins to see new possibilities that he never saw before. In retrospect, I suspect that the story was actually about me.

This dream also served as the catalyst for several life-changing decisions. I decided to take some time off from work to learn the complex art of screenwriting. For the first time, I attended writing events and befriended other aspiring writers who encouraged me to keep pursuing my creative endeavors. I connected with film executives and pitched them my story ideas. For the next five years, I would write up a storm. Even when I wanted to take a break from writing for just a few days, my creative mind would not allow me to stop. There were nights when I literally could not sleep until I wrote down the ideas that flowed into my mind. Eventually, I stopped referring to myself as a project manager and started introducing myself as a writer, which was a significant emotional paradigm shift for me.

Last year, I took a job as a copywriter and blogger. For the first time in my life, I would actually get paid to write, which was extremely gratifying. Professionally, I had started anew at the age of forty-eight. At a time when most people were planning for retirement, I was beginning a new life adventure. It felt completely terrifying—and completely right.

At this point, I have completed five full-length screenplays. I am in active discussions with a film production company; I hope to sell my screenplays and have them produced for TV or film in the near future.

My journey has been exciting and wonderful at times. At other times, it has been frightening and frustrating. But, honestly, I absolutely love being a writer, and I wouldn't change a thing. I'm still waiting for my big break, but I am hopeful because I know that this is the right path for me. Nothing worthwhile is easy. That's why accomplishments are so fulfilling; we appreciate all the blood, sweat, and tears required to achieve them.

I never thought that a dream could completely change the course of my life for the better. But then again, I suppose that when I decided not to follow my dreams, my dreams decided to follow me.

Today, when I look back at my previous career in healthcare, I often have a difficult time recalling what it felt like. This is quite surprising since I spent over twenty years working in that arena. At times, it feels as if my healthcare days were a temporary detour. Even when I thought I knew how my life was supposed to unfold, perhaps this monumental dream was meant to tell me, "Do something else. Change your life." Consequently, I believe my dream was a message from my true self because it finally awoke the writer who was always quietly living inside me.

— Kristen Mai Pham —

96

Back in Service

May the miracle you need be just around the corner.
~Vicki Reece

I had been getting many requests for the fabric facemasks that I'd been sewing during the COVID-19 crisis. Unfortunately, I had run out of the elastic for the ear loops. I tried ordering more online, but most stores were showing it as out of stock. I would have to stop offering the masks, which troubled me.

I have a huge white container where I keep all my sewing supplies and fabric. I scoured through it, and even double- and triple-checked, hoping to locate elastic left over from a prior project. Any size or color would do; I could trim it to make it work. But my searches came up empty.

I wondered how long I would have to wait for the stores to re-stock. People all over were making the masks as a way of helping out. I wanted to continue with my small contribution. I sat with idle hands and went to bed feeling dissatisfied. That night, I had a strange dream.

I was alone on some sort of ride. It was bumpy, and I was hanging on tightly. The scenery was the same no matter which direction I looked — nothing but small boxes set apart from each other. Each box was very worn looking. Then the ride suddenly reversed, and I was traveling backward. I tried to count the boxes as I passed them again. I didn't get very far before I woke up to the sound of our neighbor's lawn mower.

I told my husband about the dream. He laughed and asked, "Were the boxes practicing social distancing?" That made sense to me, but

I still had a nagging feeling about those boxes. I wondered what was in them. Or perhaps they were empty.

We were having lunch when my husband suggested I clean out the storage closet. I am a self-proclaimed "Thrift-Shop Treasure Hunter," and I often place the goodies I bring home in that closet until I have time to investigate them further. Having nothing else to do that day, I finished eating and got to work. I was eager to explore the forgotten contents of that closet. I started on the top shelf.

I found a Christmas train that I had probably placed there on a hot summer day. I was happy to find a bag of crossword-puzzle books. Those would help during the quarantine. I pulled out a stack of craft magazines and placed them near the sofa. They would be fun to browse through in the evenings. I welcomed anything to pass the time during these long days.

On the next shelf, I found a box of magnets. They were all travel souvenirs from different places. The box had a price tag on it that said, "99 cents." The magnet on top had a mountain scene and said, "Austria." I placed the box on the floor so I could look through it later. I haven't done much traveling in my life, so I looked forward to a pretend sightseeing trip. To Austria and beyond!

Toward the back of that shelf was a plastic blue box. It was the type of brittle plastic that I remembered from childhood. The box had a broken latch, but I was able to force it open. When I saw the contents, I was surprised. I had no memory of buying this box. It had been in the closet for quite a while, judging by the thin layer of dust covering it. But what a bounty it held!

It was an old sewing box. Someone had carefully arranged the spools of thread and packets of needles. There was a tiny pair of scissors and a silver thimble. A plastic crochet hook was tucked along one side, next to a worn tape measure. I sifted through the snaps and buttons and discovered a few golden safety pins. They were much sturdier than the safety pins of today.

I realized that the top tray was removable, and there was additional storage underneath. I carefully lifted it out and set it aside. I gazed at a tangle of zippers and embroidery thread. Underneath was a pair of pinking shears wrapped in yellowed tissue paper. I pushed aside more loose spools of thread and a strawberry-shaped pincushion. That's when I struck gold.

Elastic! The perfect size for the masks. Not just one package, but three! Unopened, preserved and waiting patiently to be put to use. I whispered a quick prayer of thanks and eagerly carried my sewing machine to the kitchen table.

As I worked happily on the masks, I thought back to my dream. My subconscious had been trying to tell me that there was a box that contained what I needed. I had searched the house for elastic, but not in the right place. I think my dream had been trying to communicate, "Hey, back up! You missed a spot!"

— Marianne Fosnow —

97

A Warning from the Depths

You must train your intuition — you must trust the
small voice inside you which tells you exactly
what to say, what to decide.
~Ingrid Bergman

A solid wood chest, like something you'd see in a pirate movie, rushes toward the near bank in the strong flow of the Mississippi River. It catches on some rocks in the shallows and settles in place. I'm standing near the shore with only a few flimsy reeds between me and the chest. My heart thuds and I can hardly breathe. I know people will see it. Dread washes over me. For I know that crammed inside the trunk is the body of my ex-boyfriend, murdered by me.

I woke up under a yellow-and-orange floral comforter beneath a window that looked out on the lake. I was in my family's vacation cabin in the bed my grandma used to sleep in, and before that my Great-Aunt Rosemary. My mom and sisters were also in the cabin, and we were enjoying summer break. It was the summer after my first year away at college, and I felt very wise for deciding not to get a summer internship and instead laze away the days reading novels on the pier and getting crazy tan lines.

I got out of bed and put on a swimsuit because that's what summers at the lake were all about. I had some sourdough bread and a mug of hot chocolate outside. The cabin was for sleeping. Living was done outside! At night, we would light a campfire and sit out under the wild northern stars with sweatshirts over our swimsuits. When the sky finally darkened around 10 p.m., we would listen for the haunting nighttime calls of the loons, my favorite sound.

I crawled back into bed to read a fantasy novel and dreamt again.

I walk through some brush and peer out toward the rushing waters of the Mississippi. I hold my breath in horror, and there I see—the chest. It's bumping up against the shore, and I know somebody will find it. And then everyone will know that I murdered my ex-boyfriend.

As the summer came to a close, I had to admit that I was not excited to return to school. I had this background anxiety about it. It didn't make sense to me at all. I had made more friends my freshman year at college than I had ever had in my life. Good friends. Also, I had straight A's and had been enjoying band and choir and other groups I had joined. I had a fun, busy social life. Why was I dreading sophomore year? Also, why was I having such an awful recurring dream?

About a week before I was to hop in my Jeep Wrangler and return to school, the dreams became incessant, over and over every night. Finally, I had to look deep and ask why I kept seeing that image of the locked chest. Why was the dead body of my ex inside? Why was I the murderer?

About one week before finals, I had broken up with my first boyfriend. I tried not to think about it so I could get through studying and my tests. With exams finished and A's achieved, I drove up to the lake house and didn't give it a second thought. It was a great place to relax and forget about breaking up with him.

However, it seemed like my dreaming mind wouldn't let me forget. It held a secret locked in a chest, and it was yelling at me every night—a warning from the depths of the Mississippi.

My college was located on the banks of the Mississippi River. My boyfriend and I had taken romantic walks along the river several times in an area that was dark, quiet and empty of people. This romantic setting was perverted by my boyfriend's intentions to have me do things he knew I didn't want to do.

I remembered the way he tried to manipulate me, and keep me feeling down and guilty. I remembered getting banged against the wall, his threats for displeasing things I'd said. I remembered him controlling where I went, his anger at who I talked to, his blame for all his problems. There was the coercion again and again, hits to emphasize his point, bloodstains on the carpet that embarrassed me, bloody scabs getting ripped open, and crying and pushing him off me whenever I was about to break.

That summer, I never thought about that part of freshman year—until the dream made me. Finals week had not just been about studying and testing. It had been about hiding from my stalker, running from him at night, fighting him off on a path under a lantern, and getting assaulted in a private library room I'd thought was safe. And finally, it was a struggle while locked in his dorm room where I held him in a chokehold, waiting for him to pass out so I could escape.

The meaning of my dream hit me strong. It was an epiphany; I sort of did want to kill him then! And worse, I couldn't reconcile my perception of myself as a strong, fun, intelligent woman with the girl who had been mentally tortured by her first boyfriend.

I had an entire week to run through my options. I considered transferring schools. There were great majors I could pursue at even better schools. But I had to balance that against all the friends I'd made and all the groundwork I'd laid for an amazing college experience. I was angry! Should I let him scare me away from my new home? Ultimately, I decided to return on my own terms.

The first thing I did when I got back to school that fall was to arrange a meeting with him. I told him straight to his face, with a composed body and mind, "You abused me mentally, physically, and sexually. I will never talk to you or have anything to do with you ever again." And I didn't. I said what I needed to say, and I am so grateful that I realized I needed to do that, or I would probably not be the recovered person I am today.

When I think back to that day, I imagine that chest floating far out into the water and sinking deep, deep under the waves of the Mississippi to get covered by loads of silty muck, never to surface again.

—Addison Sorenson—

98

Shoveling Snow

You may be as different as the sun and the moon,
but the same blood flows through both your hearts.
You need her, as she needs you.
~George R.R. Martin

S hoveling the snow had always been the best part about winter. Not that I thought it was fun, but my dad's reaction to a clean driveway kept me going. He hated shoveling snow more than anything. So, I took it upon myself at eight years old to do it for him. Every time I saw those white particles fall from the sky, I knew the universe was ready to put me to work.

I would run and put on my jacket, snow boots, and mittens to prepare myself for the work ahead. But every single time, before I went outside, I would stop by my older sister's room to see if she wanted to help me. I knew she would say no, but I always asked anyway.

One day there was a lot of snow, and there was no way I would be able to clean it all up myself. It was getting dark, and I hated the thought of my dad having to shovel the snow after a long day of work. So I did the routine and knocked on my sister's door. As I expected, she gave me the same old "no." Irritated, I asked again. Without saying anymore, she got up, pushed me out of the room and slammed the door in my face.

I stood there silently for a second. All I wanted was some help, and the more I recollected every "no" she had ever said to me, the more furious I became. I told her she was an awful sister and daughter, she couldn't do anything, and nobody needed her anyway.

Then, I set out in the cold to tackle the enemy that lay in my driveway. Slamming the shovel into the snow, all I could think about was my sister. I was beyond angry that she would leave me to battle this alone. I fought tirelessly, my short arms swinging back and forth while the wind cut against my cheeks. After one long hour, I was not even halfway done. Utterly defeated, I dropped the shovel into the victorious snow, and went inside to lie down on the couch.

That's when I had the dream. All I know is that it seemed like seconds until I was somehow out in my driveway again with a shovel in my hand. The feeling my chest carried was heavy, it was almost as if something had been wrong for a long time. And with every beat, I could feel my heart sink lower and lower. I kept looking to the side of me, expecting someone to be there, but I was alone.

I was drowning in the snow, and all I wanted at that moment was my sister. But, somehow, I knew she wasn't going to come. I had this understanding that she was gone. I wanted her to be there, but a part of me knew there was no way it was possible. I had no sister. I was shoveling all alone, but not with the peace of knowing she was inside my house safe and warm.

To this day, I don't know if this feeling meant that she had died in my dream or that she never existed in the first place. But I knew that not having my sister at all left me empty inside. Even though she never wanted to come and help me out, I still liked knowing she would still be there in her room when I was done. I had never really understood the significance of her in my life until I had that dream. But when I woke up, I finally was able to understand that if anything were to happen to her and she was not around anymore, nothing would feel right. And this realization came to me because of something as little as shoveling the snow.

The universe works in funny ways for reasons I cannot explain. I got up from the couch, ran to my window and looked outside. In the middle of my driveway, my sister was shoveling the snow. Maybe my dream had found its way to her at some point during my slumber, or maybe she took what I said to heart and felt bad. But after understanding what it would be like for her to be gone, the feeling of seeing her was indescribable.

I will never forget the way I felt standing at the window. And I thank all the snowflakes that fell from the sky that night because I never had to truly lose her to know how much she was worth to me.

—Uma Surampudi—

99

Pandemic Pages

One of the most important things you can do on this
earth is to let people know they are not alone.
~Shannon L. Alder

I am always looking for ways to do good and share my faith, like planting seeds. I started with a printed prayer and a five-dollar bill to give away. Then I moved on to rocks on which I painted words. I gave them to people with a prayer. Next, I painted on bathroom tiles left over from a new shower. I found cards with inspirational messages to color, and I gave away my own books when appropriate.

When we go out to eat, I let the waitress choose a card or rock and a prayer. I greet people who come to our condo and offer one of my gifts.

But when the COVID-19 pandemic came, and we were homebound, I lost those interactions with people.

So, I started cleaning and organizing our condo. The bookcase was my first project. I ended up with a pile of eighteen hardcover books. They took up a lot of space. They were piled on the table, the hallway bench, and my desk. I may be creative, but I like things to be organized, not cluttered. It makes me feel uncomfortable.

The night after I organized the books, one week before Easter, I had a dream about what to do with my books.

In my dream, it was apparent I should offer them to the residents of the thirty condos on our street. The dream even gave me a plan of how to do it, involving my husband. And it included a way to do social distancing, to stay six feet away from the neighbors, while he did his part.

The next morning, I couldn't wait to share my dream with Ron. He agreed to get involved. And when I sat down at the computer, I came up with a three-page handout that he, wearing a facemask, would attach to the front door of each condo without any personal interaction.

It was titled: "Easter: Giving Gifts with Meaning." The graphic said, "Easter is FOREVER." In addition to the book summaries, it explained various ways they could let us know which books they would like. (They could choose up to three.) Their options were to return the handout to a box outside our door, to e-mail Ron, or to give him a phone call.

The choices were from nine nonfiction books, nine fiction books and two Bibles. In addition, I also added eight of my titles. The most requested was *Angels on Duty: A Collection of Angel Encounters,* which was requested by three people.

By Wednesday, we had heard from a third of the residents. They were pleased and surprised. Some called to thank us, even if they didn't need any books at the time.

Ron wore a facemask when he delivered the books. He left them, plus one of the colored cards with an inspirational message, in a plastic bag at our neighbors' front doors.

My dream provided more than a solution for sorting out my books. It also gave my neighbors something to occupy their time as they followed the stay-at-home COVID-19 directive.

As for this Type-A woman, things are good. My bookcase is in better shape, and I was able to reach out to my neighbors. And I have a happy heart and a smile on my face, knowing that my dream helped others during this troubling time.

—Phyllis Porter Dolislager—

The Button Man

*If you feel like there's something out there that you're
supposed to be doing, if you have a passion for it,
then stop wishing and just do it.*
~Wanda Sykes

I should have been ecstatic. I was newly married and had a well-paying job at a stock-brokerage firm. I was surrounded by good friends and lived in one of the most beautiful cities in the country. But I didn't feel fulfilled. Every day, after coming home from work, I was miserable. The work itself was fine. My co-workers were wonderful. I just didn't feel like I was doing what I was supposed to be doing.

After a few weeks and many discussions with my husband, he asked "The Question." If I could do anything in the world I wanted to do, what would it be? Without hesitation, I blurted out, "I'd be a hairstylist!" He looked at me quizzically.

I was a receptionist at a hair salon when I was a teenager. I loved that job! The majority of my tasks were menial. I folded towels, made coffee, and restocked shelves. I swept hair from the floor. But, most of the time, I did what I loved best. I listened and talked to people all day long! We talked about everything. I learned about their families. Their work. Their home life. Their spouses. Their children. I loved it. Every bit of it.

Some stories were happy. Some were sad. Some clients talked because they lived alone and had no one else to talk to all day. I was always happy to listen.

But at the job I had, there was none of that. I worked with numbers. And computers. And papers. Lots and lots of papers.

And so it went. Every day, I went to work. Every day, I came home feeling unfulfilled. And each night, I thought more and more about switching careers. At the end of each daydream session, I talked myself out of the idea. It was too much work to start a new career. I would be crazy to give up my well-paying job with health insurance. I would have to go to school again. It would take too long to build a clientele. The cons outweighed the pros by a zillion!

I had all but forgotten about my wish to become a stylist until I had a dream one night.

I dreamt that I was washing a woman's hair. We were chatting away about something I don't recall. I brought her back to my chair to wrap the cape around her, and I caught a glimpse of myself in the mirror. I had a giant smile on my face. I felt happier than I had in a long time.

When I woke, the feeling stayed with me—until I remembered that I had to get up and go to work at a job that was the opposite of what I had just dreamt of.

The dream happened three nights in a row. On the third morning, I felt worse than ever, waking to the realization that I had to go to work. I dragged myself out of bed, showered, dressed, and went to work. This time, I stopped at the shop across the street from work to grab a coffee. They called my name, and I picked up my coffee. I headed out the door and waited for the walk sign. As I stood there, a man came and stood next to me. He was quite a character. He was dressed in a black suit, a white T-shirt, and a black baseball cap. His jacket and cap were covered in buttons that said things like, "Have a nice day!" "Keep smiling!" and "Just say yes!"

He caught me looking, and I gave a quick half-smile. He made eye contact and said, "Do it!"

"Excuse me?" I asked.

"You've been thinking about it, so just DO IT!" he said more emphatically this time.

The walk sign came on, and he crossed the street.

Was this strange man able to read my mind? Did he know about the dream that I had had for the last three nights? I stood there, coffee in hand, with my mouth open. And just like that, a switch in my head flipped. I was going to be a hairstylist.

I gave notice that same month, went back to school full-time, and in less than a year was working behind the chair. The very first week of work, after shampooing a woman's hair, I walked her over to my styling chair and caught a glimpse of myself in the mirror. Just as in my dream, I had a giant smile on my face. I was happier than I'd been in a long time. But this time, I didn't have to wake up. This time, I was living my dream. I lived my dream for over twenty years—thanks to a dream and the Button Man.

—Crescent LoMonaco—

The End

*Sometimes it's better to end something and try to start
something new than imprison yourself
in hoping for the impossible.*
~Karen Salmansohn

I was married over twenty years: it was rough. There seemed to be no end to the poverty and abuse. It was far from what I had grown up with. Then I never saw violence, prescription drug abuse or fraud in my family or with the people I was around.

Years went by, and no matter what I did, the abuse and poverty got worse. I was cut off from my family. I wasn't allowed to drive. My children were suffering. It was very scary, but I really believed in marriage and wanted it to work.

One cold night in January, I had a vivid dream. I usually slept very lightly, listening for my children, and also because my husband had taken to sleeping with a loaded shotgun by my pillow. He said he didn't want me to leave. I just wanted him to be normal, get a job and support his family—something he had never done and would never do.

Perhaps I was just really tired that night or had ceased to care. I had had nightmares but not dreams before. But this was a real dream, and it went like this:

My husband and I were standing in the middle of a good-sized empty room in an old building. It had a scuffed wood floor and woodwork. It seemed to be on an upper floor, so one had to go out into the hall and down the stairs to get outside. The windows were open as it was a warm, sunny day. There were no window coverings on the two large windows. The floor had a raised wooden threshold, so the door closed tight without much space under it.

We were talking close to the door, but the conversation wasn't pleasant. Suddenly, my husband had a can of stain for the floor and a brush in his hand. I stepped back, out of habit, to avoid a blow. He got down on one knee close to my feet and started to brush stain on the floor, back and forth, unknowingly moving away from me. His conversation got meaner and more frightening while he was very serious about soaking the floor with stain. Back and forth he went, covering the floor with stain and making threats. I didn't move but watched him and his brush. Sometimes, I would answer a question, but mostly I watched as he worked on the floor.

Slowly, he moved away from me toward the wall between the windows. It seemed like forever, but then he bumped into the wall. He stood up with the can in one hand and a brush in the other, still threatening me. His words had no love. It seemed then that there had never been any love or even a marriage. He looked at me and then the floor. He was up against the wall, and the entire floor was wet… a sea of stain. His words became rage. He just kept spewing hate.

I realized in that moment that I was done. There was no marriage and no future. I reached over, grabbed the door handle and started to pull it shut. He just kept talking and threatening.

I slowly kept moving until I was standing on the raised threshold of the door. I backed into the hall and finished closing the door behind me, firmly and quietly. I could still hear violence and hate coming from his mouth. He must not have even noticed I was gone.

In that moment, I was free. All the crap he threw at me all those years slid off me like water. I knew what was right, what I had to do, and I wasn't afraid. It was the end!

Then I woke up very clear-headed. It was still a cold January night, but I was done. I slept well the rest of the night.

My kids and I left in April. Only then would I see the full extent of his wrath. He could no longer physically hurt me, but he could make my life even more miserable. He filed bogus complaints with the cops, who would stop me for drugs, alcohol and weapons. I was dragged out of my church on one of his complaints. My bosses and co-workers were harassed. I had to keep changing jobs. He stalked me. My friends were threatened. He told his parents I had cheated on him, so he was leaving me. I found out he had taken loans out in my name. He faked a disability. He got government benefits for me when I wasn't living with him. The fraud was extensive, and I discovered that it had been going on for a long time.

The divorce was final some years later. Every time I would get weak from the unending battle, I would see myself (again) stepping over the threshold of that empty room and pulling the door shut as I stepped into the hall.

—Sandy Anderson—

Meet Our Contributors

Carolyn Akinyemi is a home-schooling mother of four children and author of *Superheroes Inside Me*, a book series for children teaching them about the impact of their diet on their immune system. She also loves to write music, sing, walk in the countryside, and help others achieve their potential in life.

Monica A. Andermann lives and writes on Long Island where she shares a home with her husband Bill and their little tabby Samson. Her work has been included in such publications as *Guideposts*, *Sasee* and *Woman's World* as well as many titles in the *Chicken Soup for the Soul* series.

Lainie Belcastro is thrilled to have her sixth story in the uplifting *Chicken Soup for the Soul* series! She is a children's book author and poet with Guardian Angel Publishing. Many of her poems can be viewed via the blog, "Writing In A Woman's Voice." Learn more at www.lainiebelcastro.com.

Rob L. Berry is a graduate of California State University, Bakersfield. He lives in Bakersfield, CA with his wife and three sons.

Cheri Bunch grew up on a small farm in Elma, WA. She moved to Salem, OR and received her Associate of Science degree in 1990. She is a master gardener, artist and freelance writer who has written a couple of children's books and hopes to publish them in the near future.

Jill Burns lives in the mountains of West Virginia with her wonderful family. She's a retired piano teacher and performer. She enjoys writing, music, gardening, nature, and spending time with her grandchildren.

Amy Michels Cantley is a librarian and writer in Central Florida. Ms. Cantley writes poetry, nonfiction essays, and memoir. She also leads a local writing group.

Bobbi Carducci started writing at age eight and has never stopped. She is the author of two books for caregivers, *Confessions of an Imperfect Caregiver* and *Caregiver You Are Not Alone*. Bobbi is the co-host, with her husband Mike, of the podcast "Rodger That" at www.rodgerthat. show, which is dedicated to guiding you through the haze of dementia.

Eva Carter is a freelance writer and has a background in the telecommunications industry. She is originally from Czechoslovakia, was raised in New York and now lives with her Canadian born husband, Larry, in Dallas, TX.

Brenda Cathcart-Kloke lives in Denver, CO where she enjoys writing and sharing inspirational stories. Several have been published in the *Chicken Soup for the Soul* series and in *Woman's World* magazine. Her other interests are reading and painting landscapes.

Pastor Wanda Christy-Shaner is a licensed minister. She has also done several mission trips around the world and is married and loves her five cats. Wanda is also an adrenaline freak and does anything crazy, like skydiving. She is a four-time contributor to the *Chicken Soup for the Soul* series, and has been published twice in *War Cry* magazine.

Jane Clark is an eighty-eight-year-old life coach. She enjoys reading, travel, yoga, meditation, ballet and socializing with her many friends and family members.

Debbie Cohen received her Bachelor of Arts in Theatre in 1990 and her Master of Arts in Teaching in 1991. Debbie teaches middle school reading and writing. She recently published her first children's book entitled *Lights, Camera, Action: It's Cassie Lewett!* Debbie is the mom of an amazing, funny, and creative daughter.

P.A. Cornell is a Chilean-Canadian speculative fiction writer and freelance copyeditor who believes the secret to good stories involves copious amounts of tea. She works out of her Ontario home and has published both fiction and nonfiction in various anthologies and magazines.

NancyLee Davis was a teacher for handicapped children, a farm wife and horse lover by choice. She wanted her own horse but as an adult and mother, she finally filled her barn with miniature horses, who all caught her heart and kept it. And now, as a retiree, she hooks her tiny cart to a tiny horse and she still... flies.

Denise Del Bianco is a retired widow living in her hometown, Bischwiller, France, after travelling the world with the love of her life, Pietro. After meeting in France, he and Denise raised two children in Italy and Canada. She enjoys cooking, reading, and cuddling her furry grandkids. Reach her on Twitter @DeniseBecht1.

Sergio Del Bianco has a background in fine arts and psychology. He is an artist and writer, interested in the intersection of art, psychology and the humanities. He resides in Europe with his spouse and growing family of rescue animals. E-mail him at sergiodelbianco@yahoo.com or through Twitter @DelBianco97.

Yvonne deSousa is the author of *MS Madness! A "Giggle More, Cry Less" Story of Multiple Sclerosis,* published in 2014. She shares her medical misadventures in a popular chronic illness humor blog, yvonnedesousa.com, and was previously published in *Chicken Soup for the Soul: Finding My Faith.*

Mary Alice Dixon lives and writes in Charlotte, NC. She taught architectural history and worked in the legal field, frequently helping families of abused children. She now devotes herself to reading, writing and growing a few flowers in her back yard. Occasionally people still call her by her childhood nickname, Tree.

Phyllis Porter Dolislager received a B.A. at Central Michigan University and an M.A. at Michigan State University. She was an educator until post-polio took her out of the classroom. Phyllis has published ten books. She and her husband of fifty-four years, Ron, live in East Tennessee. They have two sons and four grandchildren.

Hailing from Cleveland, OH, and a graduate of Syracuse University, **Joan Donnelly-Emery** is a freelance writer and avid gardener. She and her husband, Alan, just celebrated their twenty-fifth anniversary by viewing the Northern lights in Alta, Norway. They're enjoying life in Franklin, TN along with their Terrier, Dottie, and their pet birds.

Élise Dorsaine lives in Scotland with her husband and two sons.

She likes to read, hike, and write essays and stories.

Rhonda Dragomir is a pastor's wife and freelance writer from Kentucky. This is her fifth story published in the *Chicken Soup for the Soul* series. Rhonda has won numerous writing awards, including being named 2019 Writer of the Year by Serious Writer, Inc. Learn more at www.rhondadragomir.com.

Sharon Rosenbaum Earls loves to sew, walk, read, and write, but spending time with her grandchildren, Andrew, Ella, and Ava is her favorite thing to do.

Lut M.D. Evangelista received her Doctor of Dental Medicine degree from Centro Escolar University, Manila, Philippines. She now lives in New Jersey with her husband and daughter. Lut enjoys writing, reading, baking, and watching movies during her free time. She is currently working on her first children's book.

Kate Fellowes is the author of six mysteries, most recently *A Menacing Brew*. Her short stories and essays have appeared in several anthologies and periodicals. She blogs about work and life at katefellowes.wordpress.com and shares her home with a variety of companion animals.

Marianne Fosnow lives in Fort Mill, SC. She enjoys reading, writing and jigsaw puzzles. She loves playing with her grandchildren and reading them stories.

Surrounded by pets, farm animals, and gorgeous countryside, **Vera Frances** is a retired banker who enjoys frequenting the nearby mountains for fly fishing, hiking, and painting. She is a nature enthusiast by day, writer by night.

Pamela Freeland is a certified medium, psychic and shamanic practitioner. She received her degrees as an Integrative Healing Arts Practitioner, Spiritual Teacher and Intuitive Angel Guide through the Southwest Institute of Healing Arts. Pamela sees clients on a daily basis, teaches mediumship classes, writes and mentors.

Former newspaper columnist and poet **Lorraine Furtner** enjoys photography, the outdoors, and acting. She's a playwright and frequent contributor to Foudlinghouse.com. Her upcoming adventures include a children's picture book and a collection of poetry. Follow her on

Instagram @write_as_raine.

Renee Greene is a southerner who enjoys blogging and writing as a guest with Blogging Through the Bible, a Bible study ministry with likeminded blogging sisters. She is a member of Kingdom Called Daughters, a women's ministry on Facebook and is writing her first novel. Read her blog at hearttokens.home.blog.

Arturo Guajardo IV graduated from Texas State University with a Bachelor's in English in 2019 and will be working toward obtaining his Master's in Secondary Education from Texas State University. He currently works as a server at Gristmill River Restaurant & Bar in New Braunfels and hopes to one day be a high school principal.

Wendy Hobday Haugh's short stories, articles, and poetry have appeared in dozens of national and regional publications, including *Woman's World*, *Highlights for Children*, *Simply Saratoga*, and WritersWeekly.com. This story is her fifteenth to appear in the *Chicken Soup for the Soul* series.

Judith Victoria Hensley is a retired middle school teacher, weekly newspaper columnist for over twenty years, published author in several genres, and photographer. She describes herself as a "story gatherer" with ample opportunities for inspiration in the Kentucky Highlands region where she resides.

Melanie Holmes is a Chicago-based author of three nonfiction books; the first won a Global Media Award; the other two were released nine months apart (2019 and 2020), something she advises against for sanity's sake. The books were dedicated to her daughter, friend, and mother, respectively. Her husband's love made it all possible.

Charlotte Hopkins is a member of Steel City Creatives, a dynamic group of Pittsburgh area authors and photographers. She has written nine books including several in her *365 Days* series, and children's books featuring Pixie Trist and Bo. She opened Purple Pages Literary Services to help other writers achieve their goals.

Susan Wilking Horan is a three-time cancer survivor, wellness advocate, blogger, businesswoman and inspirational speaker. She has a Bachelor of Arts in Psychology, a Juris Doctor in Law and is an Amazon best-selling author of *The Single Source Cancer Course* and *Betty Boop's*

Guide to a Bold and Balanced Life.

Bonita Jewel moved to India when she was sixteen and lived there for twelve years. After returning to California with her husband and three children, she earned an MFA in creative writing. A freelance writer and editor, Bonita blogs irregularly, drinks homemade chai, and loves it when rain graces the arid valley she calls home.

Susan Maddy Jones is a former computer science nerd with a B.S. in computer science. She rewired her life to feed her creativity and her soul. She helped design and build her own teardrop camping trailer and makes one-of-a-kind handcrafted jewelry of wire-wrapped, wire-woven, and metal-worked components. Read her blog at TeardropAdventures. com.

Keri Kelly is an award-winning author, comedy writer, and creative writing professor at Rowan University. She earned an MFA in fiction from Rutgers University and studied comedy at Second City. When she's not writing, she can be found surfing small waves with her family at the Jersey Shore.

Catherine Kenwell is a Canadian author and qualified mediator. She recently co-authored *Not Cancelled: Canadian Caremongering in the Face of COVID-19*. Her works are featured in international horror collections, and she is now working on a horror novel and an auto-biographical brain injury memoir.

E. E. King is a painter, performer, writer, and biologist — She'll do anything that won't pay the bills, especially if it involves animals. Ray Bradbury called her stories "marvelously inventive, wildly funny and deeply thought-provoking." She's been published widely.

Kelly Kowall founded a non-profit organization called My Warrior's Place after her son was killed in 2009 while serving in Afghanistan. She is a certified Life Coach, Grief Support Provider, Fire Walking Instructor, as well as a published author and an inspirational speaker who resides in Apollo Beach, FL. E-mail her at kelly.mwp@gmail.com.

At twenty-three **Jenny Langford** left Wales to nanny in Las Vegas, where she met her husband Dan. They moved to a remote farm in Sonora, Mexico and spent forty-eight years raising eleven children. She loves her sixty-seven grandchildren and six great-grand kids as well as Jesus, gardening, reading and spending time with her family and friends.

Crescent LoMonaco is a frequent contributor to the *Chicken Soup for the Soul* series. She is an avid reader, writer, and artist. She used her experience as a previous salon owner to write the "Ask a Stylist" column for the *Santa Barbara Independent*. She lives on the California coast with her husband of twenty-two years and their son.

Diana Lynn is a writer and business owner in Washington State. This is her eleventh story published in the *Chicken Soup for the Soul* series. She is currently working on her second book.

Award recipient **Sheri Lynn** published her first chapbook entitled *Nature's Breath*. She designed postcards to go with the book, which can be found at BreatheInsights.com. A recent LIAG acceptor, her works have been published by NCPLS, PPA, Bards and LIWGs The Odyssey. Sheri plans to continue writing from her inner voice.

Emily Marszalek received her Bachelor of Arts in International Studies from Whitworth University in 2013. She likes jigsaw puzzles, rock music and playing board games with her family. Emily enjoys life's simplest pleasures in the Pacific Northwest with her boyfriend Nick and Goldendoodle Charlie Anne.

Vickie McEntire has been published in several anthologies and magazines. In 2018, she won Georgia Author of the Year for her second children's book, *Little Bird & Myrtle Turtle*. Her passion is writing and promoting literacy. She lives in Northwest Georgia with her husband and cat and is currently working on her first novel.

Danielle Soucy Mills is an award-winning author, gymnast, mom, and lifelong dreamer. Before having her two wonderful daughters, she published her books, *Tina Tumbles* and *Illusion of an Ending*, one of which miraculously appeared in *US Weekly* magazine and People. com. Learn more at daniellesoucymills.com.

Melissa Moore received a B.A. in Psychology and Biblical Studies from Azusa Pacific University and a Graduate Diploma in Pastoral Care to Women from Western Seminary. She and her husband, Chris, live in California with their boys: DJ and Oliver. Melissa enjoys baking, motivational speaking, and serving her local church.

A retired physical therapist, **Jeanne Moran** is the author of numerous articles, two historical novels, and a picture book. She reads and writes stories in which unlikely heroes make a difference in their corner of the world. In her everyday life, she strives to be one of them.

Lorraine Moran is a retired college professor. She lives in New Jersey and celebrated her fiftieth wedding anniversary in May 2020 with her high school sweetheart. She enjoys gardening, spending time with her son and grandson and animal rescue, with a soft spot for dogs.

Marya Morin is a freelance writer. Her stories and poems have appeared in publications such as *Woman's World* and Hallmark. Marya also penned a weekly humorous column for an online newsletter and writes custom poetry on request. She lives in the country with her husband. E-mail her at Akushla514@hotmail.com.

Kristen Mai Pham is thrilled to be a ten-time contributor to the *Chicken Soup for the Soul* series. When she isn't writing screenplays for television and film, she dreams of hazelnut gelato. Follow her on Instagram @kristenmaipham or e-mail her at kristenmaipham3@gmail.com.

Stephanie Pifer-Stone is an interfaith minister with a degree in Holistic Theology. She studied Religious Literacy at Harvard Divinity School. *Becoming Egg-straordinary* is her first book about releasing your inner butterfly. In addition to her husband and their furry kid, her passions include yoga, writing, and cooking.

Changing seasons, unexpected blessings, love that lasts forever... these are a few of **M. Jean Pike's** favorite things. Jean enjoys writing, cooking and gardening. She currently has nine romance novels in print.

Jillian Pretzel is an essayist, humorist, and Netflix connoisseur. She earned her MA in English and her MFA in Creative Writing from Chapman University. She loves cats, pizza, and hanging out with her husband.

Connie Kaseweter Pullen lives in rural Sandy, OR near her five children and several grandchildren. She earned a B.A. with honors at the University of Portland in 2006, with a double major in Psychology and Sociology. Connie enjoys writing, photography and exploring nature. E-mail her at MyGrandmaPullen@aol.com.

Rebecca Radicchi, her husband and crew of kids live outside Atlanta, GA where the summers are hot and the tea is sweet. She's ridden the waves of adoption, breast cancer, and being the mom of a child with complex medical needs. Learn more at rebeccaradicchi.com and on social media to talk about the wild, salty, sweetness of life.

Lori Reed graduated from a small rural high school in Western Pennsylvania in 1977. She is married and has two grown sons. Lori owns and operates a home care agency for the elderly. She enjoys reading, writing stories, swimming and time with family.

Rachel Remick majored in Film and Media Arts at Temple University in Philadelphia. Her fiction and narrative nonfiction stories have been published in several literary magazines, including *Rosebud* and *The First Line*, as well as *Sasee*. She enjoys walking dogs, swimming and ice hockey.

Nancy Campbell Renko is a retired Language Arts teacher with thirty-six years of classroom teaching experience. She and her husband of fifty years have three daughters who are also in the field of education. Nancy thanks her writing group, Trailside Writers, from the Midland, MI Senior Center for their support and encouragement.

Keisha M. Reynolds built a twenty-year career in marketing but writing remains the primary aspect of her passion. She's written for numerous publications, including *HuffPost*, and will release her debut children's book, *Sylvester Lou Goes Beyond the Mountain,* this year. She lives with her husband, Lenny, and son, Koa.

Mark Rickerby is an author, screenwriter, copyeditor, and voice actor. His stories have appeared in over twenty *Chicken Soup for the Soul* books. Links to his written works and editing service can be found at www.markrickerby.com. His greatest sources of pride and joy are his wife Claudia and their amazing daughters, Marli and Emma.

CM Riddle (Christina Riddle Deason) is the author of *One's Own Sweet Way*. She's been published in anthologies, magazines, and newspapers. She also writes rituals, ceremonies, and leads women's circles. She is a homemaker, mother, wife, and writes of everyday magic. She lives in Sonoma, CA. E-mail her at CMRiddle55@gmail.com.

Annie Riess lives with her husband on a farm in Saskatchewan.

She teaches piano, mentors a moms' group, and does freelance writing. She also enjoys spending as much time as possible with family and friends.

Donna L. Roberts is a native upstate New Yorker who lives and works in Europe. She is an Associate Professor and holds a Ph.D. in Psychology. Donna is an animal and human rights advocate and when she is researching or writing she can be found at her computer buried in rescue cats.

Ruth Rogers is a career coach and person of faith. Believing God uses dreams to speak to us, she seeks to understand their messages as important tools for life direction. She is fascinated by life and enjoys traveling in the U.S. and abroad. She and her husband have two grown sons, five grandchildren, and reside in the Midwest.

Debra Rughoo has a Bachelor of Arts degree, with honours, in English and Communications Studies, and currently works in marketing and communications in Toronto. She has previously been published in the *Toronto Star*, *The Hockey News*, *USA Hockey Magazine* and *Alive* magazine. She enjoys travel, sports, comedy and writing.

Holly Rutchik, (Minivan Matriarch) is an inspirational and humor writer. She believes in using words for encouragement. Her minivan is littered with books, magazines and coloring pages, only some of which belong to her five children. She lives in Wisconsin with Mr. Minivan Matriarch and her kids. Learn more at Hollyrutchik.com.

Kat Samworth is a dreamwork practitioner, a physical therapist and health coach living in Northern Delaware with her husband. Kat's interest in writing began when she created a blog of her experiences with dreams. She enjoys hiking, yoga, tennis and exploring the magic of dreams with her clients. E-mail her at dreamforyourlife@gmail.com.

Arthur Sanchez resides in Tampa Bay, FL with his wife of thirty-four years and their two cats. Originally an actor, Arthur stumbled onto writing and never looked back. This is Arthur's fourth appearance in the *Chicken Soup for the Soul* series, and he is very proud of being able to share his stories with the *Chicken Soup for the Soul* readers.

Margo Sanchez received her bachelor's degree in Sociology from California State University Fullerton. She has published two novels: *Departure of Reason* and *Girl on a Ledge*. You can find both fiction novels online. She is currently working on a third novel. E-mail her at writerinprogress@yahoo.com.

Judith Burnett Schneider, a research organic chemist turned writer, is the mother of three. Her work has appeared in books and magazines, on websites, and in standardized tests in the U.S. and Japan. She enjoys teaching students how to improve their writing by adding crafts and activities to make the writing process fun!

Donna Faulkner Schulte published her first book, *Santa's Search for the Perfect Child*, in 2015, *The Love Club*, and "Make a Difference" in *Chicken Soup for the Soul: The Joy of Christmas*. She is presently working on the second series of *The Love Club*, which is a four series book. She believes one person can make a difference. Let it be you.

Steve Schultz is a two-time Teacher of the Year at Fountain Valley High School where he has taught English Language Arts for the past ten years. Steve has nine other stories published in seven previous *Chicken Soup for the Soul* books. Steve is the author of *Teeter Totter Leader*. E-mail him at personalbest22@gmail.com.

Stephen Schwei is a published poet and writer with Wisconsin roots, now living in Houston, TX. A gay man with three grown children and four wonderful grandchildren, he can be a mass of contradictions. Writing helps to sort all of this out.

Florentia Scott lived and worked for many years in Canada, where most of the events related in this story happened. She now lives in California where she grew up. She enjoys hiking, gardening, music, and writing. Her poetry and short stories have been published in literary anthologies and magazines. She is currently working on a novel.

Jody Sharpe's latest novel, *Town of Angels* is third in the *Mystic Bay* series. She is an award-winning author of *The Angel's Daughter* and *To Catch an Angel*. Her children's book is *When the Angel Sent Butterflies*. She had a rewarding career as a Special Education teacher and is now writing her teaching memoir.

Tracey Sherman received her B.A. in English with teaching certification from Angelo State University in 1986. In 2020, she fulfilled a lifelong dream of earning her MFA in Writing for Children from Hamline

University. Married for forty years to her high school sweetheart, she is mother of three and grandmother of two.

Stevie Shield (born Stephen Ngao) received his Bachelor of Science from Northeastern University in 2010. Originally from Southern California, his influence as a writer comes from his itinerant upbringing. He currently works full-time as a financial analyst and lives with his pet cat, Raisa, in Los Angeles, CA.

Debbie Sistare, a retired RN/Ordained Minister with a master's in Religious Psychology, writes full-time from home where she is caretaker for her ninety-five-year-old mother. Her eleven books, including her trilogy, *In Search of the Key of David: The Symbol of Knowledge (2-Wisdom 3-Power)* can be found online under DS Sistare.

Dana D. Sterner is a retired registered nurse living and writing in Florida. She wrote this story hoping others would listen and heed God's whisper in the midst of their busy lives. Learn more at DanaSterner.com.

Uma Surampudi is going to be an incoming freshman at Lafayette College with an interest in film media studies and international affairs. From a young age, Uma believed that sharing stories had a powerful ability to bring people together. She is pursuing her dream and wants to form a connection with other readers.

Tina Szymczak received her Bachelor of Arts degree in 1995. She has two grown boys and has been married for over twenty-five years to her amazing husband Adam. Tina enjoys scrapbooking, writing and her full-time job working in early intervention. Learn more at www. spiritedblessings.com.

Jia Thomas received her Bachelor of Arts in Journalism from Southern Methodist University in 2009. She's an avid reader and enjoys nonfiction the most. She also loves gardening and music, specifically old school R&B. Jia loves the water and hopes to get her scuba certification in the future.

A 2018 Ohio Arts Foundation Individual Excellence Award winner, **Stefanie Wass's** stories have appeared in the *Los Angeles Times*, *Christian Science Monitor*, *The Seattle Times*, *The Writer*, *Cleveland Magazine*, *Akron Beacon Journal*, *This I Believe*, *Cup of Comfort*, and sixteen *Chicken Soup for the Soul* anthologies. Learn more at www.stefaniewass.com.

Dorann Weber is a freelance photographer and writer who lives in the Pine Barrens of Southern New Jersey. She's a contributor for Getty Images. Her photos and verses have been on several Hallmark cards. Writing her first story in the *Chicken Soup for the Soul* series ignited her passion for writing. She likes hiking with her family and dogs.

Vicky Webster lives in a small town in rural Missouri. She has two adult children, Cheyanne and Dalton, and is a route driver for a local pharmacy. This is her second published story in the *Chicken Soup for the Soul* series. Vicky loves spending time with her family and friends… and hugs, she loves to hug!

Aileen Weintraub is an award-winning author living in New York. She writes about women's issues and female empowerment for *The Washington Post*, *AARP*, *HuffPost*, *Glamour* and others. Her latest children's book, *We Got Game! 35 Female Athletes Who Changed the World,* is about not only listening to but following your dreams.

Susan C. Willett is a writer and blogger whose award-winning stories, poems, and humor appear in print and online, including on her website LifeWithDogsAndCats.com. She shares her home with three dogs and four cats — all rescues. Follow them all on Facebook, Twitter @WithDogsAndCats, and Instagram @LifeWithDogsAndCats.

Jamie Wilson received her Bachelor of Science, with honors, from Robert Morris University in 2000. She has two boys and works in the banking field. Jamie enjoys biking, playing piano and animal rescue. She plans to write motivational and humorous parenting books.

Bonnie Collins Wood, a paraeducator, lives in Florida with her husband Paul. She is a proud mother of two daughters and a blessed mimi to two grandchildren. Her love of reading has recently blossomed into a love of writing. Her real-life stories portray her strong faith in God.

Meet Amy Newmark

Amy Newmark is the bestselling author, editor-in-chief, and publisher of the Chicken Soup for the Soul book series. Since 2008, she has published 168 new books, most of them national bestsellers in the U.S. and Canada, more than doubling the number of Chicken Soup for the Soul titles in print today. She is also the author of Simply Happy, a crash course in Chicken Soup for the Soul advice and wisdom that is filled with easy-to-implement, practical tips for enjoying a better life.

Amy is credited with revitalizing the Chicken Soup for the Soul brand, which has been a publishing industry phenomenon since the first book came out in 1993. By compiling inspirational and aspirational true stories curated from ordinary people who have had extraordinary experiences, Amy has kept the twenty-seven-year-old Chicken Soup for the Soul brand fresh and relevant.

Amy graduated magna cum laude from Harvard University where she majored in Portuguese and minored in French. She then embarked on a three-decade career as a Wall Street analyst, a hedge fund manager, and a corporate executive in the technology field. She is a Chartered Financial Analyst.

Her return to literary pursuits was inevitable, as her honors thesis in college involved traveling throughout Brazil's impoverished northeast region, collecting stories from regular people. She is delighted to have come full circle in her writing career — from collecting stories "from the people" in Brazil as a twenty-year-old to, three decades later, collecting stories "from the people" for Chicken Soup for the Soul.

When Amy and her husband Bill, the CEO of Chicken Soup for the Soul, are not working, they are visiting their four grown children and their grandchildren.

Follow Amy on Twitter @amynewmark. Listen to her free podcast — "Chicken Soup for the Soul with Amy Newmark" — on Apple Podcasts, Google Play, the Podcasts app on iPhone, or by using your favorite podcast app on other devices.

Thank You

We owe huge thanks to all of our contributors and fans. We received thousands of submissions for this popular topic, and we spent months reading all of them. Our editors Crescent LoMonaco and Laura Dean read all of them and narrowed down the selection for Associate Publisher D'ette Corona and Publisher and Editor-in-Chief Amy Newmark.

Susan Heim did the first round of editing, D'ette chose the perfect quotations to put at the beginning of each story, and Amy edited the stories and shaped the final manuscript.

As we finished our work, D'ette Corona continued to be Amy's right-hand woman in working with all our wonderful writers. Barbara LoMonaco and Mary Fisher, along with Elaine Kimbler, jumped in at the end to proof, proof, proof. And yes, there will always be typos anyway, so feel free to let us know about them at webmaster@ chickensoupforthesoul.com, and we will correct them in future printings.

The whole publishing team deserves a hand, including our Senior Director of Marketing Maureen Peltier, our Vice President of Production Victor Cataldo, and our graphic designer Daniel Zaccari, who turned our manuscript into this beautiful, entertaining book.

Sharing Happiness, Inspiration, and Hope

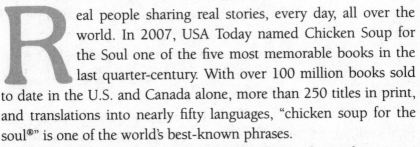

Real people sharing real stories, every day, all over the world. In 2007, USA Today named Chicken Soup for the Soul one of the five most memorable books in the last quarter-century. With over 100 million books sold to date in the U.S. and Canada alone, more than 250 titles in print, and translations into nearly fifty languages, "chicken soup for the soul®" is one of the world's best-known phrases.

Today, twenty-seven years after we first began sharing happiness, inspiration and hope through our books, we continue to delight our readers with new titles, but have also evolved beyond the bookshelves with super premium pet food, television shows, a podcast, video journalism from aplus.com, licensed products, and free movies and TV shows on our Popcornflix and Crackle apps. We are busy "changing the world one story at a time®." Thanks for reading!

Share with Us

We all have had Chicken Soup for the Soul moments in our lives. If you would like to share your story or poem with millions of people around the world, go to chickensoup.com and click on Submit Your Story. You may be able to help another reader and become a published author at the same time. Some of our past contributors have launched writing and speaking careers from the publication of their stories in our books!

We only accept story submissions via our website. They are no longer accepted via mail or fax. Visit our website, www.chickensoup.com, and click on Submit Your Story for our writing guidelines and a list of topics we are working on.

To contact us regarding other matters, please send us an e-mail through webmaster@chickensoupforthesoul.com, or fax or write us at:

Chicken Soup for the Soul
P.O. Box 700
Cos Cob, CT 06807-0700
Fax: 203-861-7194

One more note from your friends at Chicken Soup for the Soul: Occasionally, we receive an unsolicited book manuscript from one of our readers, and we would like to respectfully inform you that we do not accept unsolicited manuscripts, and we must discard the ones that appear.

Chicken Soup for the Soul

Dreams and the Unexplainable

101 Eye-Opening Stories about Premonitions and Miracles

Amy Newmark
& Kelly Sullivan Walden
Bestselling Author, National TV and Radio Dream Expert

Paperback: 978-1-61159-971-8
eBook: 978-1-61159-271-9

More guidance and insight

Dreams and Premonitions

101 Amazing Stories of Miracles, Divine Intervention, and Insight

Amy Newmark
& Kelly Sullivan Walden

Bestselling Author, National TV and Radio Dream Expert

Paperback: 978-1-61159-950-3

eBook: 978-1-61159-251-1

from incredible dream stories

Paperback: 978-1-61159-067-8
eBook: 978-1-61159-302-0

More magic for you

Chicken Soup for the Soul

for the Soul

The Magic of Cats

101 Tales of Family, Friendship & Fun

Amy Newmark

Royalties from this book go to
AMERICAN·HUMANE
FIRST TO SERVE

Paperback: 978-1-61159-066-1
eBook: 978-1-61159-301-3

from our furry family members

Chicken Soup
for the Soul

Changing lives one story at a time®
www.chickensoup.com